To Oscar

Good luck on your batism

with lots of love from

Liz, Leo & Margot.

D1583622

Oxford
ROALD
DAHL
Thesaurus

ROALD
DAHL
Approved

Oxford ROALD DAHL Thesaurus

Original text by
ROALD DAHL

Illustrated by
QUENTIN BLAKE

Compiled by
SUSAN RENNIE

OXFORD
UNIVERSITY PRESS

OXFORD
UNIVERSITY PRESS

Great Clarendon Street, Oxford OX2 6DP.
United Kingdom

Oxford University Press is a department of the University of Oxford.
It furthers the University's objective of excellence in research,
scholarship, and education by publishing worldwide

Oxford is a registered trade mark of Oxford University Press
in the UK and in certain other countries

Original text by Roald Dahl © 2019 Roald Dahl Nominee Limited
Compilation and additional material copyright © 2019 Oxford University Press
Illustrations copyright © Quentin Blake 2019
Chief Editor and lexicographer Dr Susan Rennie
Consulting Editor Vineeta Gupta
© RDLE/Quentin Blake 2019
Thanks to Michelle Porte Davies

The moral rights of the author and illustrator have been asserted
Database right Oxford University Press (maker)

First published in 2019

All rights reserved. No part of this publication may be reproduced, stored
in a retrieval system, or transmitted, in any form or by any means, without
the prior permission in writing of Oxford University Press, or as expressly
permitted by law, by licence or under terms agreed with the appropriate
reprographics rights organization. Enquiries concerning reproduction
outside the scope of the above should be sent to the Rights Department,
Oxford University Press, at the address above.

You must not circulate this book in any other binding or cover
and you must impose this same condition on any acquirer

ISBN: 978-0-19-276669-4
10 9 8 7 6 5 4 3 2 1
Printed in China

British Library Cataloguing in Publication Data
Data available

Paper used in the production of this book is a natural, recyclable product made from
wood grown in sustainable forests. The manufacturing process conforms to the
environmental regulations of the country of origin.

Illustration credits: Reproduced by permission of Penguin Books Ltd.
t = top   l = left   r = right   b = bottom

Front cover: MATILDA (Jonathan Cape, 1988) Illustrations copyright © Quentin Blake 1988.
CHARLIE AND THE CHOCOLATE FACTORY (Puffin, 1973) Written by Roald Dahl and illustrated by
Quentin Blake. Illustrations copyright © Quentin Blake 1995; **FANTASTIC MR FOX** (Puffin, 1974)
Written by Roald Dahl and illustrated by Quentin Blake. Illustrations copyright © Quentin Blake 1996.

Back cover: GEORGE'S MARVELLOUS MEDICINE (Jonathan Cape, 1981) Illustrations
copyright © Quentin Blake 1981. **MATILDA** (Jonathan Cape, 1988) Illustrations copyright
© Quentin Blake 1988.

Hardback cover with flaps: Portrait illustrations copyright © Quentin Blake 2019.

Inside pages: CHARLIE AND THE CHOCOLATE FACTORY (Puffin, 1973) Written by Roald Dahl
and illustrated by Quentin Blake. Illustrations copyright © Quentin Blake 1995. Title page; 16; 26t;
42; 43; 45r; 58; 60bl; 65t; 91t; 94; 102; 103l; 144l; 152b; 153; 154b; 157.

CHARLIE AND THE GREAT GLASS ELEVATOR (Puffin, 1973) Written by Roald Dahl and illustrated
by Quentin Blake. Illustrations copyright © Quentin Blake 1995. 20l; 41; 90-91; 104.

MATILDA (Jonathan Cape, 1988) Illustrations copyright © Quentin Blake 1988. 5; 8t; 10; 12; 15;
17; 20r; 21; 22; 25r; 26b; 31; 33; 39; 45l; 46; 47; 48; 55; 60; 61; 84; 105; 108; 109; 140; 141;
148-149; 152t; 154r; 160.

THE GIRAFFE AND THE PELLY AND ME (Jonathan Cape, 1985) Illustrations copyright © Quentin
Blake 1992. 5bl; 13; 25t; 34; 72; 78; 83; 128b; 129; 149r; 150.

JAMES AND THE GIANT PEACH (Puffin, 1961) Written by Roald Dahl and illustrated by Quentin
Blake. Illustrations copyright © Quentin Blake 1995. 8b; 18; 23; 51t; 53; 62; 68; 74; 80; 81; 86; 87;
88l; 88r; 92; 95; 96; 100; 122; 128t.

GEORGE'S MARVELLOUS MEDICINE (Jonathan Cape, 1981) Illustrations copyright © Quentin
Blake 1981. 9t; 36; 85; 108r; 110; 114.

THE BFG (Jonathan Cape, 1982) Illustrations copyright © Quentin Blake 1982. 9b; 28-29; 37;
38-39; 40; 64-65; 71; 98; 99r; 101; 124; 125; 126; 127; 130-131; 132; 133; 134-135; 136; 137;
139; 140r; 140-141b; 142; 144r; 151; 158; 158-159.

THE ENORMOUS CROCODILE (Jonathan Cape, 1978) Illustrations copyright © Quentin Blake
1978, 2000, 2010. 14; 66; 67; 76; 79; 89; 103r.

THE TWITS (Jonathan Cape, 1980) Illustrations copyright © Quentin Blake 1980. 19; 29; 32; 54;
56; 60br; 69; 73; 82; 106t; 106b; 107; 145; 156.

THE MAGIC FINGER (Puffin, 1966) Written by Roald Dahl and illustrated by Quentin Blake.
Illustrations copyright © Quentin Blake 1995. 1995. 24.

FANTASTIC MR FOX ((Puffin, 1974) Written by Roald Dahl and illustrated by Quentin Blake.
Illustrations copyright © Quentin Blake 1996. 30; 52; 77; 93; 159.

THE WITCHES (Jonathan Cape, 1983) Illustrations copyright © Quentin Blake 1983. 35; 50; 51b;
57; 59; 99l; 112-113; 116-117; 118b; 118-119; 120; 121; 146r; 147.

ESIO TROT (Jonathan Cape, 1990) Illustrations copyright © Quentin Blake 1990. 4; 70; 75; 109b;
146b.

Pedometer: Mary Evans Picture Library. 136.
Roald Dahl's hut: © 2019 The Roald Dahl Story Company Ltd. 6; 7; 73.
All other images courtesy of Shutterstock.

We have tried to contact all copyright holders, but should there be any errors or omissions,
we will be pleased to rectify them at the earliest opportunity.

Preface

If you are reading this page, you probably want to know what a thesaurus is and what to do with it. You *could* use it to stand on, to help you reach a shelf of dream-jars or gobstoppers, or to speak to a grown-up who is too rude to bend down. But that is not the BEST thing to do with it. The very best thing to do with a thesaurus is to WRITE with it. Not the way you write with a pen or that witches write with blue spit. The way to write with a thesaurus is to read it first and then IMAGINE. Imagine brain-boggling stories and creatures and characters in your head and then bring them to life with the words you find here. Words are the STUFF of STORIES and creating things out of words is every bit as magical as making waterfalls out of chocolate or dreams out of **zozimus**.

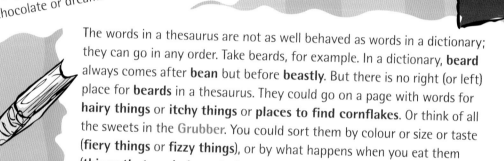

The words in a thesaurus are not as well behaved as words in a dictionary; they can go in any order. Take beards, for example. In a dictionary, **beard** always comes after **bean** but before **beastly**. But there is no right (or left) place for **beards** in a thesaurus. They could go on a page with words for **hairy things** or **itchy things** or **places to find cornflakes**. Or think of all the sweets in the Grubber. You could sort them by colour or size or taste (**fiery things** or **fizzy things**), or by what happens when you eat them (**things that explode** or **sizzle** or **turn your teeth green**). Every thesaurus is different—and THIS thesaurus is the most extra-usual of them all.

We have **hunted, gathered, rootled out** and **tracked down** the most **curious, interesting, remarkable** and **notable** words and phrases for your **pleasure, gratification** and **delight**. You can use them to describe the people, places, peaches and pelicans in Roald Dahl's stories, or to invent your very own. The only thing you **absolutely, definitely, certainly** and **positively** HAVE to do is to have . . . FUN.

Susan Rennie
CHIEF EDITOR & LEXICOGRAPHER

5

How to use this thesaurus

The word *thesaurus* originally meant 'treasure store', and browsing in a thesaurus is like rummaging through a store of precious dream-jars to find the best or *sparkiest* words to use. As with dreams, the more words (or jars) you have, the more varied and interesting your stories will be.

The *Oxford Roald Dahl Thesaurus* is ordered by **topic** —in the same way that the BFG sorts his dream-jars into dreams about flying and dreams about bathtubs. Not every word in this thesaurus is in Roald Dahl's stories, but all the words relate to Roald Dahl's world in some way.

the **section** heading tells you the wider theme to which the topic belongs

the **category** heading tells you which topic all the words on the page relate to

sub-categories divide the topic into *snipsier* sections

example sentences show you how to use the word or phrase in your own writing

related word groups list words that are related by topic

FIND OUT MORE! notes tell you where to find related words in other parts of the Thesaurus

---

• THE NATURAL WORLD

DESCRIBING LANDSCAPE

THE COUNTRYSIDE

CAN BE: fertile, green, leafy, lush, rolling, wooded

CAN HAVE: fields, forest, wood, trees, meadow, moor, river, stream, footpath, hedgerow, cottage, farm
The world I lived in consisted only of the filling-station, the workshop, the caravan, the school, and of course the woods and fields and streams in the countryside around. – DANNY THE CHAMPION OF THE WORLD

• The trees and plants that grow in an area of land are its **vegetation**. *The vegetation in Giant Country is very sparse.*

HILLS AND MOUNTAINS

CAN BE: hilly, mountainous, steep or sheer; craggy, rocky, snow-capped

CAN HAVE: cliff or crag, ridge, slope, mountain stream, fjord, rocks, boulders, cave

• A series of hills or mountains is a **range**. A low-lying area between mountains is a **valley** or (in Scotland) a **glen**.
He leaped over a dozen rivers. He went rattling through a great forest, then down into a valley and up over a range of hills as bare as concrete. – THE BFG

• The top of a mountain is the **peak** or **summit** and the bottom is the **foot** or **foothills**. The front of a cliff is the **cliff face**.
'It is a tree' called the Bristlecone Pine that grows upon the slopes of Wheeler Peak in Nevada, U.S.A.' – CHARLIE AND THE GREAT GLASS ELEVATOR

• Willy Wonka has a craggy **fudge mountain** in his factory, from which the Oompa-Loompas cut blocks of fudge.
A great, craggy mountain made entirely of fudge, with Oompa-Loompas (all roped together for safety) hacking huge hunks of fudge out of its sides. – CHARLIE AND THE GREAT GLASS ELEVATOR

• George's grandma wants him to eat **mountains** of cabbage every day, which is a **gigantuous** amount to eat!
'From now on, you must eat cabbage three times a day. Mountains of cabbage! And if it's got caterpillars in it, so much the better!' – GEORGE'S MARVELLOUS MEDICINE

DESERT OR WASTELAND

CAN BE: arid, bare, barren, desolate, parched, sandy, treeless

CAN HAVE: sand, rocks, boulders

• The extra-usual rocks in Giant Country are coloured blue.
Soon he was galloping over a desolate wasteland that was not quite of this earth. The ground was flat and pale yellow. Great lumps of blue rock were scattered around, and dead trees stood everywhere like skeletons. – THE BFG

UNDERGROUND

CAN BE: dank, damp, musty

CAN HAVE: cave or cavern, pit, tunnel

FIND OUT MORE! What might you find inside a giant's **cave**? Find out in GIANT PLACES in THE MAGICAL WORLD.

• The area under the Earth's surface is **subterranean**. The Gnoolies who inhabit Minusland are a **subterrestrial** species.
'Do any other creatures live here, Mr Wonka?' 'Plenty of Gnoolies.' 'Are they dangerous?' 'If they bite you, they are. You're a gonner, my boy, if you're bitten by a Gnooly.' – CHARLIE AND THE GREAT GLASS ELEVATOR

rocky craggy sandy arid

64

Look out for the phizz-whizzing WRITING HUT pages at the end of each section!

Extra-usual things happen in Roald Dahl's stories. Animals can speak and waterfalls are made of chocolate, so you may have to look in **extra-usual** places in this thesaurus to find the words you want. For example, in an ordinary thesaurus, an *egg-beater* would be listed in FOOD or COOKING, but in THIS thesaurus you will also find it in ALL ABOUT DREAMS.

You can start by browsing on the **Contents** page to find a topic that interests you (which will be all of them of course)—OR you can PLUNGE in, like Augustus Gloop into the chocolate river, and flick through the pages to see what words you bump into. Whichever method you choose, be sure to DILLY and DALLY on each page until you find your new Favourite Word to use in your next **buckswashling** story.

DESCRIBING LANDSCAPE

cascade gush slosh

- The land at each side of a river are its **banks**.
When she lowered herself into the chair, there was a loud squelching noise similar to that made by a hippopotamus when lowering its foot into the mud on the banks of the Limpopo River. — MATILDA

- A small stream is a **brook** or (in Scotland) a **burn**.

- A falling stream of water is a **waterfall** or **cataract**. Willy Wonka's factory has a fantabulous river and waterfall of melted chocolate (as well as a steaming **lake** of hot caramel). *'The waterfall is most important!' Mr Wonka went on. 'It mixes the chocolate! It churns it up! It pounds it and beats it! It makes it light and frothy!'* — CHARLIE AND THE CHOCOLATE FACTORY

- Other **areas of water** include: **canal, lake** or **loch, pond, pool.**

WHAT CAN WATER (AND CHOCOLATE) DO?

IT CAN: **flow** or **stream** along steadily
They were looking down upon a lovely valley. There were green meadows on either side of the valley, and along the bottom of it there flowed a great brown river. — CHARLIE AND THE CHOCOLATE FACTORY

IT CAN: **cascade, gush, pour, rush** or **surge** strongly
All the time the water came pouring and roaring down upon them, bouncing and smashing and sloshing and slashing and swashing and swirling and surging and whirling and gurgling and gushing and rushing and rushing. — JAMES AND THE GIANT PEACH

IT CAN: **dribble, drip, ooze** or **trickle** slowly
It was beginning to rain. Water was trickling down the necks of the three men and into their shoes. — FANTASTIC MR FOX

IT CAN: **slosh, splash, splish, splosh** or **swash** messily
And in every single tube the runny stuff was of a different colour, so that all the colours of the rainbow (and many others as well) came sloshing and splashing into the tub. — CHARLIE AND THE CHOCOLATE FACTORY

IT CAN: **bubble, gurgle, ripple, swirl** or **whirl** about
As we made our way out to the playground, my whole stomach began to feel as though it was slowly filling up with swirling water. — BOY

- Human beans can also **pour** and **stream** like water, when large numbers of them move quickly in the same direction.
Every day of the week, hundreds and hundreds of children from far and near came pouring into the City to see the marvellous peach stone in the Park. — JAMES AND THE GIANT PEACH

RIVERS AND STREAMS

CAN BE: **clear, muddy** (or **chocolatey** in Willy Wonka's factory), **fast-flowing** or **rapid**
In the biggest brownest muddiest river in Africa, two crocodiles lay with their heads just above the water. — THE ENORMOUS CROCODILE

- A river with a winding route might **wind its way** or **meander** (say me-*and*-er) along.

DID YOU KNOW? The word **meander** comes from the River **Maeander** in ancient Phrygia (Turkey), which was famous for its twists and turns.

parched

65

---

definitions explain the meaning of some words and phrases that relate to the topic

quotations from Roald Dahl's stories and poems show how he used certain words and phrases

synonym groups list words that mean the same, or nearly the same, as each other

DID YOU KNOW? notes tell you fantabulous facts about words and phrases, or about Roald Dahl's use of language

words in **blue** are words or names which Roald Dahl invented and used in his stories

---

These will give you lots of ideas for how to be creative with words and language, just like Roald Dahl, who wrote his **splendiferous** stories in a special **writing hut** at the bottom of his garden.

Contents

THE MAGICAL WORLD 110–111

THE WORLD OF WORDS 142–143

beard

breeches

factory

chiddler

caravan

norphanage

chocolate

beastly

window-cleaning

buckswashling

sizzlepan

blancmange

itching-powder

human-beaney

elevator

chokey

brain-power

genius

pigtails

grandmother

inventing

THE WORLD OF HUMAN BEANS

'Every human bean
is diddly and different.'
— THE BFG

ALL ABOUT CHIDDLERS

bold

adventurous

bright

daring

inquisitive

curious

DESCRIBING CHIDDLERS

YOU MIGHT BE: adventurous, **brave, bold, daring**, like Lavender
Among Matilda's new-found friends was the girl called Lavender . . . Matilda liked her because she was gutsy and adventurous. — MATILDA

OR: **bright, clever, curious, inquisitive**, like Matilda

OR: **well behaved, modest, thoughtful, loyal**, like Charlie

OR: **silly, vain, selfish, bored**, like Veruca Salt

OR: **naughty, disobedient, thoughtless, greedy**, like Augustus Gloop
'Well, well, well,' sighed Mr Willy Wonka, 'two naughty little children gone . . . I think we'd better get out of this room quickly before we lose anyone else!' — CHARLIE AND THE CHOCOLATE FACTORY

• If you **get up to mischief** (say *miss*-chiff) you do things that grown-ups think are silly or naughty but are probably a lot of fun—and if you do this A LOT you are **mischievous**. (PLEASE NOTE: grown-ups can be **mischievous** too, especially grandmas and **Oompa-Loompas**.)
George's mother said to George on Saturday morning, 'So be a good boy and don't get up to mischief.' This was a silly thing to say to a small boy at any time. — GEORGE'S MARVELLOUS MEDICINE

• A **chiddler** who is perfectly well behaved is **angelic** or **exemplary**: *Hortensia had never wanted to be angelic.*

• A **chiddler** who is **spoiled** has Very Silly parents who give them too much of everything: *Veruca Salt is as spoiled as an over-ripe banana.*

DID YOU KNOW?
The word **naughty** originally meant 'very poor' and **silly** originally meant 'blessed or holy'.

• Informal words for a **chiddler** are **youngster**, **kid** and **nipper**.
'Well, I'll be jiggered! I never would 'ave thought a little nipper like you could come up with such a fantastical brain-wave as that!' — DANNY THE CHAMPION OF THE WORLD

• A very young **chiddler** is an **infant** and one who is just learning to walk is a **toddler**.

WARNING: Note that **Wonka-Vite** can turn grown-ups into **chiddlers** if they take too many doses.
'The Wonka-Vite worked perfectly! She is now precisely three months old! And a plumper rosier infant I've never set eyes on!' — CHARLIE AND THE GREAT GLASS ELEVATOR

• A **chiddler** like Charlie who has no brothers or sisters is an **only child**. A **chiddler** like Sophie who has no parents is an **orphan** or **norphan**.

DID YOU KNOW?
The word **chiddler** sounds a bit like **childer**, an old dialect word for 'children'.

DID YOU KNOW?
The word **infant** comes from a Latin word meaning 'unable to speak', because babies are too young to talk.

WHAT DO CHIDDLERS DO?

YOU MIGHT: **make friends** with a giant, a giraffe or **gigantuous** insects. A friend that you play with is a **playmate**.

And James Henry Trotter, who once . . . had been the saddest and loneliest little boy that you could find, now had all the friends and playmates in the world.
— JAMES AND THE GIANT PEACH

YOU MIGHT: **go exploring** outdoors or have a **buckswashling adventure**

He had made it! He had got there! And now the forest was all his to explore!
— THE MINPINS

YOU MIGHT: **climb a tree** or **build a tree-house** or **hide some treasure**

This, we decided, would be our secret hiding place for sweets and other small treasures such as conkers and monkey-nuts and birds' eggs. — BOY

YOU MIGHT: **keep a pet** or **start a collection** of Interesting Things

'I think the next thing I must get Should be a most peculiar pet The kind that no one else has got—A giant ANT-EATER! Why not?' — DIRTY BEASTS

YOU MIGHT: **ride a bicycle** or **tricycle** or **bounce on a trampoline**

James began thinking about all the other children in the world and what they might be doing at this moment. Some would be riding tricycles in their gardens.
— JAMES AND THE GIANT PEACH

YOU MIGHT: **walk on stilts** or **slide down a banister** (**extra-usual** grown-ups like Willy Wonka do this too)

They came to a long flight of stairs. Mr Wonka slid down the banisters. The three children did the same. — CHARLIE AND THE CHOCOLATE FACTORY

YOU MIGHT: **invite** friends to your **birthday party** and **blow out the candles** on your cake

'Let's have a party this time, Danny. We can write out invitations and I'll go into the village and buy chocolate éclairs and doughnuts and a huge birthday cake with candles on it.' — DANNY THE CHAMPION OF THE WORLD

YOU MIGHT: **keep a secret** or **share it** with friends

No child has ever had such an exciting young life as Little Billy, and no child has ever kept such a huge secret so faithfully. — THE MINPINS

FIND OUT MORE!
You can **play** at the seaside too! Find out more in ALL ABOUT THE SEA in THE NATURAL WORLD.

YOU MIGHT: **read a book** or **borrow** one from a library. Someone who loves to read books as much as Matilda is a **bookworm** or **bibliophile**.

'I'm wondering what to read next,' Matilda said. 'I've finished all the children's books.' — MATILDA

YOU MIGHT: **use your brain-power** to **teach a lesson** to silly grown-ups

Matilda's wonderfully subtle mind was already at work devising yet another suitable punishment for the poisonous parent. — MATILDA

YOU MIGHT: **watch television** (if you must) like Mike Teavee—but it could **turn your brain to mush**

The nine-year-old boy was seated before an enormous television set, with his eyes glued to the screen. — CHARLIE AND THE CHOCOLATE FACTORY

YOU MIGHT: **have a bath** (but not too often, as witches can sniff you if you are too clean)

'I shall never have a bath again,' I said. 'Just don't have one too often,' my grandmother said. 'Once a month is quite enough for a sensible child.' — THE WITCHES

YOU MIGHT: **stay up to the witching hour** like Sophie, to see if magic happens

have a buckswashling adventure

PLAYING GAMES

YOU MIGHT PLAY: conkers, hide-and-seek
(or hide-and-sneak), hopscotch,
marbles, snakes and ladders,
tiddlywinks

*Never once, even on her
best days, had she smiled
at George and said, 'Well,
how are you this morning,
George?' or 'Why don't you
and I have a game of Snakes
and Ladders?'* – GEORGE'S
MARVELLOUS MEDICINE

DID YOU KNOW?
The word **conker** was originally a dialect word for 'snail shell', because the game of **conkers** was first played with snail shells.

YOU MIGHT: blow up a balloon or
fly a kite or make a fire-balloon like Danny
*'You can fly the kite all by yourself any time you like,'
my father said. 'But you must never fly the fire-balloon
unless I'm with you.'* – DANNY THE CHAMPION OF THE WORLD

YOU MIGHT PLAY WITH: ball, boomerang, catapult,
compass, doll, kaleidoscope, magnet,
puppet, toboggan, toy car, yo-yo

*A tuck-box would also
contain all manner of
treasures such as a
magnet, a pocket-knife,
a compass, a ball of string,
a clockwork racing-car,
half-a-dozen lead soldiers,
a box of conjuring-tricks,
some tiddly-winks, a
Mexican jumping bean,
a catapult, some foreign
stamps, a couple of
stink-bombs.* – BOY

DID YOU KNOW?
A **catapult** was originally a large war machine used by the ancient Greeks and Romans to fire darts or hurl stones at the enemy.

• If you feel **hopscotchy** you feel happy and excited, as
if you are playing a game of **hopscotch**. If you **leapfrog**
over something, it means that you leap or vault over it,
as in a game of **leapfrog**.

YOU MIGHT: ride on a **roundabout**, **slide down a chute**,
or play on a **see-saw** or **swings** at a **fair** or **playground**

BEWARE: A crocodile might **masquerade** as a
see-saw before gobbling you up.
*The Enormous Crocodile
found a large piece of wood and placed
it in the middle of the playground.
Then he lay across the piece of
wood and tucked in his feet
so that he looked almost
exactly like a see-saw.*
– THE ENORMOUS
CROCODILE

• If you enjoy playing
team games or **sports**, like
running, football and cricket, you
are **athletic** or **sporty**: *Agatha Trunchbull
had been very sporty in her youth.*

GOING TO SCHOOL

• When you are at school, you are
a **pupil** or **school-chiddler** and
the other pupils in your class
are your **classmates**: *Matilda
is popular with all of her
classmates.*

FIND OUT MORE!
Why is the centre of your eye called a **pupil**? Find out in DESCRIBING FACES.

YOU MIGHT SEE: **classroom**,
corridor, **blackboard**, **chalk**
(sometimes writing by itself), **desks**,
jug of water (with or without a newt)
*Nigel, at the other end of the room, jumped to his
feet and started pointing excitedly at the blackboard
and screaming, 'The chalk! The chalk! Look at
the chalk!'* – MATILDA

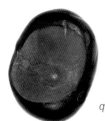

YOU MIGHT BRING: pencil, sharpener, pencil-box or pencil-case (for pencils and amphibians), exercise book or jotter, schoolbag or satchel

Quick as a flash, Lavender got her pencil-box from her satchel and slid open the lid just a tiny bit. The newt was lying quite still. — MATILDA

YOU MIGHT: have lessons or do homework (unless you happen to have been turned into a mouse)

'No more school!' said Bruno, grinning a broad and asinine mouse-grin. 'No more homework! I shall live in the kitchen cupboard and feast on raisins and honey!' — THE WITCHES

YOU MIGHT LEARN: spelling, maths or sums, times table or multiplication table (both backwards and forthwards)

'Recite the three-times table backwards!' the Trunchbull barked. 'Backwards?' stammered Wilfred. 'But I haven't learnt it backwards.' — MATILDA

YOU MIGHT: recite a poem or write a limerick—or do both, like Matilda

'I insist upon hearing this limerick,' Miss Honey said, smiling one of her rare smiles. 'Stand up and recite it.' — MATILDA

YOU MIGHT: wear a uniform or put on a gym kit. Miss Trunchbull wears old-fashioned gym knickers which she keeps in a special drawer.

YOU MIGHT: play games in a gym or on a playing-field or put on a school play or concert

Games-playing at school is always fun if you happen to be good at it, and it is hell if you are not. — BOY

YOU MIGHT: stay off school if you are sick or unwell, or see a nurse or matron

'What's the matter with you?' the Matron shouted, and the sheer force of her voice caused that massive bosom to quiver like a gigantic blancmange. — BOY

• The time during the year when you are at school is **term-time** and the weeks at the end of the school year are the **summer holidays**.

The summer holidays! Those magic words! The mere mention of them used to send shivers of joy rippling over my skin. — BOY

• You might get a **report** at the **end of term** to say how well (or not) you are doing at school.

School teachers suffer a good deal from having to listen to this sort of twaddle from proud parents, but they usually get their own back when the time comes to write the end-of-term reports. — MATILDA

• A **boarding-school** is a school where the pupils live away from home. A room with lots of beds where pupils sleep in a boarding-school is a **dormitory**.

Unless you have been to boarding-school when you are very young, it is absolutely impossible to appreciate the delights of living at home. — BOY

• Very young **school-chiddlers** go to a **nursery school** or **kindergarten**. (PLEASE NOTE: only human **chiddlers** go to school, as there are no schools in Giant Country.)

'There never was any schools to teach me talking in Giant Country,' the BFG said sadly. — THE BFG

THINGS THAT MIGHT GET YOU INTO TROUBLE

INCLUDE: sneaking a newt into class, setting off a stink-bomb, sprinkling itching-powder in the headmistress's gym knickers or pouring syrup on the seat of her chair

'I had sent away by post, you see, for this very powerful itching-powder,' Hortensia said. 'It cost fifty pence a packet and was called The Skin-Scorcher.' — MATILDA

WARNING: At a school like **Crunchem Hall**, such behaviour is Very Risky and might lead to you being put in the **Chokey**.

'And the Trunchbull put you in The Chokey for a whole day?' Matilda asked, gulping. 'All day long,' Hortensia said. 'I was off my rocker when she let me out.' — MATILDA

• You might get **found out** by a teacher, or might **own up** or **confess** yourself. Someone might **tell** or **sneak on** you to get you into trouble. (PLEASE NOTE: anyone who **tells on** Hortensia will come to a Very Sticky End.)

'But how did she know it was you?' Lavender asked. 'A little squirt called Ollie Bogwhistle sneaked on me,' Hortensia said. 'I knocked his front teeth out.' — MATILDA

THINGS THAT WON'T GET YOU INTO TROUBLE

INCLUDE: eating Wonka's Invisible Chocolate Bars or sucking a Sugar-Coated Pencil, using telekinetic powers (so long as no one can tell it is you)

'Who did it?' she roared. 'Come on! Own up! Step forward! You won't escape this time! Who is responsible for this dirty job? Who pushed over this glass?' Nobody answered. — MATILDA

DID YOU KNOW?
The word **dormitory** comes from Latin and means 'a sleeping place'—and **lavatory** means 'a washing place'.

ALL ABOUT GROWN-UPS

DESCRIBING AGE

• Another word for a grown-up is an **adult**. Grown-ups like Mrs Silver, who are neither young nor old, are **middle-aged**.
The balcony immediately below Mr Hoppy's . . . belonged to an attractive middle-aged lady called Mrs Silver. — ESIO TROT

• Charlie's grandparents are **old aged** or **elderly**. Someone who is as old as a witch or giant is **ancient**.
'You ancient vuns have served me vell over many years . . . and I do not vish to deny you the pleasure of bumping off a few thousand children each just because you have become old and feeble.' — THE WITCHES

• A very old tree or building can be **ancient** too, and an old object or furniture is **historical** or **antique**: *The BFG lived in an ancient cave.*

• An **elderly** grown-up might be **frail** and **feeble**, with **aches and pains**—but they will feel **frisky as a ferret** after taking Wonka-Vite or George's medicine. Grandpa Joe also feels **younger** or **rejuvenated** when he is with Charlie.
In a way, the medicine had done Grandma good. It . . . seemed to have cured all her aches and pains, and she was suddenly as frisky as a ferret. — GEORGE'S MARVELLOUS MEDICINE

• If you take too much Vita-Wonk you will **age** rapidly and end up **wrinkly** or **wizened**, like Grandma Georgina.

• Before she takes Wonka-Vite, Grandma Georgina is a **septuagenarian** (between 70 and 79 years old) and Grandpa Joe is a **nonagenarian** (between 90 and 99).

• A grown-up who looks or acts like a younger person is **youthful** and a young person who acts like a grown-up is **mature**.
A grown-up who acts in a silly and selfish way is said to be **childish** or **juvenile** (although they are usually being far sillier than **chiddlers**).

MEMBERS OF A FAMILY

INCLUDE: **brother, sister, cousin, parents, mother** or **mum, father** or **dad, aunt** or **auntie, uncle, grandfather, granddad** or **grandpa, grandmother, grandma** or **granny**
Grandpa Joe was the oldest of the four grandparents. He was ninety-six and a half, and that is just about as old as anybody can be. — CHARLIE AND THE CHOCOLATE FACTORY

• The people who belong to your family are your **relations** or **relatives**.
'Didn't you have any other relations?' Matilda asked. 'Any uncles or aunts or grannies who would come and see you?' — MATILDA

• Another word for a **brother** or a **sister** is a **sibling**. An older brother or sister is an **elder** sibling and the oldest child in a family is the **eldest**: *Matilda has an elder brother who is just like her dad.*

• A woman like Mrs Silver whose husband has died is a **widow**.
Mrs Silver was a widow who also lived alone. And although she didn't know it, it was she who was the object of Mr Hoppy's secret love. — ESIO TROT

• Words that mean 'like a mother' and 'like a father' are **maternal** and **paternal**. A formal word meaning 'kindly, like an uncle' is **avuncular**: *The BFG is a gentle avuncular creature.*

DID YOU KNOW?
Roald Dahl called his Norwegian grandparents *Bestemama* and *Bestepapa*, which are Norwegian words for 'grandma' and 'grandpa.'

In Shakespeare's time, the word *nuncle* was used as a short form of *mine uncle.*

DID YOU KNOW?
An old word for a **wrinkle** is a **frumple.**

FIND OUT MORE!
There are more words for **wrinkles** and **creases** in DESCRIBING FACES.

septuagenarian

rejuvenate

elderly

JOBS FOR GROWN-UPS

INCLUDE: astronaut, chef or cook, chocolatier or confectioner, doctor, farmer, fireman or firefighter, gardener, inventor, lexicographer, librarian, mechanic, nurse, pilot, policeman or police officer, scientist, shopkeeper, sweet-shop owner, teacher, waiter or waitress, window-cleaner, writer

• PLEASE NOTE: monkeys, pelicans and giraffes make far better **window-cleaners** than **human beans**.
'We are the Window-Cleaners!' sang out the Monkey. 'We will polish your glass Till it's shining like brass And it sparkles like sun on the sea!' – THE GIRAFFE AND THE PELLY AND ME

• People who work in a **factory**, like the **Oompa-Loompas**, are **factory workers**. Someone like Mr Bucket who works long hours is **hard-working**.
Mr Bucket . . . worked in a toothpaste factory, where he sat all day long at a bench and screwed the little caps on to the tops of the tubes of toothpaste after the tubes had been filled. – CHARLIE AND THE CHOCOLATE FACTORY

• Someone with a **part-time** job, like Mrs Silver, works only part of the day or week, and someone like Mr Hoppy, who is old enough to stop working for a living, is **retired**.
Mrs Silver had a part-time job. She worked from noon until five o'clock every weekday afternoon in a shop that sold newspapers and sweets. – ESIO TROT

• The person in charge of a company is the **head** or **boss**. The head of a school is a **headmistress**, **headmaster** or **head teacher**.
The head teacher, the boss, the supreme commander of this establishment, was a formidable middle-aged lady whose name was Miss Trunchbull. – MATILDA

• The head of a whole country is a **prime minister** or **president** and the head of a town or city is a **mayor**.
Everyone who had come over on the peach was a hero! They were all escorted to the steps of City Hall, where the Mayor of New York made a speech of welcome. – JAMES AND THE GIANT PEACH

• Other words for a job are **profession** and **career**.
'I have discovered, Miss Honey, during my long career as a teacher that a bad girl is a far more dangerous creature than a bad boy.' – MATILDA

OTHER THINGS THAT GROWN-UPS DO

THEY MIGHT: go shopping or play bingo, like Mrs Wormwood
Nearly every weekday afternoon Matilda was left alone in the house . . . Her father went to work and her mother went out playing bingo in a town eight miles away.
– MATILDA

THEY MIGHT: do some knitting or read a newspaper, like the Jenkinses, or watch television all evening, like the Wormwoods
The Jenkinses were the only couple sitting alone. Mr Jenkins was reading a newspaper. Mrs Jenkins was knitting something large and mustard-coloured.
– THE WITCHES

THEY MIGHT: fall in love and live happily ever after, like Mr Hoppy and Mrs Silver, or get on each other's nerves like Mr and Mrs Twit

THEY MIGHT: make rules that are asinine, baffling, biffsquiggling, nonsensical or propsposterous
But the fact remained that any five-year-old girl in any family was always obliged to do as she was told, however asinine the orders might be. – MATILDA

DID YOU KNOW?
The word **asinine** (say **ass**-i-nine) means 'very stupid' and comes from the Latin word for a donkey or ass, because asses were thought to be stupid and stubborn animals (rather like some grown-ups).

DESCRIBING FACES

WHAT DO FACES LOOK LIKE?

THEY CAN BE: craggy, crinkly, crumpled, gnarled, wizened, wrinkly

That face of hers was the most frightful and frightening thing I have ever seen. . . . It was so crumpled and wizened, so shrunken and shrivelled, it looked as though it had been pickled in vinegar. — THE WITCHES

THEY CAN BE: blotched, chubby, flabby, pasty, pimply or spotty, podgy, puffy, warty

Aunt Sponge . . . had small piggy eyes, a sunken mouth, and one of those white flabby faces that looked exactly as though it had been boiled. — JAMES AND THE GIANT PEACH

THEY CAN BE: gaunt, haggard, hollow, pinched

And every day, Charlie Bucket grew thinner and thinner. His face became frighteningly white and pinched. The skin was drawn so tightly over the cheeks that you could see the shapes of the bones underneath. — CHARLIE AND THE CHOCOLATE FACTORY

THEY CAN BE: hairy, bearded, bristly, nailbrushy

And how often did Mr Twit wash this bristly nailbrushy face of his? The answer is NEVER, not even on Sundays. — THE TWITS

DID YOU KNOW?
Roald Dahl invented the idea of **spotty powder** (which makes you come out in spots so that you can miss school) for an early version of *Charlie and the Chocolate Factory.*

THEY CAN HAVE: blotches, spots, pimple, wart, creases, lines, scar, wrinkles, freckles, facial hair

Her tiny face was like a pickled walnut. There were such masses of creases and wrinkles that the mouth and eyes and even the nose were sunken almost out of sight. — CHARLIE AND THE GREAT GLASS ELEVATOR

HAIRY FACES

CAN HAVE: beard, bristles or spikes, bushy eyebrows, moustache, whiskers, tufts

Mr Twit was one of these very hairy-faced men. The whole of his face except for his forehead, his eyes and his nose was covered with thick hair. The stuff even sprouted in revolting tufts out of his nostrils and ear-holes. — THE TWITS

- A formal word meaning 'very hairy' is **hirsute**: *Mr Twit is exceedingly hirsute.*

- A face that is not hairy at all is **unhairy** or **clean-shaven**.
  As you know, an ordinary unhairy face like yours or mine simply gets a bit smudgy if it is not washed often enough, and there's nothing so awful about that. But a hairy face is a very different matter. — THE TWITS

FIND OUT MORE! Mice and foxes have **whiskers** too! Find out more in ALL ABOUT ANIMALS in THE NATURAL WORLD.

pasty puffy podgy blotched chubby warty flabby spotty

bristles bushy whiskers spikes tufts drooping pointed straggly

DID YOU KNOW?
The word **hirsute** comes from a Latin word meaning 'rough or shaggy'.

Roald Dahl had **pogonophobia**, which means 'a strong dislike of beards'.

BEARDS AND MOUSTACHES

CAN BE: bushy, clipped, drooping or droopy, pointed, straggly

The driver was an oldish man with a thick black drooping moustache. The moustache hung over his mouth like the roots of some plant. — THE WITCHES

• Willy Wonka has a short pointed beard called a **goatee** beard.

• You can **clip** or **trim** a beard or moustache to keep it neat. A beard that is never trimmed, like Mr Twit's, is **unkempt**.

• You can **stroke** a beard thoughtfully, or **twirl** a moustache around your finger.
'Well,' said Mr Wonka, stroking his beard and gazing thoughtfully at the ceiling, 'I must say that's a wee bit trickly.' — CHARLIE AND THE CHOCOLATE FACTORY

WHAT CAN FACES DO?

THEY CAN: beam, glow or light up with happiness
James's little face was glowing with excitement, his eyes were as big and bright as two stars. — JAMES AND THE GIANT PEACH

THEY CAN: flush or blush with embarrassment, or turn red, purple or lava-coloured with rage
The Trunchbull stood motionless on the platform. Her great horsy face had turned the colour of molten lava and her eyes were glittering with fury. — MATILDA

THEY CAN: frown with anger or puzzlement, or grimace, wince or scrunch up with pain

THEY CAN: turn blue with cold, or white with fear.
The Ladderless Window-Cleaners work so hard they **go blue in the face** (or **blue in the beak**).
'We will polish your glass Till it's shining like brass And it sparkles like sun on the sea! We will work for Your Grace Till we're blue in the face, The Giraffe and the Pelly and me!' — THE GIRAFFE AND THE PELLY AND ME

• When you **keep a straight face** you try Really Hard not to laugh (especially at the Queen).
'What does he mean?' the Queen said, frowning at Sophie. 'What is whizzpopping?' Sophie kept a very straight face. — THE BFG

FACIAL EXPRESSIONS

CAN BE: cheerful, radiant, smiling, sunny

OR CAN BE: grave, grim, serious, sulky, sullen

• An expression can also be **frozen** in shock or surprise.
The sheet-white faces of Shuckworth, Shanks and Showler were pressed against the glass of the little windows, terror-struck, stupefied, stunned, their mouths open, their expressions frozen like fish fingers. — CHARLIE AND THE GREAT GLASS ELEVATOR

• A face with no expression is **blank**, **expressionless** or **vacant**.
Mr Wonka had not moved. He was still gazing straight ahead, still quite cool, perfectly expressionless. — CHARLIE AND THE GREAT GLASS ELEVATOR

FACIAL FEATURES

• **Cheeks** can be: **chubby**, **flushed**, **rosy**, or **hollow** and **sunken**.
I could just make out his face under the peak of his cap, the lips pale, the cheeks flushed, the eyes shining bright. — DANNY THE CHAMPION OF THE WORLD

• **Chins** and **jaws** can be: **square-set** or **chiselled**. A **double chin** has a fold of flesh underneath it.
You can have a wonky nose and a crooked mouth and a double chin and stick-out teeth, but if you have good thoughts they will shine out of your face like sunbeams and you will always look lovely. — THE TWITS

• The faces of **Cloud-Men** are **shapeless** and almost **featureless**, apart from their eyes.
There were no noses, no mouths, no ears, no chins—only the eyes were visible in each face, two small black eyes glinting malevolently through the hairs. — JAMES AND THE GIANT PEACH

• **Vermicious Knids** have an **ovoid** face with only one **facial feature**: their eyes. Their entire body is their face.

ovoid

EARS

CAN: **stick out** or **protrude**, **flap**, **wave**, **wiggle** or **swiggle** back and forth. In extreme situations (as when pulled by Miss Trunchbull) they can also **stretch**.
'Ears never come off!' the Trunchbull shouted. 'They stretch most marvellously, like these are doing now, but I can assure you they never come off!' — MATILDA

CAN: **pick up** or **listen** to sounds, or **prick up** if they hear something interesting. The BFG has **extra-usually sensitive** ears which can hear far more than **human-beaney** ears.

• If you are **all ears**, it means that you are listening very carefully, but if you **stick your fingers in your ears** then you are trying NOT to listen to someone (such as a droning grown-up).
I was all ears now. I edged a bit further round the garbage-bin so that I could see everything that was going on in the kitchen. — THE WITCHES

NOSES

CAN BE: **bulbous**, **crooked**, **hooked**, **pointed**, **shapely**, **wonky**
'I look and smell,' Aunt Sponge declared, 'as lovely as a rose! Just feast your eyes upon my face, observe my shapely nose!' — JAMES AND THE GIANT PEACH

FIND OUT MORE!
Witches have extra-usual nostrils! Find out more in ALL ABOUT WITCHES in THE MAGICAL WORLD.

• A **button nose** is small and roundish, and a **snub nose** is short and with a turned-up end.

• You can **blow** or **pick** or **wipe** your nose, or **breathe**, **sneeze**, **snore** or **snort** through it. If you have a cold your nose might be **runny**.
'We may see a Creature with forty-nine heads Who lives in the desolate snow, And whenever he catches a cold (which he dreads) He has forty-nine noses to blow. — JAMES AND THE GIANT PEACH

• The two openings in your nose are your **nostrils**. A word meaning 'to do with your nose' is **nasal**:
Tufts of nasal hair tickled Mr Twit's nostrils.

MOUTHS AND LIPS

CAN BE: **pursed** or **puckered**, **thin**, **tight-lipped**
George couldn't help disliking Grandma. She was a selfish grumpy old woman. She had pale brown teeth and a small puckered-up mouth like a dog's bottom. — GEORGE'S MARVELLOUS MEDICINE

• You can **purse**, **pucker** or **press** your lips together. Mouths can also **open wide** in amazement or **clamp shut** in silence—or sometimes both.
The woman's face had turned white as snow and her mouth was opening and shutting like a halibut out of water and giving out a series of strangled gasps. — MATILDA

• If someone **licks their lips**, it means they are looking forward to tasting something **delumptious**.
'A big fat earwig is very tasty,' Grandma said, licking her lips. 'But you've got to be very quick, my dear, when you put one of those in your mouth.' — GEORGE'S MARVELLOUS MEDICINE

DID YOU KNOW?
The word **earwig** means 'ear insect', because people used to believe that earwigs crawled into their ears.

EYES

CAN BE: **beady, curranty, piercing, piggy, steely, twinkly**
Mr Hazell did not look at him. He sat quite still in the seat of his Rolls-Royce, his tiny piggy eyes staring straight ahead.
— DANNY THE CHAMPION OF THE WORLD

OR CAN BE: **bulbous, bulging, protuberant, saucer-like**

OR CAN BE: **deep-set, glassy** or **glazed, moist, sunken, tearful, watery**
Captain Lancaster sat up front at his desk, gazing suspiciously round the class with his watery-blue eyes.
— DANNY THE CHAMPION OF THE WORLD

• If someone is **sharp-eyed** or has **sharp eyes**, like **Mr Fox**, they have very good eyesight.
Just then, his sharp night-eyes caught a glint of something bright behind a tree not far away. It was a small silver speck of moonlight shining on a polished surface. — FANTASTIC MR FOX

blaze flash bulge stare pop out of their sockets twinkle glitter sparkle

• The dark circular opening in your eye is called the **pupil**. **Vermicious Knids** have bright red pupils in their fearsome eyes.
About three-quarters of the way up, in the widest part, there were two large round eyes as big as tea-cups. The eyes were white, but each had a brilliant red pupil in the centre. — CHARLIE AND THE GREAT GLASS ELEVATOR

• The ball of your eye is the **eyeball**. Mrs Twit has an artificial **glass eye** which she uses to scare Mr Twit.
You can play a lot of tricks with a glass eye because you can take it out and pop it back in again any time you like. You can bet your life Mrs Twit knew all the tricks. — THE TWITS

WHAT CAN EYES DO?

THEY CAN: **glitter, shine, sparkle** or **twinkle** with excitement or glee
His eyes were most marvellously bright. They seemed to be sparkling and twinkling at you all the time. The whole face, in fact, was alight with fun and laughter. — CHARLIE AND THE CHOCOLATE FACTORY

THEY CAN: **stare** or **widen** in amazement, or **bulge** or **pop out of their sockets** with surprise
'Stop!' Aunt Spiker said quickly. 'Hold everything!' She was staring up into the branches with her mouth wide open and her eyes bulging as though she had seen a ghost. — JAMES AND THE GIANT PEACH

THEY CAN: **blaze** or **flash** with anger, or even **shoot sparks** like Matilda's super-powered eyes
She felt the electricity beginning to flow inside her head, gathering itself behind the eyes, and the eyes became hot and millions of tiny invisible hands began pushing out like sparks towards the cigar. — MATILDA

FIND OUT MORE!
Find out how **eyes** can see in ALL ABOUT LOOKING, and how **ears** can hear in ALL ABOUT SOUNDS.

DID YOU KNOW?
The word **pupil** comes from a Latin word meaning 'little girl or doll' because of the tiny images you can see reflected in them.

THEY CAN: **sting, smart** or **water,** or **well up** with tears
The wind stung Sophie's cheeks. It made her eyes water. It whipped her head back and whistled in her ears. — THE BFG

THEY CAN: **blink** or **wink**. If someone **does not bat an eyelid**, it means they do not care about something.
A minute later, they were out in the open, standing on the very top of the peach, near the stem, blinking their eyes in the strong sunlight and peering nervously around. — JAMES AND THE GIANT PEACH

• Your **eyelids** can also **droop** or **flicker**.
The small girl smiles. One eyelid flickers. She whips a pistol from her knickers. She aims it at the creature's head And bang bang bang, she shoots him dead. — REVOLTING RHYMES

• If you are surprised or alarmed, you might **raise your eyebrows**.
He saw the Giraffe, the Pelly, the Monkey and me all staring down at him from above, but not a muscle moved in his face, not an eyebrow was raised. — THE GIRAFFE AND THE PELLY AND ME

ALL ABOUT BODIES

DESCRIBING BODIES

• The shape of your body is your **build**, **figure** or **physique** (say fi-*zeek*).

A formidable figure she was too, in her belted smock and green breeches. Below the knees her calf muscles stood out like grapefruits inside her stockings. — MATILDA

• Tall bodies can be **lanky**, **lofty** or **towering** like the BFG.

• Thin bodies can be **bony**, **gaunt**, **scrawny**, **skinny** or **wiry**. Thin arms or legs are **spindly**.

It was a truly fantastic sight, this ancient scrawny old woman getting taller and taller, longer and longer, thinner and thinner, as though she were a piece of elastic being pulled upwards by invisible hands. — GEORGE'S MARVELLOUS MEDICINE

• Old bodies can be **saggy**, **scraggy**, **shrivelled** or **wrinkly** like Charlie's grandparents.

Every one of these old people was over ninety. They were as shrivelled as prunes, and as bony as skeletons. — CHARLIE AND THE CHOCOLATE FACTORY

• Small bodies can be: **petite**, **slender** and **slim**, or **dumpy**, **squat** and **stocky**.

And behold, within half a minute, another twenty years had fallen away from his face and body and he was now a slim and sprightly young Oompa-Loompa of thirty. — CHARLIE AND THE GREAT GLASS ELEVATOR

• Strong bodies can be **beefy**, **burly**, **brawny**, **hulking** or **muscular**: *Miss Trunchbull has a muscular physique.*

• Fat bodies can be **chubby**, **flabby**, **plump**, **portly**, **stout** or **thickset**. Someone like Farmer Bunce, with a stomach that sticks out, is **pot-bellied**.

The tall skinny Bean and dwarfish pot-bellied Bunce were driving their machines like maniacs, racing the motors and making the shovels dig at a terrific speed. — FANTASTIC MR FOX

• Folds of fat can **bulge** or **sag** and muscles can **ripple**. Giants' stomachs also **bulge** after a night of hunting **human beans**.

Great flabby folds of fat bulged out from every part of his body, and his face was like a monstrous ball of dough with two small greedy curranty eyes peering out upon the world. — CHARLIE AND THE CHOCOLATE FACTORY

BODY PARTS

• The main part of your body, except your head, arms and legs, is your **trunk** or **torso**:
The giant had a humungously hairy torso.

• Another word for a stomach is a **belly** and an informal word is **tummy**.
Mrs Twit . . . lay there in the dark scratching her tummy. Her tummy was itching. Dirty old hags like her always have itchy tummies. — THE TWITS

• The insides of your stomach are your **guts** and the inside of your throat is your **gullet**. If you say someone **has guts** it means that they are very brave.
The Queen went absolutely wild. She yelled, 'I'm going to scrag that child! I'll cook her flaming goose! I'll skin'er! I'll have her rotten guts for dinner!' — REVOLTING RHYMES

• Another word for a woman's breasts is her **bosom** (say *boo*-zum).
The Trunchbull, her face more like a boiled ham than ever, was standing before the class quivering with fury. Her massive bosom was heaving in and out. — MATILDA

hulking muscular

burly brawny

beefy burly

- Your arms and legs are your **limbs**, and your fingers, thumbs and toes are your **digits**.

- The back part of your foot is the **heel** and the part where your foot joins your leg is your **ankle**. Miss Trunchbull likes to dangle pupils by their ears or ankles.
'Eight threes,' the Trunchbull shouted, swinging Wilfred from side to side by his ankle, 'eight threes is the same as three eights and three eights are twenty-four!' – MATILDA

- If you **pull someone's leg**, it means that you are joking or teasing them.
'Walnuts!' screamed the Monkey. 'Not walnuts? You don't really mean walnuts? You're pulling my leg! You're joking!' – THE GIRAFFE AND THE PELLY AND ME

DID YOU KNOW?
The word **digit** comes from the Latin word for a finger or toe. It later came to mean 'a number' because people used their fingers and toes for counting.

DID YOU KNOW?
Someone who can twist and bend their body like a human **Vermicious Knid** is called a **contortionist**.

WHAT CAN BODIES DO?

THEY CAN: **sprout** upwards when they grow, or **shrink** downwards with **The Dreaded Shrinks**
As soon as Mrs Twit sat down, Mr Twit pointed at her and shouted, 'There you are! You're sitting in your old chair and you've shrunk so much your feet aren't even touching the ground!' – THE TWITS

THEY CAN: **sweat** in the heat or break into a **cold sweat** with fear. Sweat can **run** or **trickle** down your skin.
I could feel a trickle of cold sweat running down one side of my forehead and across my cheek. I didn't dare lift a hand to wipe it away. – DANNY THE CHAMPION OF THE WORLD

bony gaunt skinny wiry

THEY CAN:
shiver or **tingle** with cold or excitement, or **quiver** or **tremble** with fear
And then all at once, little shivers of excitement started running over the skin on James's back. – JAMES AND THE GIANT PEACH

THEY CAN: **ache, throb** or **wince** with pain
'Oh, wouldn't it be wonderful,' said Mrs Bucket, 'to be twenty years younger and not have aching feet any more!' – CHARLIE AND THE GREAT GLASS ELEVATOR

THEY CAN: **crouch** or **squat down, curl up** or **stretch out**. You can also **crane** your neck forwards or upwards.
Charlie and Grandpa Joe both craned their necks to read what it said on the little label beside the button. – CHARLIE AND THE CHOCOLATE FACTORY

THEY CAN: **bend, curve, twist** or go into **contortions**, like the **elastic** body of a **Vermicious Knid**
Then the three remaining creatures began stretching themselves all at the same time, each one elongating itself slowly upward, growing taller and taller, thinner and thinner, curving and twisting, stretching and stretching, curling and bending. – CHARLIE AND THE GREAT GLASS ELEVATOR

THEY CAN: **flip, jerk** or **turn somersaults** in the air, like George's grandma
Grandma's body gave a sudden sharp twist and a sudden sharp jerk and she flipped herself clear out of the chair and landed neatly on her two feet on the carpet. – GEORGE'S MARVELLOUS MEDICINE

FIND OUT MORE!
Bodies can also **zippfizz** along! Find out more in DESCRIBING MOVEMENT.

- Your limbs can **flail, thrash, wave** or **writhe** about, like giants having a **rumpledumpus**.
One of the Fleshlumpeater's flailing fists caught the still-fast-asleep Meatdripping Giant smack in the mouth. At the same time, one of his furiously thrashing legs kicked the snoring Gizzardgulping Giant right in the guts. – THE BFG

- You can also **stand on your toes, balance on one leg**, or **stand on your head** like Mr and Mrs Twit.
'I've got it!' cried Mr Twit. 'I know what we'll do! We'll stand on our heads, then anyway we'll be the right way up!' – THE TWITS

WHAT CAN HANDS AND FEET DO?

THEY CAN: **stretch** out or **reach** up or down
Suddenly, Mr Wonka . . . reached down into the bottom of the boat, picked up a large mug, dipped it into the river, filled it with chocolate, and handed it to Charlie. 'Drink this,' he said. — CHARLIE AND THE CHOCOLATE FACTORY

THEY CAN: **grab**, **grabble**, **grasp**, **pick up** or **hold** onto something
'And I knows where there is a bogglebox for boys!' shouted the Gizzardgulper. 'All I has to do is reach in and grab myself a handful!' — THE BFG

THEY CAN: **touch**, **stroke** or **caress** gently. You can also **cup** your hands around something.
Charlie put out his hand and touched the screen, and suddenly, miraculously, the bar of chocolate came away in his fingers. — CHARLIE AND THE CHOCOLATE FACTORY

THEY CAN: **kick**, **punch**, **scratch**, **swipe** or **bungswoggle** wildly, like **squarreling** giants
'He is swiping me right in the mouth!' yelled the Meatdripper. 'He is bungswoggling me smack in the guts!' shouted the Gizzardgulper. — THE BFG

• Fingers can also **jab**, **poke** or **prod** roughly.
Mr Wonka jabbed a button. The doors closed and the Great Glass Elevator shot upwards for home. — CHARLIE AND THE GREAT GLASS ELEVATOR

• A **Magic Finger** will also **tingle** and **flash** like lightning with the power to make **extra-usual** things happen.
Then the tip of the forefinger of my right hand begins to tingle most terribly . . . And suddenly a sort of flash comes out of me, a quick flash, like something electric. — THE MAGIC FINGER

jab
flash
prod
tingle

DESCRIBING HAIR

IT CAN BE: **thick**, **flowing**, **glossy**, **shiny**, **silky** or **silken**

OR CAN BE: **thin**, **dry**, **stringy**, **wispy**

OR CAN BE: **greasy**, **matted**, **shaggy**, **straggly**, **tangled**
The Bloodbottler was a gruesome sight . . . There was black hair sprouting on his chest and arms and on his stomach. The hair on his head was long and dark and tangled. — THE BFG

• A single piece of hair is a **strand** and a bunch of hair is a **lock** or **tress**.
The Trunchbull . . . took a firm grip on Rupert's long golden tresses with her giant hand and then, by raising her muscular right arm, she lifted the helpless boy clean out of his chair and held him aloft. — MATILDA

• Hair can **grow** or **sprout** on your head (especially after taking **Hair Toffee**). A full amount of hair is a **crop**, **head** or **shock** of hair.
'That's Hair Toffee!' cried Mr Wonka. 'You eat just one tiny bit of that, and in exactly half an hour a brand-new luscious thick silky beautiful crop of hair will start growing out all over the top of your head!' — CHARLIE AND THE CHOCOLATE FACTORY

• Someone with no hair at all is **bald** or has a **bald scalp**. A covering of false hair is a **wig** or **toupee** (say *too*-pay).

FIND OUT MORE!
Why do witches wear **wigs**? Find out in ALL ABOUT WITCHES in THE MAGICAL WORLD.

• If someone tells you to **keep your hair on**, it means that you should calm down and not panic.
'Now now now now now!' said Mr Wonka . . . 'If everyone will keep their hair on and leave this to Charlie and me, we shall have them exactly where they used to be in the flick of a fly's wing!' — CHARLIE AND THE GREAT GLASS ELEVATOR

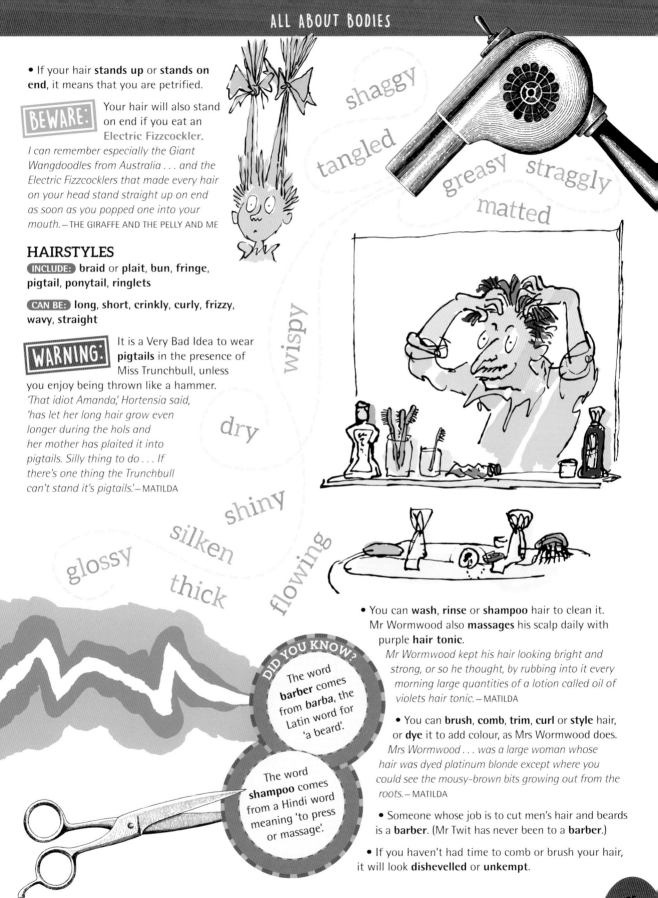

• If your hair **stands up** or **stands on end**, it means that you are petrified.

BEWARE: Your hair will also stand on end if you eat an **Electric Fizzcockler.**
I can remember especially the Giant Wangdoodles from Australia . . . and the Electric Fizzcocklers that made every hair on your head stand straight up on end as soon as you popped one into your mouth. — THE GIRAFFE AND THE PELLY AND ME

HAIRSTYLES

INCLUDE: **braid** or **plait**, **bun**, **fringe**, **pigtail**, **ponytail**, **ringlets**

CAN BE: **long**, **short**, **crinkly**, **curly**, **frizzy**, **wavy**, **straight**

WARNING: It is a Very Bad Idea to wear **pigtails** in the presence of Miss Trunchbull, unless you enjoy being thrown like a hammer.
'That idiot Amanda,' Hortensia said, 'has let her long hair grow even longer during the hols and her mother has plaited it into pigtails. Silly thing to do . . . If there's one thing the Trunchbull can't stand it's pigtails.' — MATILDA

shaggy
tangled
greasy straggly
matted
wispy
dry
shiny
silken
glossy
thick
flowing

• You can **wash**, **rinse** or **shampoo** hair to clean it. Mr Wormwood also **massages** his scalp daily with purple **hair tonic**.
Mr Wormwood kept his hair looking bright and strong, or so he thought, by rubbing into it every morning large quantities of a lotion called oil of violets hair tonic. — MATILDA

• You can **brush**, **comb**, **trim**, **curl** or **style** hair, or **dye** it to add colour, as Mrs Wormwood does.
Mrs Wormwood . . . was a large woman whose hair was dyed platinum blonde except where you could see the mousy-brown bits growing out from the roots. — MATILDA

• Someone whose job is to cut men's hair and beards is a **barber**. (Mr Twit has never been to a **barber**.)

• If you haven't had time to comb or brush your hair, it will look **dishevelled** or **unkempt**.

DID YOU KNOW?
The word **barber** comes from *barba*, the Latin word for 'a beard'.

The word **shampoo** comes from a Hindi word meaning 'to press or massage'.

25

• **Breeches** are short trousers that fit tightly at the knee. An **apron** or **overall** protects clothes from getting messy. (Miss Trunchbull prefers to wear an old-fashioned **smock** to cover her outlandish **breeches**.)

The massive thighs which emerged from out of the smock were encased in a pair of extraordinary breeches, bottle-green in colour and made of coarse twill. — MATILDA

• Other words for clothing are **attire**, **dress** and **garb**: *The Oompa-Loompas were wearing the strangest attire.*

• An item of clothing is a **garment** and a set of clothes that go together is an **outfit**. A style of clothes that **school-chiddlers** (and some grown-ups) wear is a **uniform**.

ALL ABOUT CLOTHES

CLOTHES TO WEAR

FIND OUT MORE! The words **cardigan** and **wellingtons** are **eponyms**. Find out more in NAMES AND NAMING in THE WORLD OF WORDS.

INCLUDE: blazer, cardigan, cloak, coat, dress or gown, jacket, jumper or sweater, shirt, shorts, skirt, suit, tie, trousers, waistcoat

All these arrangements were only just completed when the Queen, now fully dressed in a trim skirt and cashmere cardigan, entered the Ballroom holding Sophie by the hand. — THE BFG

CAN HAVE: belt, bow, buckle, buttons, collar, cuffs, hem, pocket, sleeves, zip

• A dress without sleeves is **sleeveless** and a shirt without a collar, like the one the BFG wears, is **collarless**.
Sophie saw that under the cloak he was wearing a sort of collarless shirt and a dirty old leather waistcoat that didn't seem to have any buttons. — THE BFG

• A **tail coat** has two long hanging **coat-tails** at the back. Tail coats are usually worn on formal occasions, but Willy Wonka wears one every day (so he probably has more than one).
And on he rushed, down the endless pink corridors, with his black top hat perched on the top of his head and his plum-coloured velvet coat-tails flying out behind him like a flag in the wind. — CHARLIE AND THE CHOCOLATE FACTORY

NIGHTCLOTHES

INCLUDE: nightdress or nightie, nightcap, nightgown or nightshirt, pyjamas, dressing-gown

'I can fly faster than any of you!' cried Grandpa George, whizzing round and round, his nightgown billowing out behind him like the tail of a parrot. — CHARLIE AND THE GREAT GLASS ELEVATOR

• If you say that someone is **the cat's pyjamas**, you mean that they are as **wondercrump** as Willy Wonka!
The Mirror answered every time, 'Oh Madam, you're the Queen sublime. You are the only one to charm us, Queen, you are the cat's pyjamas.' — REVOLTING RHYMES

UNDERWEAR

INCLUDES: knickers, pants or underpants, petticoat, socks, stockings, vest

As she floated gently down, Mrs Twit's petticoat billowed out like a parachute, showing her long knickers. — THE TWITS

DID YOU KNOW? The word **pyjamas** comes from Urdu and Persian words that mean 'leg clothing'.

The word **knickers** is short for **knickerbockers**, a type of knee-length trousers.

DESCRIBING CLOTHES

• Clothes that fit well are **comfortable, comfy, neat** or **smart**.

• Clothes that do not fit well are **ill-fitting**. Those that are too big are **baggy** or **loose**, and those that are too small are **tight** or **uncomfortable**.

• A style of clothes may be **dapper, fashionable** or **stylish**, or **dowdy, drab** or **old-fashioned**.
All of them were wearing these old-fashioned clothes from hundreds of years ago, and several had on very peculiar hats and bonnets. — THE MINPINS

• Old clothes may be **faded, frayed, ragged, shabby, tattered, threadbare** or **worn**.

• Thick clothes may be **cosy** or **warm**, and thin clothes may be **light** or **flimsy**. Clothes made from wool are **knitted, woollen** or **woolly**. Rough clothes that make you itch are **scratchy** or **tickly**.
'Human beans from Jersey has a most disgustable woolly tickle on the tongue,' the Giant said. 'Human beans from Jersey is tasting of cardigans.' — THE BFG

• If your clothes and hair are in a mess (after being spat out of a giant's mouth, for example) you may look **bedraggled** or **dishevelled**: *Sophie stood there bedraggled and dripping with giant's spit.*

WHAT ELSE CAN YOU WEAR?

TYPES OF HAT
INCLUDE: bonnet, cap, helmet
The Oompa-Loompas were all dressed in the most extraordinary way. They were wearing bright-red space suits, complete with helmets and goggles. — CHARLIE AND THE CHOCOLATE FACTORY

• A hat with a tall stiff top, like the one that Willy Wonka wears, is a **top hat**.

TYPES OF SHOE
INCLUDE: boots, gym shoes, sandals, slippers, suction-boots, wellington boots or wellies
'Suction-boots,' the Minpin said. 'We all wear them. You can't live in trees without suction-boots.' On his feet he was wearing tiny green boots rather like miniature wellies. — THE MINPINS

• Clean shoes may be **polished** or **shiny**. Dirty shoes may be **grimy, muddy** or **encrusted** with dirt. A small-sized shoe, like Cinderella's glass slipper, is **dainty**.
At once, one of the Ugly Sisters, (The one whose face was blotched with blisters) Sneaked up and grabbed the dainty shoe, And quickly flushed it down the loo. — REVOLTING RHYMES

OTHER ACCESSORIES
INCLUDE: glasses or spectacles, gloves, goggles, handbag, jewellery, scarf, umbrella, walking-stick or cane
Aunt Spiker, on the other hand, was lean and tall and bony, and she wore steel-rimmed spectacles that fixed on to the end of her nose with a clip. — JAMES AND THE GIANT PEACH

• Most people use a **walking-stick** to help them to walk, but Mrs Twit uses hers to hit small animals and children.

• Some items of **jewellery** to wear are: **bracelet, brooch, earrings, necklace, ring.** A **tiara** (say tee-*ah*-ra) is a **jewelled** headband.
A lady with an enormous chest and flaming orange hair came flying out of the house screaming, 'My jewels! Somebody's stolen my jewels! My diamond tiara! My diamond necklace! My diamond bracelets! My diamond earrings! My diamond rings!' — THE GIRAFFE AND THE PELLY AND ME

• The **pin** of a **brooch** can also be used in an emergency as a weapon against giants.
When she was right up close to the great naked hairy legs, she rammed the three-inch-long pin of the brooch as hard as she could into the Fleshlumpeater's right ankle. — THE BFG

WEARING CLOTHES

• When you wear clothes you are **dressed** and when you take them off you are **undressed**. An old-fashioned word meaning 'dressed' is **clad**: *The BFG was clad in shabby, ill-fitting clothes.*

• You can also say that someone **sports** a type of clothing.
These breeches reached to just below the knees and from there on down she sported green stockings with turn-up tops, which displayed her calf muscles to perfection. — MATILDA

• You can be **draped, layered, muffled, swathed** or **wrapped** in clothing.
She was no more than a shadow. They could see her face and just the faintest outline of her body swathed in a sort of gown. — CHARLIE AND THE GREAT GLASS ELEVATOR

• Clothes can **hang** loosely, or can **billow, flap, fly** or **stream** behind you when you move.

• Rain, sweat or water can **drench** or **soak** your clothes, or can **trickle** down inside your collar.

DID YOU KNOW?
In Scotland a **top hat** is called a *lum hat* which means 'chimney hat'.

ALL ABOUT HOMES

TYPES OF HOME

INCLUDE: caravan, castle, cave, cottage, farmhouse, flat, house, mansion, palace, tent, tree-house

The caravan was our house and our home. It was a real old gipsy wagon with big wheels and fine patterns painted all over it in yellow and red and blue. — DANNY THE CHAMPION OF THE WORLD

• A home for orphans like Sophie is an **orphanage** or **norphanage**.

• A large home, like a palace, may be **grand, imposing** or **stately**. A smaller home, like a cottage, may be **compact, cosy** or **homely**.

It was a modern brick house that could not have been cheap to buy and the name on the gate said Cosy Nook. Nosey cook might have been better, Miss Honey thought. — MATILDA

• A home that has not been well looked after may be **dilapidated, ramshackle** or **rundown**.

They lived—Aunt Sponge, Aunt Spiker, and now James as well—in a queer ramshackle house on the top of a high hill in the south of England. — JAMES AND THE GIANT PEACH

• Willy Wonka once crafted an entire **palace** out of chocolate for Prince Pondicherry—although it melted on the first hot sunny day and became a lake thereafter.

And what a palace it was! It had one hundred rooms, and everything was made of either dark or light chocolate! The bricks were chocolate, and the cement holding them together was chocolate. — CHARLIE AND THE CHOCOLATE FACTORY

OUTSIDE A HOUSE

THERE MAY BE: balcony, bricks, chimney, fence, front door, garage, garden, gate, hedge, path, roof, slates or roof tiles, steps, windows

Matilda saw a narrow dirt-path leading to a tiny red-brick cottage. The cottage was so small it looked more like a doll's house than a human dwelling. — MATILDA

• The front door may have a **doormat, doorstep, keyhole** or **latch,** and a **letterbox.**

Mrs Twit got the key from under the doormat (where Muggle-Wump had carefully replaced it) and into the house they went. — THE TWITS

• If someone **goes through the roof** it usually means they get very cross and shout a lot—but if they take **Marvellous Medicine Number One**, they will grow so tall they really *will* burst through the roof!

'I'm still going!' came the old screechy voice from up above. 'Give me another dose, my boy, and let's go through the roof!' — GEORGE'S MARVELLOUS MEDICINE

INSIDE A HOUSE

THERE MAY BE: ceiling, cupboard, curtains, doors, fireplace, floor, floorboards, furniture, hallway, rooms, staircase, walls, windows

It looked as though some madman was ripping out the whole of the inside of the house, because now pieces of staircase and bits of the banisters and a whole lot of old floorboards came whistling through the windows.
— THE GIRAFFE AND THE PELLY AND ME

DID YOU KNOW? The word **window** comes from Old Norse (Viking) words meaning 'wind eye'.

IT MAY FEEL: airy, bright, cosy, homely, spacious, welcoming

OR: cluttered, cramped, damp, dark, forbidding

• Walls may be covered with **paint, pictures** or **wallpaper** (including Willy Wonka's **lickable** variety).

LICKABLE WALLPAPER FOR NURSERIES, it said on the next door. 'Lovely stuff, lickable wallpaper!' cried Mr Wonka, rushing past. — CHARLIE AND THE CHOCOLATE FACTORY

• Most doors have **doorknobs** or **door-handles,** but some have special **door-openers** for **human-beaney** mice.

Soon every door in the house had a door-opener on it. All I had to do was to press my front paws on to a tiny wooden platform and hey presto, a spring would stretch and a weight would drop and the door would swing open. — THE WITCHES

carpet *ceiling* *rug* *sofa* *armchair* *cabinet*

• Doors can **swing** or be **flung** open or shut. They can **creak** open slowly, or can **slam** shut noisily. You might hear a **knock**, a loud **rap** or a quiet **tap** on a door.
Inside the room, beyond the curtains, Sophie suddenly heard what was obviously a knock on the door. She heard the doorknob being turned. She heard someone entering the room. – THE BFG

• A series of stairs or steps is a **flight**, and a long rail at the side of a staircase, for holding onto or sliding down, is a **banister**.
The door was at the top of a flight of stone steps leading down from the house to the cellar. And now someone was starting to come down those steps. – FANTASTIC MR FOX

• The ledge underneath a window, where birds or **chiddlers** can perch, is a **window-sill**.
With all the patience of a small girl who has something important to wait for, Sophie sat motionless on the window-sill. – THE BFG

ROOMS IN A HOUSE

INCLUDE: **bathroom, bedroom, dining-room, kitchen, lavatory** or **toilet, living-room, sitting-room**
Mr Hoppy turned and ran from the balcony into the living-room, jumping on tip-toe like a ballet-dancer between the sea of tortoises that covered the floor. – ESIO TROT

FIND OUT MORE! Willy Wonka's factory also has an **Inventing Room!** Find out more in MAKING AND INVENTING.

• A room or space at the top of a house is an **attic** and one underground is a **basement** or **cellar**.
There was a big hole in the floor and another in the ceiling, and sticking up like a post between the two was the middle part of Grandma. Her legs were in the room below, her head in the attic. – GEORGE'S MARVELLOUS MEDICINE

• A bedroom with lots of beds in a boarding school or **norphanage** is called a **dormitory**.

• An old-fashioned word for a sitting-room is a **parlour**.
Seated in a comfortable armchair in Mrs Silver's parlour, sipping his tea, Mr Hoppy was all of a twitter. – ESIO TROT

DID YOU KNOW? The word **parlour** comes from French **parler** 'to speak' and was originally a room in a monastery where people could talk.

An old word for an **attic** was a sky-parlour.

ITEMS OF FURNITURE

INCLUDE: **armchair, bathtub, bed, bookcase** or **bookshelf, cabinet, carpet, chair, chest-of-drawers** (or **chest-of-drawers-piano**), **desk, dressing-table, lamp, rug, sofa, table, wardrobe**

• Furniture is usually placed on the **floor**, but in **extra-usual** circumstances, it may be glued to the **ceiling** with Very Strong Glue.
All the furniture, the big table, the chairs, the sofa, the lamps, the little side tables, the cabinet with bottles of beer in it, the ornaments, the electric fire, the carpet, everything was stuck upside down to the ceiling. – THE TWITS

BEWARE: In the absence of gravity (or glue), **furniture** will start to float.
'There's a bed in it,' said Shanks. 'A big double bed and that's floating too.' 'A bed!' barked the President. 'Whoever heard of a bed in a spacecraft!' – CHARLIE AND THE GREAT GLASS ELEVATOR

• In an emergency, **grandfather clocks, pianos** and **ping-pong tables** can also be used to make makeshift dining furniture for giants.
The BFG sat down on the chest-of-drawers-piano and gazed in wonder around the Great Ballroom. 'By gumdrops!' he cried. 'What a spliffling whoppsy room we is in!' – THE BFG

FIND OUT MORE! Animals have **homes** too. Find out what they are called in ALL ABOUT ANIMALS in THE NATURAL WORLD.

BEASTLY (AND NOT-SO-BEASTLY) HUMAN BEANS

cruel evil nasty spiteful mean horrid detestable odious

BEASTLY HUMAN BEANS

CAN BE: cruel, unkind, nasty, mean, detestable, spiteful, hateful, horrid, ghastly or odious, like Aunts Spiker and Sponge
And there they sat, these two ghastly hags, sipping their drinks, and every now and again screaming at James to chop faster and faster. — JAMES AND THE GIANT PEACH

OR: evil-minded, wicked, foul, monstrous, malevolent, vicious or malicious, like Farmers Boggis, Bunce and Bean

OR: bad-tempered, disagreeable, irritable, tetchy, grumpy or cantankerous, like George's grandma. Another word for a grumpy person is a **grouch**.
Most grandmothers are lovely, kind, helpful old ladies, but not this one . . . She was a miserable old grouch. — GEORGE'S MARVELLOUS MEDICINE

DID YOU KNOW?
The word **cranky** means 'quirky or eccentric', but in America it also means 'grumpy or bad-tempered'.

OR: arrogant, conceited, haughty (rhymes with *naughty*), superior, stuck-up, snooty or smug, like Mr Hazell
Mr Hazell did not look at him. He sat quite still in the seat of his Rolls-Royce, his tiny piggy eyes staring straight ahead. There was a smug superior little smile around the corners of his mouth. — DANNY THE CHAMPION OF THE WORLD

OR: sneaky, devious, scheming or underhand, like Mr Wormwood

• A bad person can be a **rogue**, **rascal** or **scoundrel**. A mean old woman who reminds you of a witch is a **hag** or **harridan**.

• A nasty character in a book or film is a **villain** and someone who acts like a villain is **villainous**. An informal word for a villain is a **baddy**.

• Someone who commits a crime is a **criminal** or **culprit** and someone who steals valuable things is a **robber** or **thief**.
'This clot . . . that you see before you is none other than a disgusting criminal, a denizen of the underworld, a member of the Mafia!' – MATILDA

• Someone who is famous for being bad is **infamous** or **notorious**: *Goldilocks is a notorious porridge thief.*

• Someone who kills another human bean is a **murderer**. A murderer has **murderous** or **murderful** thoughts.

• Someone who tries to defeat or harm you is an **enemy** or **adversary** and a chief enemy is an **arch enemy**: *The farmers are Mr Fox's arch enemies.*

• Other words for **beastliness** and **nastiness** are **malice** and **villainy**: *What villainy will Bunce get up to this evening?*

• Other words for a mean human bean are **grinksludger**, **squifflerotter** and **rotrasper**.
'Grown-up human beans is not famous for their kindnesses. They is all squifflerotters and grinksludgers.' – THE BFG

WHAT DO MEAN HUMAN BEANS DO?

THEY DO: awful, dreadful, terrible, appalling, shocking, vile, ghastly, monstrous, hideous, horrible or unspeakable things

THEY MIGHT: bully, scold, berate, chide or tell you off: *James's aunts are always scolding him for being lazy.*

THEY MIGHT: mock, jeer, laugh or sneer at you, make faces or call you names
The boys laughed and made faces at me, and Mr Gregg told me to go home and mind my own P's and Q's. Well, that did it!
– THE MAGIC FINGER

THEY MIGHT: scowl, frown, snarl, snap or bark at you
Mr Coombes was looking grim. His hammy pink face had taken on that dangerous scowl which only appeared when he was extremely cross and somebody was for the high-jump. – BOY

THEY MIGHT: grouse, grouch, grumble or gripe at you
George couldn't help disliking Grandma. She was a selfish grumpy old woman . . . and she was always complaining, grousing, grouching, grumbling, griping about something or other. – GEORGE'S MARVELLOUS MEDICINE

THEY MIGHT: dangle you by the ears or swing you by the pigtails
It really was a quite extraordinary sight to see this giant Headmistress dangling the small boy high in the air and the boy spinning and twisting like something on the end of a string and shrieking his head off. – MATILDA

THEY MIGHT: lower you down a deep dark well, or lock you in a cellar or the **Chokey** as a **punishment**
'Why don't we just lower the boy down the well in a bucket and leave him there for the night? . . . That ought to teach him not to laze around like this the whole day long.'
– JAMES AND THE GIANT PEACH

THEY MIGHT: mistreat animals or hunt or shoot birds, like the Greggs or Twits
'Let's go inside and load our lovely new guns and then it'll be bang bang bang and Bird Pie for supper.' – THE TWITS

THEY MIGHT: tear up, rip, destroy or deface something precious, like a library book
With frightening suddenness he now began ripping the pages out of the book in handfuls and throwing them in the waste-paper basket. – MATILDA

grinksludger squifflerotter rotrasper

THEY MIGHT: **play nasty tricks** on each other, like Mr and Mrs Twit, to **get revenge** or **pay each other back**
The next day, to pay Mr Twit back for the frog trick, Mrs Twit sneaked out into the garden and dug up some worms. — THE TWITS

THEY MIGHT: **grow jealous** (say *jell*-us) or **envious** and **spy** on each other
All the other chocolate makers, you see, had begun to grow jealous of the wonderful sweets that Mr Wonka was making, and they started sending in spies to steal his secret recipes. — CHARLIE AND THE CHOCOLATE FACTORY

THEY MIGHT: **cheat, deceive, dupe, fool, swindle** or **hoodwink** each other

• Someone who swindles other people, like Mr Wormwood, is a **cheat, fraud, swindler** or **crook.** His behaviour is **fraudulent, dishonest, corrupt** or **crooked** (say *kroo*-kid).
'But that's dishonest, Daddy,' Matilda said. 'It's cheating.' 'No one ever got rich being honest,' the father said. — MATILDA

BEASTLY INSULTS

• Beastly grown-ups like to **hurl insults** at **chiddlers** (or at each other if there are no **chiddlers** about).

• They might call you a: **nasty, useless, lazy, indolent, disobedient** or **disrespectful little beast, brat, brute, clot, twerp, maggot, wart** or **worm.**

'You're a nasty little maggot!' the voice screeched back. 'You're a lazy and disobedient little worm, and you're growing too fast.' — GEORGE'S MARVELLOUS MEDICINE

'Shut up, you little twerp!' Aunt Spiker snapped, happening to overhear him. 'It's none of your business!' — JAMES AND THE GIANT PEACH

• Miss Trunchbull also calls her pupils: **blithering idiot, clotted carbuncle, empty-headed hamster, festering gumboil, fleabitten fungus, glob of glue, poisonous pustule, witless weed.**

• When grown-ups insult each other, they might say: **filthy old frumpet, grizzly old grunion, miserable old mackerel, rotten old turnip, whiskery old warthog.**
Mrs Twit . . . suddenly called out at the top of her voice, 'Here I come, you grizzly old grunion! You rotten old turnip! You filthy old frumpet!' — THE TWITS

DID YOU KNOW?
To **insult** someone means literally to 'jump on' them. It comes from the Latin word **salire** meaning 'to leap'.

FIND OUT MORE!
Giants love to hurl **insults** (as well as rocks). Find out more in GIANT LANGWITCH in THE MAGICAL WORLD.

Learn more about **lickswishy alliteration** in ALL ABOUT WRITING in THE WORLD OF WORDS.

'Here I come, you grizzly old grunion! You rotten old turnip! You filthy old frumpet!'

NOT-SO-BEASTLY HUMAN BEANS

ARE: **good**, **kind** or **kindly**, **friendly**, **gentle**, jumbly, **generous**, **kind-hearted**, **loving**, **sweet-natured**

'I do have one extra special little wish.'
'And what might that be?' said the Duke in a kindly voice. — THE GIRAFFE AND THE PELLY AND ME

OR: **patient**, **helpful**, **sympathetic** or **understanding**, like Miss Honey

OR: **honest**, **decent**, **honourable**, **noble**, **worthy**, **virtuous**, **trustworthy**, unlike Mr and Mrs Wormwood

Matilda longed for her parents to be good and loving and understanding and honourable and intelligent. — MATILDA

• A good character in a book or film is a **hero** or **heroine** and someone who acts like a hero is **heroic**: *Is Charlie or Willy Wonka the hero of the story?*

WHAT DO FRIENDLY HUMAN BEANS DO?

THEY DO: **nice**, **lovely**, **pleasant** or **agreeable** things and have **good thoughts**

If you have good thoughts they will shine out of your face like sunbeams and you will always look lovely. — THE TWITS

THEY MIGHT: **welcome**, **greet** or **smile** at you.

 If a grown-up smiles TOO MUCH they might be a witch wearing a face mask.
When he was three-quarters way down the stairs he caught sight of Mrs Silver already standing at the open door waiting to welcome him with a huge smile on her face. — ESIO TROT

THEY MIGHT: **help**, **assist**, **encourage** or **praise** you, like Mrs Phelps

'I am reading other books,' Matilda said. 'I borrow them from the library. Mrs Phelps is very kind to me. She helps me to choose them.' — MATILDA

THEY MIGHT: **invite you to tea** or **offer you breakfast**, like the Queen

'Have either of you had breakfast?' the Queen said.
'Oh, could we?' Sophie cried. 'Oh, please! I haven't eaten a thing since yesterday!' — THE BFG

FIND OUT MORE! Giants can be **jumbly** too! Find out more in ALL ABOUT GIANTS in THE MAGICAL WORLD.

sweet-natured loving generous jumbly kind-hearted friendly

ALL ABOUT FEELINGS

FEELING HAPPY

YOU MIGHT FEEL: cheerful, joyful, jolly, merry, delighted, light-hearted, contented, gleeful, hopscotchy, dory-hunky

'Whenever I is feeling a bit scrotty,' the BFG said, 'a few gollops of frobscottle is always making me hopscotchy again.' – THE BFG

YOU MIGHT BE: full of joy, in high spirits, ecstatic, elated, overjoyed, thrilled to bits

'Are you happy?' I asked him. 'I'm ecstatic!' he cried, jumping up and down. 'I'm happy as a horse in a hay-field!' – CHARLIE AND THE GREAT GLASS ELEVATOR

YOU MIGHT: beam, smile, grin, laugh, leap or jump for joy

Her Ladyship leaps high with joy And cries, 'Well done, my scrumptious boy! The old goat's clobbered once for all! Now you and I can have a ball!' – RHYME STEW

• Something that **makes you happy** is: **delightful, enjoyable, joyous, heart-warming**. It will: **delight** you, **cheer you up, lift your spirits, put a smile on your face.**

• If you are **over the moon** you feel so happy that you could jump right over the moon with joy: *Charlie was over the moon when he found a Golden Ticket.*

WAYS TO LAUGH

YOU MIGHT:

chuckle, giggle or griggle quietly

'I'm joking,' said Mr Wonka, giggling madly behind his beard. 'I didn't mean it. Forgive me. I'm so sorry.' – CHARLIE AND THE CHOCOLATE FACTORY

YOU MIGHT: cackle, chortle or churgle loudly, or snort or hoot with laughter

The Roly-Poly Bird was up there as well, and the monkeys were in the cage and the whole lot of them were hooting with laughter at Mr Twit. – THE TWITS

• Something that **makes you laugh** is: amusing, comical, funny, hilarious, witty.

Of course the whole class started screaming with laughter, and then Mrs Winter said, 'Will you be so kind as to tell me what you find so madly funny, all of you?' – THE MAGIC FINGER

DID YOU KNOW? Some old-fashioned words meaning the same as **glum** are *glumpy* and *glumpish.*

FEELING SAD

YOU MIGHT FEEL: unhappy, gloomy, glum, miserable, depressed, dejected, downhearted, downcast, broken-hearted, melancholy, mournful, sorrowful, forlorn, upset, scrotty

Suddenly, we all became very quiet and melancholy, and the Monkey looked as though he was about to cry as he sang me a little song of farewell. – THE GIRAFFE AND THE PELLY AND ME

YOU MIGHT BE: full of woe, in despair, in low spirits, down in the dumps

YOU MIGHT: cry, sob, sigh, shed a tear, shake your head

'I told you I hadn't got it quite right,' sighed Mr Wonka, shaking his head sadly. – CHARLIE AND THE CHOCOLATE FACTORY

• Something that **makes you sad** is **depressing, dispiriting, heartbreaking**. It might: **depress, sadden** or **upset** you, **break your heart.**

And all through the night we could hear her calling to us, saying 'Help! help! help!' and it was heartbreaking to listen to her. But what could we do? – JAMES AND THE GIANT PEACH

cheerful merry jolly gleeful

DID YOU KNOW? The word **chortle** was invented by Lewis Carroll, who used it in Alice *Through the Looking-Glass.* It is probably a blend of **chuckle** and **snort.**

forlorn sorrowful gloomy glum

WAYS TO CRY

YOU MIGHT: weep, sob, blubber or snivel softly
Mrs Gregg began to cry. 'Oh, dear! Oh, dear!' she sobbed. 'They have taken our house. What shall we do? We have no place to go!' — THE MAGIC FINGER

YOU MIGHT: bawl or wail loudly
Grandma Josephine . . . was sitting in the middle of the huge bed, bawling her head off. 'Wa! Wa! Wa!' she said. 'Wa! Wa! Wa! Wa!' — CHARLIE AND THE GREAT GLASS ELEVATOR

• When you start to cry, your eyes **well up** with tears and you feel **tearful**. A single tear is a **teardrop**.

• Tears can **run** or **stream** or **trickle** down your face. If you are **in floods of tears** you cannot stop crying.
Very softly, the Old-Green-Grasshopper started to play the Funeral March on his violin, and by the time he had finished, everyone, including himself, was in a flood of tears. — JAMES AND THE GIANT PEACH

FEELING ANGRY

YOU MIGHT FEEL: cross, furious, irate, enraged, incensed, annoyed, exasperated, indignant
The Grand High Witch glared around the room. 'I hope nobody else is going to make me cross today,' she remarked. — THE WITCHES

YOU MIGHT BE: fuming, raging, seething with rage

YOU MIGHT: lose your temper, fly into a rage, go red or purple in the face
The Trunchbull was in such a rage that her face had taken on a boiled colour and little flecks of froth were gathering at the corners of her mouth. — MATILDA

• If you **hit the roof** you become suddenly very angry, as if you had exploded upwards like George's grandma after a dose of Marvellous Medicine.

• If you are **nettled** by something it means you are annoyed by it, as if you had been stung by one of Mrs Twit's **nettles**.

• Something that **makes you angry** is annoying, **maddening, exasperating** or **irksome**. It might: **make your blood boil, make you see red, make steam come out of your ears.**

• An outburst of anger is a **fit of temper** or a **tantrum**. If someone goes completely mad with rage, they **go berserk**: *Miss Trunchbull will go berserk when she finds out who ate her cake.*

• If you have a Magic Finger, it will **tingle** and **flash sparks** when you get angry at silly grown-ups.
Well, that did it! I saw red. And before I was able to stop myself, I did something I never meant to do. I PUT THE MAGIC FINGER ON THEM ALL! — THE MAGIC FINGER

FEELING AFRAID

DID YOU KNOW?
The word **petrify** means literally 'to turn into stone'. It comes from Greek **petra** meaning 'rock or stone' and is related to petrol.

YOU MIGHT FEEL: fearful, frightened, scared, petrified, terrified, alarmed, anxious, nervous, apprehensive
Charlie climbed on to the bed and tried to calm the three old people who were still petrified with fear. 'Please don't be frightened,' he said. 'It's quite safe.' — CHARLIE AND THE CHOCOLATE FACTORY

YOU MIGHT: go or turn pale, break into a cold sweat, quiver, shake, shudder, tremble, stutter
'My m-m-mummy thinks I look lovely, Miss T-T-Trunchbull,' Amanda stuttered, shaking like a blancmange. — MATILDA

• Something that **makes you afraid** is: scary, fearsome, frightsome or frightswiping. It might: give you goosepimples, make your hair stand on end, send shivers down your spine, make your blood run cold.
The Grand High Witch took a quick step forward, and when she spoke again, it was in a voice that made my blood run cold. — THE WITCHES

DID YOU KNOW?
The word **berserk** comes from the **Berserkers**, Viking warriors who wore bearskins and went into a frenzy during battle.

FIND OUT MORE!
There are fearsome **frightswiping** creatures to find in *THE MAGICAL WORLD!*

DESCRIBING MOVEMENT

fly *dash* *speed*
dart *flit*
scurry
zippfizz *bootle*

MOVING ALONG

• The speed at which you move is your **pace** and if you **pace** up and down, you take slow steps while you are thinking or waiting.
My father stood up and began pacing the floor of the caravan. 'Here's the plan of action,' he said.
— DANNY THE CHAMPION OF THE WORLD

• A long step is a **stride** and the **gait** of a **human bean** or giant is the way that they walk or run.
I saw this tremendous tall person running along the crest of the hill. He had a queer long-striding lolloping gait.
— DANNY THE CHAMPION OF THE WORLD

YOU MIGHT: **bounce**, **bound** or **skip** merrily
The BFG went bouncing off the ground as though there were rockets in his toes and each stride he took lifted him about a hundred feet into the air. — THE BFG

YOU MIGHT: **jog** or **trot** along briskly
'Here we are!' cried Mr Wonka, trotting along in front of the group. 'Through this big red door, please! That's right! It's nice and warm inside!' — CHARLIE AND THE CHOCOLATE FACTORY

YOU MIGHT: **march** or **stride** purposefully
A moment later, Mr and Mrs Twit came marching into the garden, each carrying a fearsome-looking gun. — THE TWITS

YOU MIGHT: **tramp**, **stamp**, **stomp** or **clump** heavily
The creature came clumping into the cave and stood towering over the BFG. — THE BFG

YOU MIGHT: **lope**, **pad** or **shuffle** softly
The keeper came loping softly down the track with the dog padding quick and soft-footed at his heel. — DANNY THE CHAMPION OF THE WORLD

YOU MIGHT: **lumber**, **lollop** or **galumph** clumsily:
Sophie heard the giants galumphing towards the cave.

• If you move **in spurts**, you move with occasional bursts of speed, like a giant trying not to be seen during the witching hour.

• If you are **injured**, you might **hobble** or **limp** along.

GOING FAST

YOU MIGHT: **dash**, **dart**, **flit**, **fly**, **hurry**, **race**, **run**, **rush**, **hasten**, **hurtle**, **bootle**, **career**, **speed**, **sprint**, **streak**, **rocket**, **whizz**, **zippfizz**, **zoom**
The three old people . . . came sprinting after Mr Wonka, shouting, 'Wait for us! Wait for us!' . . . They leaped across paths and over little bushes like gazelles in spring-time.
— CHARLIE AND THE GREAT GLASS ELEVATOR

YOU MIGHT: **scamper**, **scumper**, **scurry**, **scuttle**, **scuddle**, **skaddle**, **skedaddle**, **skiddle**, **skididdle** or **skittle** away hastily
Here goes, I thought, and like a flash I skittled out from under the table and made for the wall. — THE WITCHES

FIND OUT MORE!
What do you call a group of zippfizzing giants? Find out in ALL ABOUT GIANTS in THE MAGICAL WORLD.

DID YOU KNOW?
The word **galumph** was invented by Lewis Carroll, who used it in Alice *Through the Looking-Glass*. It is probably a blend of *gallop* and *triumph*.

DID YOU KNOW?
The word **whizz** was first used over 400 years ago. William Shakespeare described meteors *whizzing in the ayre* in his play *Julius Caesar*.

zoom

sprint

whizz

skididdle

scuddle

scumper

DID YOU KNOW?
The word **corridor** comes from Latin and means 'running place' (so it is odd that grown-ups tell you not to run in them).

YOU MIGHT: speed up until you reach **top speed** or **top gear**. If you move very fast, you go **at a furious** or **terrific pace**.
The BFG changed into his famous top gear and all at once he began to fly forward as though there were springs in his legs and rockets in his toes. — THE BFG

YOU MIGHT: run away from someone, or **chase after** them to **catch up**
'We've absolutely got to stop them!' Sophie cried. 'Put me back in your pocket quick and we'll chase after them and warn everyone in England they're coming.' — THE BFG

• If you **run rings around** someone, you show you are much better or cleverer than they are.
The only power Matilda had over anyone in her family was brain-power. For sheer cleverness she could run rings around them all. — MATILDA

GOING SLOW

YOU MIGHT: walk, amble, stroll or saunter slowly
'Thank you, my dear child,' the Centipede said, opening his eyes. Then he got down off the sofa and ambled across the room and crawled into his hammock.
— JAMES AND THE GIANT PEACH

YOU MIGHT: slouch casually or **drift** or **wander** aimlessly

YOU MIGHT: dawdle, dally or dilly-dally lazily
'Come on!' cried Mr Wonka. 'Get a move on, please! We'll never get round today if you dawdle like this!'
— CHARLIE AND THE CHOCOLATE FACTORY

YOU MIGHT: creep, crawl, edge, inch or slink stealthily
Mr Fox crept up the dark tunnel to the mouth of his hole. He poked his long handsome face out into the night air and sniffed once. He moved an inch or two forward and stopped.
— FANTASTIC MR FOX

YOU MIGHT: glide, slide or skate gracefully, or **skim** lightly over the ground
He would glide—that was the only word to describe his way of moving—he would glide noiselessly from one dark place to another, always moving, always gliding forward through the streets of London, his black cloak blending with the shadows of the night. — THE BFG

YOU MIGHT: slow down until you are going **at a slow** or **leisurely pace**. If you move **at a snail's pace** you move as slowly as a snail slithering, or a grobe slimeing, along the ground.

creep crawl edge inch slink

OTHER WAYS TO MOVE

YOU MIGHT: **stagger**, **stumble**, **teeter** or **totter** unsteadily
The cook disappeared. Almost at once she was back again staggering under the weight of an enormous round chocolate cake on a china platter. – MATILDA

YOU MIGHT: **slip**, **trip**, **bump** or **crash** into something by accident
Grandma Georgina . . . was trumpeting and spitting like a rhinoceros and flying from one side of the Elevator to the other, shouting 'Out of my way! Out of my way!' and crashing into poor Mr and Mrs Bucket with terrible speed. – CHARLIE AND THE GREAT GLASS ELEVATOR

YOU MIGHT: **overbalance**, **tumble** or **topple** over
'Now stay there till we come back!' Mr Twit ordered. 'Don't you dare to move! And don't overbalance!' – THE TWITS

YOU MIGHT: **jump**, **leap**, **pounce** or **spring** out suddenly
The Pelican opened his gigantic beak and immediately the policemen pounced upon the burglar, who was crouching inside. – THE GIRAFFE AND THE PELLY AND ME

YOU MIGHT: **bob** up and down, or **dance** or **hop** about in excitement
Both aunts were now hopping round and round the tree, clapping their hands and shouting all sorts of silly things in their excitement.
– JAMES AND THE GIANT PEACH

YOU MIGHT: **twist**, **turn**, **twitch**, **churn** or **choggle** about
Mr Twit wriggled and squirmed, and he squiggled and wormed, and he twisted and turned, and he choggled and churned, but the sticky glue held him to the floor. – THE TWITS

YOU MIGHT: **fidget**, **figgle**, **squirm**, **squiggle**, **wriggle** or **writhe** furiously
The Fleshlumpeater . . . rolled and he wriggled, he fought and he figgled, he squirmed and he squiggled. But there was not a thing he could do. – THE BFG

YOU MIGHT: **lean** or **lurch** to one side, or **lunge** or **pitch** forwards
Suddenly the Trunchbull lunged forward and grabbed the large empty china platter on which the cake had rested. – MATILDA

YOU MIGHT: **roll**, **rock**, **sway**, **swing** or **waddle** from side to side
Aunt Sponge, fat and pulpy as a jellyfish, came waddling up behind her sister to see what was going on. – JAMES AND THE GIANT PEACH

YOU MIGHT: **spin** or **twirl** around or do a **pirouette** (say pirr-oo-*ett*)
And now the Trunchbull was leaning back against the weight of the whirling girl and pivoting expertly on her toes, spinning round and round. – MATILDA

MOVING THINGS

YOU MIGHT: **pull** or **tug** something towards you, or **push**, **shove** or **thrust** it away
A ghoulish snarling ghastly sound Came up from somewhere underground, Then slimy tendrils tugged his coat And tried to fasten round his throat. – RHYME STEW

FIND OUT MORE!
What creatures **slither** and **swoop**? Find out in THE NATURAL WORLD.

squirm

choggle

fidget

figgle

YOU MIGHT: lift, hoist, heave or carry something, or drag it behind you
With the monkeys and the birds all pulling and puffing, the carpet was dragged off the floor and finally hoisted up on to the ceiling. — THE TWITS

YOU MIGHT: throw, pitch or hurl something, or drop it by mistake

• Matilda can move things just by thinking because she has special **telekinetic** powers.
Six days later, by the following Wednesday evening, she was able not only to lift the cigar up into the air but also to move it around exactly as she wished. — MATILDA

recline rest comatose stationary motionless

squiggle writhe wriggle

STAYING STILL

YOU MIGHT: stop, halt or come to a standstill
'Wait!' cried Mr Wonka, skidding suddenly to a halt.
— CHARLIE AND THE CHOCOLATE FACTORY

YOU MIGHT: lie or rest in bed, recline on a sofa, or sit cross-legged on a floor
The creatures, some sitting on chairs, others reclining on a sofa, were all watching him intently. — JAMES AND THE GIANT PEACH

• If you stay completely still, you are **motionless** or **stationary**.
With all the patience of a small girl who has something important to wait for, Sophie sat motionless on the window-sill. — THE BFG

• Someone who is **comatose** (say *koh*-ma-toes) is unable to move, as if they are in a coma.
Bruce Bogtrotter . . . was sitting on his chair like some huge overstuffed grub, replete, comatose, unable to move or to speak. — MATILDA

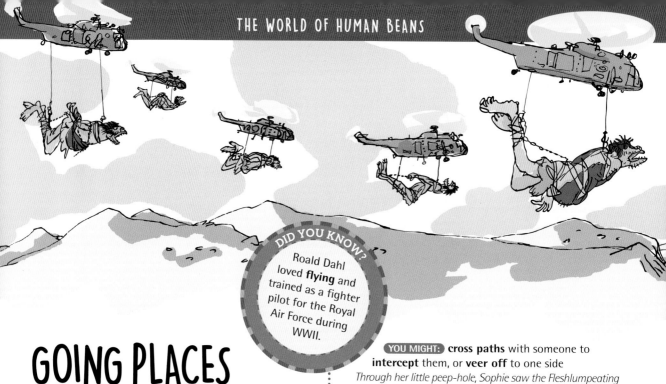

DID YOU KNOW?
Roald Dahl loved **flying** and trained as a fighter pilot for the Royal Air Force during WWII.

GOING PLACES

COMING AND GOING

YOU MIGHT: travel or proceed on a journey, or go exploring. Someone who goes on a journey is a traveller or an explorer.

YOU MIGHT: advance, approach or come towards a place
Matilda and Lavender glanced round and saw the gigantic figure of Miss Trunchbull advancing through the crowd of boys and girls with menacing strides. – MATILDA

YOU MIGHT: back away, retreat or withdraw from a place
I stared at the great orange beak and backed away. 'Go ON!' the Monkey shouted from up in his window. 'The Pelly isn't going to swallow you! Climb IN!' – THE GIRAFFE AND THE PELLY AND ME

YOU MIGHT: leave, depart from, quit or vacate a place
The Ladybird . . . came over and stood beside him. 'In case you don't know it,' she said, 'we are about to depart for ever from the top of this ghastly hill that we've all been living on for so long.' – JAMES AND THE GIANT PEACH

YOU MIGHT: descend, fall, roll or slide downwards
Matilda, who was mesmerized by the whole crazy affair, saw Amanda Thripp descending in a long graceful parabola on to the playing-field beyond. – MATILDA

YOU MIGHT: ascend, climb or clamber upwards
'The Cobra is the cleverest and most dangerous cat-burglar in the world!' said the Chief of Police. 'He must have climbed up the drainpipe.' – THE GIRAFFE AND THE PELLY AND ME

YOU MIGHT: cross paths with someone to intercept them, or veer off to one side
Through her little peep-hole, Sophie saw the Fleshlumpeating Giant moving over to intercept them. – THE BFG

• To move in a line is to file in or out. A line of people going in one direction is a trail.
Soon, there was a trail of children a mile long chasing after the peach as it proceeded slowly up Fifth Avenue. – JAMES AND THE GIANT PEACH

WAYS TO TRAVEL

INCLUDE: on foot, on horseback, by air or by plane, by car or by road, by train or by rail. You might also travel by ear or by pocket, tucked snugly in the BFG's ear or waistcoat.

YOU MIGHT: cycle or pedal on a bicycle, or ride a bicycle or horse. You mount a bicycle or horse to get onto it, and dismount to get off.
Then Sergeant Samways mounted his bicycle and waved us goodbye and pedalled away down the road in the direction of the village. – DANNY THE CHAMPION OF THE WORLD

YOU MIGHT: row or steer a boat, or fly in a plane, Giant Peach, hot-air balloon or spaceship
The river of chocolate was flowing very fast inside the pipe, and the Oompa-Loompas were all rowing like mad, and the boat was rocketing along at a furious pace. – CHARLIE AND THE CHOCOLATE FACTORY

• You board a plane or ship to get onto it, and disembark to get off. A plane or spacecraft takes off to start a journey and lands to finish it.
So off we set, my mother and I and my trunk and my tuck-box, and we boarded the paddle-steamer and went swooshing across the Bristol Channel in a shower of spray. – BOY

DID YOU KNOW?

The word **ambulance** comes from Latin *ambulare* 'to walk' and originally meant a mobile hospital drawn by horses.

ALL ABOUT CARS

• Parts of a car include: **engine, wheels, tyres, brakes, bonnet, bumper, roof, petrol tank, steering-wheel, speedometer, headlights** or **headlamps, horn**

The pheasants . . . were all over the roof and the bonnet, sliding and slithering and trying to keep a grip on that beautifully polished surface. – DANNY THE CHAMPION OF THE WORLD

• An old car with a noisy engine is a **banger**, and a car or caravan for going on a journey is a **tourer**.

The canvas hood had been folded back because of the mild weather, converting the car into a magnificent open tourer. – BOY

FIND OUT MORE!

What noises does a **car engine** make? Find out in ALL ABOUT SOUNDS.

• A car might **cruise** along at a leisurely pace, or **chug** along slowly.

Two minutes later we were safely inside the taxi and cruising slowly down the bumpy track towards the road. – DANNY THE CHAMPION OF THE WORLD

DID YOU KNOW?

In North America, the **bonnet** of a car is called the *hood* and **petrol** is called *gasoline*.

• It might **bump** along an uneven road or **skid** on a slippery road. It might **brake** or **swerve** to avoid something in its path.

The little car swerved violently off the road, leaped through the gap, hit the rising ground, bounced high in the air, then skidded round sideways behind the hedge and stopped.

– DANNY THE CHAMPION OF THE WORLD

• A car (or giant) going as fast as it can is going **at top speed** or **in top gear**.

• A **speedometer** is a dial which shows the speed at which a car is travelling. The **mileage** is the total number of miles a car has travelled.

BEWARE: The mileage in any car that Mr Wormwood sells is NOT accurate, as he fiddles the dial using an electric drill.

• Someone who repairs cars, like Danny's father, is a **mechanic** (say me-*kan*-ick). A place where cars are repaired or stored is a **garage** and somewhere to buy **petrol** or fuel for a car is a **filling-station**.

My father owned the filling-station and the caravan and a small field behind, but that was about all he owned in the world. – DANNY THE CHAMPION OF THE WORLD

• Someone whose job is to **drive** a car for someone else is a **chauffeur** (say *show*-fur).

At exactly that moment, a huge white Rolls-Royce pulled up right below us, and a chauffeur in a blue and gold uniform got out. – THE GIRAFFE AND THE PELLY AND ME

OTHER ZIPPFIZZING VEHICLES

INCLUDE: ambulance, bicycle, bus, taxi, caravan, boat, ship, plane, helicopter or bellypopper, fire-engine, Great Glass Elevator, spaceship or Space Hotel

• A cycle with three wheels is a **tricycle**.

I can remember oh so vividly how the two of us used to go racing at enormous tricycle speeds down the middle of the road. – BOY

• Formal words for a boat, ship or spaceship are **craft** and **vessel**.

The splendid little vessel with its single tall funnel would move out into the calm waters of the fjord and proceed at a leisurely pace along the coast. – BOY

• A **lorry** or **tractor** might **clank** or **trundle** (not zippfizz) along.

Soon, two enormous caterpillar tractors with mechanical shovels on their front ends came clanking into the wood. Bean was driving one, Bunce the other. – FANTASTIC MR FOX

• An **emergency vehicle**, like an **ambulance, fire-engine** or **police car**, has a **siren** which **screams** or **wails** as it zippfizzes past.

Someone must have called the police because suddenly no less than four squad cars came racing towards us with their sirens screaming.

– THE GIRAFFE AND THE PELLY AND ME

FIND OUT MORE!

Who **travels** in Outer Space? Find out in THE SKY AND OUTER SPACE in THE NATURAL WORLD.

zippfizzing

MAKING AND INVENTING

ALL ABOUT INVENTORS

THEY ARE: brainy, bright, clever, intelligent, curious, inquisitive

'Brilliant! Sensational! Marvellous! You are a genius, O Brainy One! It is a thrilling invention, this Delayed Action Mouse-Maker!' – THE WITCHES

OR: creative, imaginative, inspired, sparky

OR: eccentric, quirky, whimsical

THEY: create, invent, imagine, dream up, concoct, devise or design ingenious things, like unmeltable ice cream

'Did you know that he's invented a way of making chocolate ice cream so that it stays cold for hours and hours without being in the refrigerator?' – CHARLIE AND THE CHOCOLATE FACTORY

OR: discover or unearth something new, or make an amazing discovery

I tell you, I felt exactly like that other brilliant fellow must have felt when he discovered penicillin. 'Eureka!' I cried. 'I've got it!' – MATILDA

- Their brain might buzz, fizz, spark, whirr or phizz-whizz with ideas.

It was impossible to be bored in my father's company. He was too sparky a man for that. Plots and plans and new ideas came flying off him like sparks from a grindstone. – DANNY THE CHAMPION OF THE WORLD

THEY MIGHT: build, construct or assemble a machine, device or gadget

But after a few days, my grandmother began to invent gadgets for me in order to make life a bit easier. – THE WITCHES

THEY MIGHT: do calculations, draw up a plan, sketch a design, make a model

THEY MIGHT: experiment or run a test, then analyse results

- If things don't go to plan they may have to start afresh or have a rethink.

- Other words for an inventor are creator and discoverer. Some people who invent are: artist, designer, engineer, mathematician, scientist, storyteller, chocolate maker or chocolatier (say chocolate-*ear*).

'My dear boy,' said Grandpa Joe . . . 'Mr Willy Wonka is the most amazing, the most fantastic, the most extraordinary chocolate maker the world has ever seen!' – CHARLIE AND THE CHOCOLATE FACTORY

- Someone with brilliant ideas or with a lot of brain-power is a genius or brainbox.

Being very small and very young, the only power Matilda had over anyone in her family was brain-power. – MATILDA

- Someone who can think quickly is quick-witted or sharp-witted. Someone with no ideas or spark at all is dull or dim-witted.

DID YOU KNOW?
Roald Dahl was an **inventor** too! He invented a type of valve used in brain surgery, originally to help one of his sons who was ill.

unearth analyse discover experiment imagine

FIND OUT MORE!
You can **concoct** magic potions too! Find out more in ALL ABOUT MAGIC in THE MAGICAL WORLD.

Eye of newt

splutter

steam

buzz

whirr

clank

MACHINES AND GADGETS

MAY HAVE: buttons to press, levers to pull, handles to crank, knobs to turn, lights that blink or flash
'Retro-rockets!' bellowed Mr Wonka. 'I mustn't forget to fire the retro-rockets!' He flew over to another series of buttons and started playing on them like a piano. — CHARLIE AND THE GREAT GLASS ELEVATOR

MAY BE: intricate, complex, fiddly, finicky, gleaming, shiny
Mr Wonka led the party over to a gigantic machine that stood in the very centre of the Inventing Room. It was a mountain of gleaming metal that towered high above the children and their parents. — CHARLIE AND THE CHOCOLATE FACTORY

MIGHT: whirr, buzz, clank, splutter, give off steam, light up
All about him . . . strange iron machines were clanking and spluttering, and there were pipes running all over the ceiling and walls. — CHARLIE AND THE CHOCOLATE FACTORY

MIGHT: go wonky, break down, fall apart, melt down, catch fire, explode

YOU MIGHT: tweak or tinker with it, or disassemble or take it apart

YOU MIGHT: start or fire it up, switch it on or off, shut it down

IDEAS AND INVENTIONS

MAY BE: brilliant, bright, ingenious, fantabulous, fantastic or fantastical, marvellous, phizz–whizzing, splendiferous, staggering, stupendous, wondercrump
'But it isn't only chocolate bars that he makes. Oh, dear me, no! He has some really fantastic inventions up his sleeve, Mr Willy Wonka has!'
— CHARLIE AND THE CHOCOLATE FACTORY

OR: crazy, crackpot, hare-brained, madcap, wacky, zany, seemingly impossible

• An eccentric inventor might seem: barmy, batty, cracked, crazy, daffy, dippy, dotty, nutty, potty
'This man,' shouted Grandma Josephine, 'is crazy as a crumpet!' 'He's cracked as a crayfish!' cried Grandma Georgina.
— CHARLIE AND THE GREAT GLASS ELEVATOR

• A brilliant idea is a **brainwave** or **brainstorm**. A completely new idea is **novel, original, groundbreaking** or **unique**.

• An idea that is not well thought out is said to be **half-baked** (like a cake that is not properly cooked).

DID YOU KNOW?
The word **hare-brained** means 'as mad as a hare' because hares behave in a crazy way in springtime. You can also say *as mad as a March hare.*

FIND OUT MORE!
You can **invent wondercrump** words too! Find out more in THE WORLD OF WORDS.

ALL ABOUT SOUNDS

LOUD NOISES

clang
crash
whizzpop
wham

INCLUDE: bang, blare, boom, clang, clank, clash, clatter, crash, thud, wham
By golly, what a place that kitchen was! The noise! And the steam! And the clatter of pots and pans! — THE WITCHES

CAN BE: noisy, blaring, deafening, earbursting or ear-splitting, thunderous
Suddenly there was an ear-splitting BANG and the Pelican leaped twenty feet into the air. — THE GIRAFFE AND THE PELLY AND ME

OR CAN BE: grating, harsh, jarring, piercing, raucous, shrill
The rushing whooshing sound of the wind outside grew louder and louder and shriller and shriller until it became a piercing shriek. — CHARLIE AND THE GREAT GLASS ELEVATOR

• Loud music or a loud television will **blare** or **blast** out sound, especially in the Wormwood household.

• Other words for loud noises are: **din, racket, cacophony, clamour**. A loud explosion might go **kaboom!**

• A noisy disturbance is a **row** (rhymes with *cow*), **commotion, tumult, uproar, hullabaloo, pandemonium** or **rumpledumpus**.

SOFT SOUNDS

INCLUDE: fizz, hiss, hum, murmur, patter, rustle, sizzle, tinkle, whiffle, whisper
He heard . . . a tiny noise, a soft rustling sound, as though someone had moved a foot ever so gently through a patch of dry leaves. — FANTASTIC MR FOX

• A quiet sound is **faint, low, muffled** or **muted**, and a pleasantly soft sound is **silvery, sweet, mellifluous** or **dulcet** (say *dull*-sit).
'A dream . . . is making a tiny little buzzing-humming noise. But this little buzzy-hum is so silvery soft, it is impossible for a human bean to be hearing it.' — THE BFG

• Something that makes no sound at all is **silent** and a very deep silence is **deathly** silent or quiet.

DID YOU KNOW?
The word **pandemonium** means literally 'place of all demons', and was invented by the poet John Milton over 300 years ago.

FIND OUT MORE!
Words like **crash, fizz** and **tinkle** are **onomatopoeic**. Find out more in ALL ABOUT WRITING in THE WORLD OF WORDS.

BODY NOISES

INCLUDE: burp, gasp, gurgle, hiccup, huff, puff, pant, sigh, sniff, snore or snortle, snort, splutter, wheeze, whistle, whizzpop
The Ladybird was making whistling noises as she breathed, and the Earthworm was coiled up like a spring at one end of his hammock, wheezing and blowing through his open mouth. — JAMES AND THE GIANT PEACH

• If you like something you might **clap** or **applaud**, or give a **whoop** of joy. If you don't like something you might **boo** or **blow a raspberry**. Giants like to **whizzpop** to show they are happy—but PLEASE NOTE that this noise is only acceptable in Giant Country.

OTHER SOUNDS

INCLUDE: beep, bleep, boing, bong, buzz, click, clink, chink, clunk, crack, crackle, creak, crunch, jingle, jangle, ping, plink, plop, pop, rattle, rumble, scrunch, snap, squeak, swish, swoosh, tick, tinkle, twang, whoosh, zap
'The mouse-trrraps have a powerful spring, The springs go crack and snap and ping! Is lovely noise for us to hear! Is music to a vitch's ear!' — THE WITCHES

Scrunch, scrunch, scrunch went the shovels above their heads. Small stones and bits of earth began falling from the roof of the tunnel. – FANTASTIC MR FOX

• Cars and engines can also **chug, drone, hum, purr, putter, roar** or **whirr**.

• You can also use ALL these buckswashling sound words as **verbs** (*The newt plopped into the jug of water*), **nouns** (*The newt fell in with a plop*) or **exclamations** (*Plop! In fell the newt*).

HEARING SOUNDS

YOU MIGHT: hear, listen to or **pick up** sounds
Down in the tunnel the foxes crouched, listening to the terrible clanging and banging overhead.
– FANTASTIC MR FOX

YOU MIGHT: catch something said quickly or **make out** something faint or unclear. You might **strain your ears** to hear something very faint or far away
Up above us, the Giraffe was beginning to sing a little song, but she sang so softly I could hardly catch the words.
– THE GIRAFFE AND THE PELLY AND ME

YOU MIGHT: overhear something secret or **eavesdrop** on a private conversation

• A sound that you can hear is **audible** or **within earshot**, and one you cannot hear is **inaudible**. Every thingalingaling is audible to the BFG because of his super-sensitive ears.

• When a sound **echoes**, it bounces off a wall or ceiling and you hear it repeated.
'Wait!' shrieked one of the witches in the back row. 'Hold everything!' Her shrieking voice echoed through the Ballroom like a trumpet.
– THE WITCHES

DID YOU KNOW?
The word *eavesdrop* originally meant the ground outside a house where water dropped from the eaves (the overhanging part of the roof).

An *eavesdropper* was someone who stood there to listen in secret.

MAKING MUSIC

• A musical sound is **harmonious, melodious** or **tuneful**. The beat in a piece of music is the **rhythm** and music with a strong beat, like the **chants** of the Oompa-Loompas, is **rhythmical**.
BOOM-BOOM! BOOM-BOOM! And all the Oompa-Loompas . . . began to sway and hop and dance to the rhythm of the music. – CHARLIE AND THE GREAT GLASS ELEVATOR

• You might **play, blow, drum, beat, pluck** or **strum** a musical instrument. A flourish of trumpets is a **fanfare**.

• You might **sing a song** or **hum** or **whistle a tune**. If you suck a Pishlet you will be able to whistle expertly (even if you couldn't before).

• You might **burst into song** suddenly or start to **strike up** a tune.
Far away down on the bank of the chocolate river, Charlie could see the Oompa-Loompa band striking up once more.
– CHARLIE AND THE GREAT GLASS ELEVATOR

• A group of musicians is a **band** or an **orchestra** and a group of singers is a **choir** (rhymes with *fire*).
The Old-Green-Grasshopper became a member of the New York Symphony Orchestra, where his playing was greatly admired. – JAMES AND THE GIANT PEACH

MUSICAL INSTRUMENTS

INCLUDE: bagpipes or bagglepipes, **banjo, drums, piano, trumpet, violin** or **fiddle**
And what a wonderful instrument the Old-Green-Grasshopper was playing upon. It was like a violin! It was almost exactly as though he were playing upon a violin! – JAMES AND THE GIANT PEACH

• Extra–usual instruments that are played in Giant Country are curly crumpets and thunderous thrumpets.
'Save our souls!' bellowed the Fleshlumpeater. 'Sound the crumpets! I is bitten by a septicous venomsome vindscreen viper!' – THE BFG

• Bells can **chime, peal, ring** or **toll** (rhymes with *roll*). A **peal of laughter** is a loud outburst of laughing like a round of bells ringing out.
The Oompa-Loompa took one look at Mrs Gloop and exploded into peals of laughter. – CHARLIE AND THE CHOCOLATE FACTORY

DESCRIBING VOICES

WHAT DO VOICES SOUND LIKE?

• The way that a voice sounds is its **tone**.
He heard the Giant mutter twice, 'By gosh, that tasted very nice. Although' (and this in grumpy tones) 'I wish there weren't so many bones.' – REVOLTING RHYMES

• A deep-sounding voice is **gruff, husky** or **throaty**. A broken voice is **croaky** or **hoarse**.
All at once she was leaning forward in her chair and whispering in a throaty sort of voice George had never heard her use before. – GEORGE'S MARVELLOUS MEDICINE

• A high-sounding voice is **high-pitched, piercing, screechy, shrill** or **squeaky**.
'George!' came the screechy voice from the next room. 'Who are you talking to in there? What are you up to?' – GEORGE'S MARVELLOUS MEDICINE

• A loud and powerful voice is **booming, thunderous** or **stentorian**:
Miss Trunchbull has a stentorian voice.

• A quiet voice is **low, hushed** or **hushy quiet, muffled, muted, soft, soft-spoken** or **whispery**.

 When grown-ups like Miss Trunchbull speak *softly* it is a sign of DANGER.
When she spoke again her voice was suddenly softer, quieter, more friendly, and she leaned towards the boy, smiling. 'You like my special chocolate cake, don't you, Bogtrotter?' – MATILDA

• Even a **hushy quiet** voice can sound **like thunder and thrumpets** to the BFG's extra-sensitive ears.
'Your voice is sounding like thunder and thrumpets!' 'I'm so sorry,' Sophie whispered. 'Is that better?' 'No!' cried the BFG. 'It sounds as though you is shootling off a bunderbluss!' – THE BFG

• A nervous voice is **shaky, trembly, wavery** or **wobbly**.
After a time, my voice began to go all trembly. I started to say silly things like, 'Oh Dad, please tell me where you are! Please answer me!' – DANNY THE CHAMPION OF THE WORLD

• A voice that is unpleasant to hear is **harsh, grating, metallic** or **rasping**, like nails scraping on metal.
Her voice, I noticed, had that same hard metallic quality as the voice of the witch I had met under the conker tree, only it was far louder and much much harsher. It rasped. It grated. It snarled. It scraped. It shrieked. And it growled. – THE WITCHES

• If someone is **sharp-tongued** or has a **sharp tongue**, they are always making harsh or unkind comments. George's grandma is an expert at insults and has a **razor-sharp** tongue.
'Grandma may not have a hoarse throat,' George said, 'but she's certainly got a sharp tongue.' – GEORGE'S MARVELLOUS MEDICINE

DID YOU KNOW?
The word **stentorian** comes from *Stentor*, the name of an ancient herald in the Trojan War who had a VERY LOUD voice.

WHAT CAN VOICES DO?

THEY CAN: talk, speak, chatter, chitter or jabbel to others
The creature came clumping into the cave and stood towering over the BFG. 'Who was you jabbeling to in here just now?' he boomed. – THE BFG

THEY CAN: babble, burble, prattle, twitter or **gossip** excitedly
All I could hear were the voices of the ancient witches burbling their silly sentences about 'How kind Your Grandness is' and all the rest of it. – THE WITCHES

THEY CAN: cry, shout, scream, shriek, yell or cheer loudly
The crowds went wild with excitement. They lined the streets and they leaned out of the windows of the skyscrapers, cheering and yelling and screaming and clapping. – JAMES AND THE GIANT PEACH

THEY CAN: shake, tremble, quaver, quiver, waver or **wobble** nervously
'That . . . that . . . that isn't the reason, ma'am.' The maid's voice was quivering terribly. – THE BFG

THEY CAN: sing, chant, lilt, trill or warble musically
The Centipede was dancing around the deck and turning somersaults in the air and singing at the top of his voice: 'Oh, hooray for the storm and the rain!' – JAMES AND THE GIANT PEACH

THEY CAN: chirp or chirrup eagerly, or **harrumph** with disapproval
'Have you got the message?' 'Yes, Miss Honey,' chirruped nineteen eager little voices. – MATILDA

THEY CAN: hoot with laughter or **whoop** with delight
'The little man gave a great whoop of joy and threw his bowl of mashed caterpillars right out of the tree-house window.' – CHARLIE AND THE CHOCOLATE FACTORY

THEY CAN: drone or ramble on boringly, or **murmur** unclearly. A confused sound of many voices speaking is a **babble** or **hubbub**.
The sound grew louder. It swelled into a great babble of speech from many throats. – THE WITCHES

THEY CAN: echo or reverberate around a room or cave
'Wait!' shrieked one of the witches in the back row. 'Hold everything!' Her shrieking voice echoed through the Ballroom like a trumpet. – THE WITCHES

• Voices can also **grow louder** as they get nearer, or can **fade** or **trail away** into the distance.

When a group of people suddenly stop talking there is a **hush**.
'Dad!' I called out. 'Dad, are you there?' My small high voice echoed through the forest and faded away. – DANNY THE CHAMPION OF THE WORLD

DID YOU KNOW?
The word **gossip** comes from an Old English word meaning 'godfather'. It later came to mean a friend invited to the birth of a child (where there was a lot of chattering).

USING YOUR VOICE

• You **utter** sounds with your voice, using your **voicebox** or **larynx** (say *larr*-inks). A word meaning to do with your voice is **vocal**: *Miss Trunchbull has very powerful vocal cords.*

• You **raise your voice** so that people can hear you, and **lower your voice** or **keep your voice down** so that they can't.
Don Mini stood up to make a speech. 'Minpins of the forest!' he cried, raising his small voice so that it could be heard all over the tree. – THE MINPINS

• If you speak **at the top of your voice**, you speak AS LOUDLY AS POSSIBLE. If you do this too often you might **lose your voice** and go hoarse.

• If someone screams **blue murder**, they are screaming for help as loud as they can—which often happens with Miss Trunchbull's pupils.
Amanda was screaming blue murder and the Trunchbull was yelling, 'I'll give you pigtails, you little rat!' – MATILDA

• Someone who chatters a lot is a **chatterbox** or **natterbox**. Matilda's parents think she is a **chatterbox**, when really she is a **brainbox**.
The parents, instead of applauding her, called her a noisy chatterbox and told her sharply that small girls should be seen and not heard. – MATILDA

• When someone **yodels** they sing while making their voice alternate between very high and low notes.
'I cannot possibly allow anyone, even little girls, to be seeing me and staying at home. The first thing you would be doing, you would be scuddling around yodelling the news that you were actually seeing a giant.' – THE BFG

DID YOU KNOW?
An old-fashioned word for a **chatterbox** is a **flibbertigibbet**.

ALL ABOUT SPEAKING

WAYS TO SPEAK

YOU CAN: shout, yell, bawl, bellow, boom, roar or thunder loudly
'SPEAK!' boomed the voice, getting louder and louder and ending in a fearful frightening shout that rattled Charlie's eardrums. 'SPEAK! SPEAK! SPEAK!' – CHARLIE AND THE GREAT GLASS ELEVATOR

YOU CAN: snap, bark, rant, rave, spit, snort or explode angrily
'Don't be a fool, Shuckworth!' snapped Ground Control. 'Pull yourself together, man! This is serious!' – CHARLIE AND THE GREAT GLASS ELEVATOR

YOU CAN: whisper or murmur softly, or speak under your breath
'What's the matter?' Sophie whispered in her under-the-breath voice. 'I is in a bit of a puddle,' he said. – THE BFG

YOU CAN: mumble, mutter, stammer or stutter unclearly
'I do wish you wouldn't mumble,' said Mr Wonka. 'I can't hear a word you're saying.' – CHARLIE AND THE CHOCOLATE FACTORY

YOU CAN: cry, howl, scream, screech, shriek, squeal or yelp in horror or fright
You could hear Mrs Jenkins's shrill voice all over the room. 'Herbert!' it was screaming. 'Herbert, get me out of here!' – THE WITCHES

YOU CAN: groan, moan, sigh, wail, whimper or whine in pain or sadness
'I'm a wreck!' groaned the Centipede. 'I am wounded all over!' 'It serves you right,' said the Earthworm. – JAMES AND THE GIANT PEACH

YOU CAN: blurt out suddenly or gasp with surprise
'Oh, my sainted souls!' gasped the Giraffe. 'Oh, my naked neck! I cannot believe what I am seeing!' – THE GIRAFFE AND THE PELLY AND ME

YOU CAN: make a speech, read out loud or recite a poem or limerick
'I insist upon hearing this limerick,' Miss Honey said, smiling one of her rare smiles. 'Stand up and recite it.' – MATILDA

• If someone wants you to be quiet, they will say **Sh!** or **Shush!**—but if they are as rude as Aunt Spiker, they will shout **Shut up!**
'Ssshh!' said Grandpa Joe. 'Listen, Charlie! The drums are starting up! They're going to sing.' – CHARLIE AND THE CHOCOLATE FACTORY

'Shut up, you little twerp!' Aunt Spiker snapped, happening to overhear him. 'It's none of your business!' – JAMES AND THE GIANT PEACH

DID YOU KNOW?
The word **whisper** is almost as ancient as a Bristlecone Pine. It was first recorded in Old English over a thousand years ago.

A formal word for 'whispering' is **susurration**, which comes from the Latin word *susurrus* meaning 'muttering or whispering'.

suggest
propose
assert
announce
exclaim declare

SAYING THINGS

YOU CAN: **comment, mention, note, observe** or **remark** something casually
The Grand High Witch glared around the room. 'I hope nobody else is going to make me cross today,' she remarked. – THE WITCHES

YOU CAN: **announce, exclaim, assert, declare** or **insist** something strongly
'This isn't just an ordinary up-and-down lift!' announced Mr Wonka proudly. 'This lift can go sideways and longways and slantways and any other way you can think of!' – CHARLIE AND THE CHOCOLATE FACTORY

YOU CAN: **ask, enquire** or **pose** a question, or **demand** an answer
'What's the matter with you?' Aunt Sponge demanded. 'It's growing!' Aunt Spiker cried. 'It's getting bigger and bigger!' – JAMES AND THE GIANT PEACH

YOU CAN: **propose** or **suggest** an idea
'We could try peeling him like a banana,' the Old-Green-Grasshopper suggested. 'Or rubbing him with sandpaper,' the Ladybird said. – JAMES AND THE GIANT PEACH

YOU CAN: **answer, reply** or **respond** to something, or **retort** with a sharp or funny reply
'You have a lot of boots,' James murmured. 'I have a lot of legs,' the Centipede answered proudly. 'And a lot of feet. One hundred, to be exact.' – JAMES AND THE GIANT PEACH

YOU CAN: **beg, entreat, implore, plead** or **urge** someone to do (or NOT do) something *'Let him go, Miss Trunchbull, please,' begged Miss Honey. 'You could damage him, you really could!'* – MATILDA

YOU CAN: **repeat** or **reiterate** a point again
'I think you speak beautifully,' Sophie said. 'You do?' cried the BFG, suddenly brightening. 'You really do?' 'Simply beautifully,' Sophie repeated. – THE BFG

• Words can also **pour, stream** or **tumble out** in a **torrent** as you speak.
The words poured out of Mr Hazell's mouth like hot lava from an erupting volcano.
– DANNY THE CHAMPION OF THE WORLD

FIND OUT MORE! What kind of **insults** do beastly grown-ups use? Find out in BEASTLY (AND NOT-SO-BEASTLY) HUMAN BEANS.

Giants are experts in explosive **expletives**! Find out more in GIANT LANGWITCH in THE MAGICAL WORLD.

⚠ EXCELLENT EXCLAMATIONS

INCLUDE: **great whistling whangdoodles!**, **snorting snozzwangers!**, **gunghummers and bogswinkles!**, **screaming scorpions!**
'Great whistling whangdoodles!' cried Mr Wonka, leaping so high in the air that when he landed his legs gave way and he crashed on to his backside. 'Snorting snozzwangers!' – CHARLIE AND THE GREAT GLASS ELEVATOR

• If you are **surprised** or **excited**, you might exclaim: **by golly!, by gosh!, by gumdrops!** or **by gumfrog!**, **goodness me!, crikey!, oh my!** A Geraneous Giraffe will also say **Oh, my naked neck!**
Sophie was silent for a few moments. Then suddenly, in a voice filled with excitement, she cried out, 'I've got it! By golly, I think I've got it!' – THE BFG

• If you are **happy**, you might shout **hooray!, hurrah!** or **hurray!** or **whoopee!** or **yippee!** If you discover something you might shout **Ha!**
'Whoopee!' cried the witches, clapping their hands. 'You are brilliant, O Your Grandness! You are fantabulous!' – THE WITCHES

• If you are **hurt**, you might shout: **ayee!, ouch!, ow!,** or even **eeeow!**
'Eeeow!' roared the Fleshlumpeater. 'Ayeee! Oooow!' 'He's still asleep,' the BFG whispered. 'The terrible trogglehumping nightmare is beginning to hit him.' – THE BFG

• If you are **scared** or in a **panic**, you might shout **help!** or **mince my maggots!** or **swipe my swoggles!** If you want to scare someone you might suddenly shout **boo!**
'Oh help!' screamed Mrs Twit. 'Help help help! I'm beginning to feel giddy!' – THE TWITS

'Oh no!' he cried. 'Oh mince my maggots! Oh swipe my swoggles! . . . It's a trogglehumper!' – THE BFG

• If you taste something as **disgusterous** as a **snozzcumber**, you might shout **ugh!**
Sophie took a small nibble. 'Uggggggggh!' she spluttered. 'Oh no! Oh gosh! Oh help!' She spat it out quickly. – THE BFG

• Grown-ups who are **angry**, like furious farmers, might exclaim: **dang and blast!**
'Dang and blast that lousy beast!' cried Boggis. 'I'd like to rip his guts out!' said Bunce. – FANTASTIC MR FOX

• An **exclamation** that you shout when you are angry is called an **expletive**: *The giants shout a string of expletives when they are caught.*

ALL ABOUT LOOKING

HOW TO LOOK AT THINGS

YOU CAN: **glance, glimpse, peek** or **peep** quickly. You can also **catch** or **get a glimpse of** something briefly
By lunchtime, the whole place was a seething mass of men, women, and children all pushing and shoving to get a glimpse of this miraculous fruit. — JAMES AND THE GIANT PEACH

YOU CAN: **catch sight of, notice, spot, sight** or **spy** something accidentally or casually
Watch the birds as they fly above your heads and, who knows, you might well spy a tiny creature riding high on the back of a swallow or a raven. — THE MINPINS

YOU CAN: **make out** or **distinguish** something vaguely or gradually
They came to an enormous billowing cloud that was shining in a pale golden light, and in the folds of this cloud Little Billy could make out creatures of some sort moving around. — THE MINPINS

YOU CAN: **observe** or **watch** something for a while, or **keep watch** overnight
'You'd better be careful,' Mrs Twit said, 'because when I see you starting to plot, I watch you like a wombat.' — THE TWITS

YOU CAN: **peer at, examine** or **inspect** something closely, or **pore over** it carefully. You can also **take a good look at** something.
There was a short silence. They all peered down anxiously at the sharks who were cruising slowly round and round the peach. — JAMES AND THE GIANT PEACH

YOU CAN: **glare, glower, frown, scowl** or **grimace** angrily
James glanced up and saw Aunt Spiker standing over him, grim and tall and bony, glaring at him through her steel-rimmed spectacles. — JAMES AND THE GIANT PEACH

YOU CAN: **gaze** or **stare** steadily, or can **gape** or **goggle** in amazement
The Queen was still staring at Sophie. Gaping at her would be more accurate. Her mouth was slightly open, her eyes were round and wide as two saucers. — THE BFG

FIND OUT MORE!
You can find *squillions* of ways to describe **eyes** in DESCRIBING FACES.

peer pore gaze gape goggle

YOU CAN: **scan** or **survey** something over a wide area
Mr Tibbs stood back to survey the new furniture. 'None of it is in the classic style,' he whispered, 'but it will have to do.' — THE BFG

• If your eyes are **glued to** something, you cannot stop watching or looking at it.
Mrs Wormwood sat munching her meal with her eyes glued to the American soap-opera on the screen. — MATILDA

• When you **squint** you look at something with your eyes half-shut.
Sophie, squinting through the glare of the sun, saw several tremendous tall figures moving among the rocks about five hundred yards away. — THE BFG

• An old-fashioned word for seeing something is to **behold** it.
Every one of these 'creatures' was at least as big as James himself, and in the strange greenish light that shone down from somewhere in the ceiling, they were absolutely terrifying to behold. — JAMES AND THE GIANT PEACH

THINGS THAT HELP YOU SEE

INCLUDE: **binoculars** or **biciruclers**, **camera**, **glasses** or **spectacles**, **magnifying glass**, **telescope** or **telescoop**

The First Officer handed the telescope to the Captain. The Captain put it to his eye. 'There's birds everywhere!' he cried. 'The whole sky is teeming with birds! What in the world are they doing?' — JAMES AND THE GIANT PEACH

• A **telescope** (boiled until it is soft) is also an essential ingredient in **Delayed Action Mouse–Maker Formula**, as it causes **chiddlers** to shrink to the size of a mouse.
'All you have to do if you are vishing to make a child very small is to look at him through the wrrrong end of a telescope.' — THE WITCHES

• A word meaning 'to do with your eyes' is **optical** and a word meaning 'to do with your sight' is **visual**.

• **Optical** instruments, like telescopes and cameras, have a glass **lens** which makes things look bigger to your eye.
At one of these ends there was an enormous camera on wheels, and a whole army of Oompa-Loompas was clustering around it, oiling its joints and adjusting its knobs and polishing its great glass lens. — CHARLIE AND THE CHOCOLATE FACTORY

• You **focus** a telescope or camera by adjusting the lens until what you see looks clear and sharp.
'Quick! Give me the telescope!' yelled Shuckworth. With one hand he focused the telescope and with the other he flipped the switch connecting him to Ground Control. — CHARLIE AND THE GREAT GLASS ELEVATOR

survey focus scan

peep peek glower

DID YOU KNOW?
The word **lens** comes from a Latin word meaning 'lentil', because of its similar shape.

WHAT DO CAMERAS DO?

THEY CAN: **click**, **flash**, **focus**, **take a photograph** or **picture**, **zoom** in or out

There was great excitement in the Beauregarde household when our reporter arrived to interview the lucky young lady—cameras were clicking and flashbulbs were flashing and people were pushing and jostling and trying to get a bit closer to the famous girl. — CHARLIE AND THE CHOCOLATE FACTORY

• You use a camera to **photograph** or **shoot** an image. Film or TV cameras can also **film** or **record** a scene.

• You **point** or **aim** a camera at what you want to photograph.
Half a mile back, Shuckworth, Shanks and Showler were keeping the television camera aimed all the time at the Glass Elevator. — CHARLIE AND THE GREAT GLASS ELEVATOR

DID YOU KNOW?
The word **camera** comes from a Latin phrase meaning 'dark chamber', because early cameras were dark boxes with a lens.

feast gorge gobble gollop guzzle

DID YOU KNOW?
An old English dialect word meaning 'to nibble' is to **chumble.**

EATING AND DRINKING

WAYS TO EAT

`YOU CAN:` **chew**, **gnaw** or **suck** food slowly—and you can suck an **Everlasting Gobstopper** FOREVER
'You can put an Everlasting Gobstopper in your mouth and you can suck it and suck it and suck it and suck it and it will never get any smaller!'—CHARLIE AND THE CHOCOLATE FACTORY

`YOU CAN:` **nibble**, **peck** or **pick at** food gently
'Nonsense!' shouted the Prince. 'I'm not going to eat my palace! I'm not even going to nibble the staircase or lick the walls! I'm going to live in it!'—CHARLIE AND THE CHOCOLATE FACTORY

`YOU CAN:` **gobble** or **gollop** or **gulp** food quickly
'Whenever I see a live slug on a piece of lettuce,' Grandma said, 'I gobble it up quick before it crawls away. Delicious.'
— GEORGE'S MARVELLOUS MEDICINE

`YOU CAN:` **guzzle** or **wolf** food greedily, or **tuck into** it hungrily. If you eat a huge amount of food at one time, you **feast** or **gorge** on it.
Charlie went on wolfing the chocolate. He couldn't stop. And in less than half a minute, the whole thing had disappeared down his throat.—CHARLIE AND THE CHOCOLATE FACTORY

`YOU CAN:` **crunch** or **munch** or **chomp** food noisily
They were ravenous. So for a while there was no conversation at all. There was only the sound of crunching and chewing as the animals attacked the succulent food.
— FANTASTIC MR FOX

• You might **lick your lips** if you feel hungry. If you feel REALLY hungry, you are **famished**, **ravenous** or **starving**.
'We've got to earn some more money quickly. The Pelly is starving, the Monkey is famished and I am perishing with hunger.'—THE GIRAFFE AND THE PELLY AND ME

• Someone who enjoys eating has a good **appetite**, and someone who eats too much food, like Augustus Gloop, is a greedy **glutton**. Someone who enjoys eating fancy food, like the **Centipede**, is a **gourmet** (say *goor*-may) or an **epicure**.

• The type of food that someone eats is their **diet**:
The Oompa-Loompas used to live on a diet of mashed caterpillars.

THINGS TO EAT WITH

• You eat food with **cutlery**, such as a knife, fork and spoon. (The BFG uses a sword, garden fork and spade for **cutlery** when he has breakfast at the Palace.) Dishes such as cups, saucers and plates are called **crockery**.
There was suddenly a crash and a clatter of crockery which could only have meant that the tray the maid was carrying had fallen out of her hands. — THE BFG

• When you serve food, you **ladle**, **scoop**, **spoon** or **dish it out**.

• An amount of food to serve is a **dollop** or **spoonful**, and an amount on a plate is a **plateful**.
A real witch gets the same pleasure from squelching a child as you get from eating a plateful of strawberries and thick cream. — THE WITCHES

• Someone with terrible **table manners**, like Mr Twit, **shovels** food into his mouth.
Mr Twit started eating, twisting the long tomato-covered strings around his fork and shovelling them into his mouth. Soon there was tomato sauce all over his hairy chin. — THE TWITS

EATING MEALS

• A small portion of food is a **morsel** and a tiny amount is a **crumb**. An amount that you eat at one time is **bite**, **nibble** or **mouthful**.
Mr Twit never went really hungry. By sticking out his tongue and curling it sideways to explore the hairy jungle around his mouth, he was always able to find a tasty morsel here and there to nibble on. — THE TWITS

• Parts of a meal that you keep to eat later (or that stick in Mr Twit's beard) are **leftovers**.

• A small meal is a **snack** and a huge meal is a **feast** or **banquet** (say *bang*-kwit). A meal that you enjoy with friends in the middle of the night is called a **midnight feast**.

DID YOU KNOW?
The silent letter **k** at the start of **knife** was pronounced centuries ago—just like the **k** in **Knid**!

FIND OUT MORE!
A **spoonerism** has nothing to do with spoons! Find out more in THE WORLD OF WORDS.

DID YOU KNOW?
The word **morsel** comes from an old French word meaning 'little bite'.

• An amount of food that you eat at a meal is a **portion** or **helping**. The BFG has such a **squackling** appetite that he needs at least five helpings of **human–beaney** food.
A whole relay of footmen were kept busy hurrying to and from the kitchen carrying third helpings and fourth helpings and fifth helpings of fried eggs and sausages for the ravenous and delighted BFG. — THE BFG

• Willy Wonka's magical gum tastes of three **courses** of a meal one after the other (with no washing-up).
'That tiny little strip of gum lying there is a whole three-course dinner all by itself! . . . Just a little strip of Wonka's magic chewing-gum —and that's all you'll ever need at breakfast, lunch, and supper!' — CHARLIE AND THE CHOCOLATE FACTORY

FIND OUT MORE!
Giants are very messy eaters! Find out more in GIANT FOOD AND DRINK in THE MAGICAL WORLD.

WAYS TO DRINK

YOU CAN: **sip** a drink slowly, or take a **sip**
Grandma sipped the tea. 'It's not sweet enough,' she said. 'Put more sugar in.' — GEORGE'S MARVELLOUS MEDICINE

YOU CAN: **gulp** or **swallop** a drink quickly, or take a large **gulp** or **swig**
The ancient beanpole had already put the cup to her lips, and in one gulp she swallowed everything that was in it. — GEORGE'S MARVELLOUS MEDICINE

YOU CAN: **slurp** a drink noisily: *Farmer Bean was slurping his cider.*

• A fizzy drink also **bubbles**, **fizzes** or **froths** —as does water when you add **Wonka-Vite**.
Mr Wonka tipped all fourteen pills into the glass. The water bubbled and frothed. 'Drink it while it's fizzing,' he said. — CHARLIE AND THE GREAT GLASS ELEVATOR

• You can drink from a **cup**, **mug**, **glass** or **tumbler** (although giants drink straight from the **bottle**).
'Have some yourself!' cried the BFG, tipping the neck of the enormous bottle towards her. 'Don't you have a cup?' Sophie said. 'No cups. Only bottle.' — THE BFG

sip slurp gulp swig swallop

ALL ABOUT FOOD

DESCRIBING FOOD

• Food comes in **dillions** of **flavours**. It can taste: **buttery, cabbagey, cheesy, chocolatey, curranty, fruity, lemony, milky, minty, nutty, salty, sugary, vinegary.**
'The grass you are standing on, my dear little ones, is made of a new kind of soft, minty sugar that I've just invented! I call it swudge!'– CHARLIE AND THE CHOCOLATE FACTORY

IT CAN BE: **sweet, juicy, tender** or **succulent** like a ripe peach
And they all went over to the tunnel entrance and began scooping out great chunks of juicy, golden-coloured peach flesh. – JAMES AND THE GIANT PEACH

IT CAN BE: **bitter, sour, sharp** or **tangy** like a gooseberry
Her name was Mrs Pratchett. She was a small skinny old hag with a moustache on her upper lip and a mouth as sour as a green gooseberry. – BOY

IT CAN BE: **tough, chewy** or **stringy** like **chiddlers** (to a crocodile)
'I never eat children,' the Notsobig One said. 'Only fish . . . Children are too tough and chewy.' – THE ENORMOUS CROCODILE

IT CAN BE: **fiery, hot, peppery** or **spicy** like **Devil's Drenchers**
To the Monkey I gave a bag of Devil's Drenchers, those small fiery black sweets that one is not allowed to sell to children under four years old. – THE GIRAFFE AND THE PELLY AND ME

IT CAN BE: **crumbly** and **flaky**, or **crispy, crunchy** and **crusty** like **Giant Wangdoodles**
I can remember especially the Giant Wangdoodles from Australia, every one with a huge ripe red strawberry hidden inside its crispy chocolate crust. – THE GIRAFFE AND THE PELLY AND ME

crunchy crusty crispy crumbly

IT CAN BE: **smooth, creamy, rich** or **velvety** like chocolate
Charlie put the mug to his lips, and as the rich warm creamy chocolate ran down his throat into his empty tummy, his whole body from head to toe began to tingle with pleasure. – CHARLIE AND THE CHOCOLATE FACTORY

IT CAN BE: **gooey, gloopy, sticky** or **syrupy** like treacle
The saucepan was full of a thick gooey purplish treacle, boiling and bubbling. – CHARLIE AND THE CHOCOLATE FACTORY

IT CAN BE: **slimy, sloppy, mushy, slushy** or **squishy** like **Squiggly Spaghetti**
Mrs Twit waited until Mr Twit had eaten the whole plateful. Then she said, 'You want to know why your spaghetti was squishy?' – THE TWITS

stringy

DID YOU KNOW?
The word **spaghetti** comes from Italian and means literally 'little strings'.

slimy sloppy slushy squishy

IT CAN BE: **thin, runny** or **watery** like the Bucket family's cabbage soup
In the evenings, after he had finished his supper of watery cabbage soup, Charlie always went into the room of his four grandparents to listen to their stories. – CHARLIE AND THE CHOCOLATE FACTORY

• A **cake** can also be: **light, airy, spongy** or **splongy**, or **heavy, doughy, soggy** or **stodgy**.
'If you is putting the right amounts of all the different things into it, you is making the cake come out any way you want, sugary, splongy, curranty, Christmassy or grobswitchy.' – THE BFG

• An informal word for food is **grub**. The BFG also calls it **grabble**.
'Just feast your eyes on that!' cried Mr Fox, dancing up and down. 'What d'you think of it, eh? Pretty good grub!' – FANTASTIC MR FOX

DELUMPTIOUS FOOD

CAN BE: appetising, delectable, delicious, delunctious, flavory-savory, glumptious, guzzly, jumbly, lickswishy, luscious, mouth-watering, scrumdiddlyumptious, scrumptious or scrumptious-galumptious, tasty, yummy
'A walnut fresh from the tree is scrumptious-galumptious, so flavory-savory, so sweet to eat that it makes me all wobbly just thinking about it!'—THE GIRAFFE AND THE PELLY AND ME

• A piece of **delumptious** food is a **delicacy** or **titbit**: *The Centipede eats earwigs as a delicacy.*

• If something is **a piece of cake** it is very easy to do: *School work is a piece of cake for Matilda.*

lickswishy
delunctious
scrumdiddlyumptious
delectable
scrumptious
luscious

WHAT TASTES DELUMPTIOUS?
• Some tasty things are: **caramel, fudge, marshmallow, toffee** and **toffee apples,** Miss Trunchbull's **chocolate cake**, every **Wonka bar** ever made, all the **lickswishy sweets** sold in the **Grubber.**
'Mr Willy Wonka can make marshmallows that taste of violets, and rich caramels that change colour every ten seconds as you suck them.'—CHARLIE AND THE CHOCOLATE FACTORY

• The **Oompa-Loompas** love to guzzle **cacao beans** (say kak-*ah*-oh), which are used to make **chocolate**—just as the **Fleshlumpeater** loves to gobble **human beans**!

ALL ABOUT CHOCOLATE
• Chocolate can be **creamy, milky, smooth** and **silky,** or **dark, rich** and **velvety.**

• You can **lick, melt, mix, mould, pour, swirl** or **whip** chocolate (as well as **guzzle** it of course).
'The creamiest loveliest chocolate I've ever tasted!' said Grandpa Joe, smacking his lips. 'That's because it's been mixed by waterfall,' Mr Wonka told him.—CHARLIE AND THE CHOCOLATE FACTORY

• A block of chocolate to eat is a **bar** and a humungous bar is a **slab.** The most scrumdiddlyumptious **Wonka bar** of all is **Whipple-Scrumptious Fudgemallow Delight.**
Walking to school in the mornings, Charlie could see great slabs of chocolate piled up high in the shop windows, and he would stop and stare and press his nose against the glass, his mouth watering like mad.—CHARLIE AND THE CHOCOLATE FACTORY

• Most chocolate bars have a **wrapper**, but only SOME wrappers hide a **Golden Ticket** underneath. You might **rip** or **tear off** a wrapper, just to check.
Fully grown women were seen going into sweet shops and buying ten Wonka bars at a time, then tearing off the wrappers on the spot and peering eagerly underneath for a glint of golden paper.—CHARLIE AND THE CHOCOLATE FACTORY

• A word meaning chocolate and sweets is **confectionery** and Willy Wonka is a **confectioner** or **chocolatier** (say chocolate-*ear*).

DID YOU KNOW?
The word **chocolate** comes from the Nahuatl (Mexican) word **chocolatl**, because chocolate was first created and drunk in ancient Mexico.

Roald Dahl loved **chocolate**! He collected foil **wrappers** from the bars he ate and made them into a silver ball which he kept in his writing hut.

repulsive

rotsome

uckyslush

grobswitchy

disgustive

DISGUSTEROUS FOOD

CAN BE: **disgusting** or **disgustive**, **grobswitchy**, **repulsive** or **repulsant**, **rotsome**, **uckyslush**

• Food that has gone **rotten** (like the **leftover** food in Mr Twit's beard) is **maggoty** or **mouldy**.
You would probably see much larger objects . . . that had been there for months and months, like a piece of maggoty green cheese or a mouldy old cornflake or even the slimy tail of a tinned sardine. — THE TWITS

• Food with no taste is **bland** or **tasteless** and food that is too **disgusterous** to eat is **inedible**. Willy Wonka's chewing-gum is never bland as it never loses its flavour.

• Food that is so **repulsant** it makes you feel ill is **nauseating**, **sickly** or **sickable**: *a spoonful of sickable snozzcumber soup.*

WHAT TASTES DISGUSTEROUS?
• Some things that taste nasty are: **cabbage** with **caterpillars**, **snozzcumbers**, **Squiggly Spaghetti**.
'From now on, you must eat cabbage three times a day. Mountains of cabbage! And if it's got caterpillars in it, so much the better!' — GEORGE'S MARVELLOUS MEDICINE

'It's a new kind,' Mrs Twit said, taking a mouthful from her own plate which of course had no worms. *'It's called Squiggly Spaghetti.'* — THE TWITS

ALL ABOUT DRINKS

• Some drinks are: **hot chocolate** or **cocoa**, **juice**, **lemonade**, **milk**, **tea**, **coffee**, **water**.
Aunt Sponge and Aunt Spiker were sitting comfortably in deck-chairs near by, sipping tall glasses of fizzy lemonade and watching him to see that he didn't stop work for one moment. — JAMES AND THE GIANT PEACH

• Willy Wonka also keeps **extra-usual** cows who produce **chocolate milk**.

• Some drinks for grown-ups are **beer** (which Mr Twit likes), **cider** (which Farmer Bean makes) and **gin**. The **Oompa-Loompas** also like **butterscotch** and **buttergin**.
On his way back to the kitchen, George saw a bottle of gin standing on the sideboard. Grandma was very fond of gin. She was allowed to have a small nip of it every evening. — GEORGE'S MARVELLOUS MEDICINE

• A drink with bubbles, like Willy Wonka's **Fizzy Lifting Drink**, is **bubbly**, **fizzy**, **frothy** or **effervescent**.
FIZZY LIFTING DRINKS, it said on the next door. 'Oh, those are fabulous!' cried Mr Wonka. 'They fill you with bubbles . . . and up you go until your head hits the ceiling—and there you stay.' — CHARLIE AND THE CHOCOLATE FACTORY

FIND OUT MORE!
How do you eat a snozzcumber? Find out in GIANT FOOD AND DRINK in THE MAGICAL WORLD.

FIND OUT MORE!
Frobscottle is **effervescent** too! Find out more in GIANT FOOD AND DRINK in THE MAGICAL WORLD.

COOKING FOOD

fry frizzle
simmer sizzle
stew squizzle

YOU CAN: blend, chop, cut, grate, grind, knead, mash, mince, mix, peel, pickle, pulp, slice, stir, whip, whisk, whizz or squizzle food to prepare it
'A hundred knives go slice, slice, slice; We add some sugar, cream, and spice; We boil him for a minute more, Until we're absolutely sure That all the greed and all the gall Is boiled away for once and all.' — CHARLIE AND THE CHOCOLATE FACTORY

YOU CAN: bake, boil, frizzle, fry, grill, melt, poach, roast, simmer, sizzle or stew food to cook it
'What do we do with all those mice who have had their tails chopped off?' asked the audience. 'You simmer them in frog-juice for vun hour,' came the answer. — THE WITCHES

• If you are not careful, you might **burn, overcook, spill** or **spoil** the food. It might **boil over** or **bubble over** when it is cooking.
Place chocolate in very large cauldron and melt over red-hot furnace. When melted, lower the heat slightly so as not to burn the chocolate, but keep it boiling. — CHARLIE AND THE GREAT GLASS ELEVATOR

• When you prepare food, you sometimes follow a **recipe**. The items in a recipe are the **ingredients**.
'All the other chocolate makers, you see, had begun to grow jealous of the wonderful sweets that Mr Wonka was making, and they started sending in spies to steal his secret recipes.' — CHARLIE AND THE CHOCOLATE FACTORY

• A small amount of an **ingredient** that you add is a **drop**, **pinch**, **splash** or **sprinkle**.
'I've eaten fresh mudburgers by the greatest cooks there are . . . And pails of snails and lizards' tails, And beetles by the jar. (A beetle is improved by just a splash of vinegar.)' — JAMES AND THE GIANT PEACH

• If you **cook someone's goose**, it means that you spoil their plans.
'Now you've done it!' cried Mrs Kranky, glaring at her husband. 'You've cooked the old girl's goose!' — GEORGE'S MARVELLOUS MEDICINE

THINGS TO COOK WITH
INCLUDE: chopping board, egg-beater, frying-pan or sizzlepan, kettle, kitchen knife, mixer, pot, rolling-pin, saucepan, wooden spoon
The next moment, one of the cooks came along with a gigantic saucepan of steaming green soup and poured the whole lot into the silver basin. — THE WITCHES

• You can cook food in an **oven** or on a **stove**. Witches **roast** telescopes and alarm-clocks in their ovens (which is Not Recommended for non-witches).
'Next,' said The Grand High Witch, 'you take your boiled telescope and your frrried mouse-tails and your cooked mice and your rrroasted alarm-clock and all together you put them into the mixer.' — THE WITCHES

FIND OUT MORE!
Why does the BFG need an **egg-beater**? Find out in ALL ABOUT DREAMS in THE MAGICAL WORLD.

DID YOU KNOW?
An old word for an **egg-beater** is a froth-stick.

DESCRIBING SMELLS

fragrant *perfumed* *pungent* *aromatic*

GLORIUMPTIOUS SMELLS

CAN BE: aromatic, fragrant, perfumed, scented, sweet or sweet-smelling
The Globgobbler is an especially delicious sweet that is made somewhere near Mecca, and the moment you bite into it, all the perfumed juices of Arabia go squirting down your gullet one after the other. — THE GIRAFFE AND THE PELLY AND ME

• Other words for pleasant smells are **aroma, fragrance, perfume** and **scent**. A slight smell is a **whiff**.
The rich scent of chicken wafted down the tunnel to where the foxes were crouching.
— FANTASTIC MR FOX

• Scrumptious food smells **appetising** or **mouth-watering**:
A mouth-watering smell drifted from the Fudge Room.

• A strong smell is **heady, heavy, pungent** or **rich**.
And outside the walls, for half a mile around in every direction, the air was scented with the heavy rich smell of melting chocolate! — CHARLIE AND THE CHOCOLATE FACTORY

• A smell or taste that is a mixture of sweet and sour is **bittersweet**.
The tunnel was damp and murky, and all around him there was the curious bittersweet smell of fresh peach. — JAMES AND THE GIANT PEACH

WHAT SMELLS GLORIUMPTIOUS?
• Some **sweet-smelling** things are: Willy Wonka's **factory** (which smells of all his scrumptious **ingredients**), **perfume, tinkle-tinkle tree blossom**.
All the most wonderful smells in the world seemed to be mixed up in the air around them—the smell of roasting coffee and burnt sugar and melting chocolate and mint and violets and crushed hazelnuts and apple blossom and caramel and lemon peel. — CHARLIE AND THE CHOCOLATE FACTORY

• Chickens also smell **mouth-watering** to foxes, and **chiddlers** smell **irresistible** to giants.

• Most **perfumes** are sweet-smelling, except the one that George's mother uses, which is made from turnip flowers.
There was a bottle of perfume called flowers of turnips. It smelled of old cheese. In it went. — GEORGE'S MARVELLOUS MEDICINE

REPULSANT SMELLS

CAN BE: disgusting or disgustive, evil-smelling, filthy, foul, icky, malodorous, repellent, repulsive, smelly, stinking
The shoe was long and very wide. (A normal foot got lost inside.) Also it smelled a wee bit icky. (The owner's feet were hot and sticky.) — REVOLTING RHYMES

• Something rotten smells **fetid** or **rancid**:
The Bloodbottler's breath smelled rotsomely rancid.

• A damp place smells **dank, mildewed, mouldy** or **musty**.
James could feel breath blowing on his cheeks. The breath smelled musty and stale and slightly mildewed, like air in an old cellar. — JAMES AND THE GIANT PEACH

• Other words for nasty smells are **fumes, odour, stench, stink, reek**.
The smell was disgusting. It was the stench that comes from deep inside the tummy of a meat-eating animal. — THE MINPINS

• When something smells **repulsant**, it **reeks, stinks** or **gives off** a nasty smell.
'Boggis gives off a filthy stink of rotten chicken-skins. Bunce reeks of goose-livers, and as for Bean, the fumes of apple cider hang around him like poisonous gases.' — FANTASTIC MR FOX

> **DID YOU KNOW?**
> The word **aroma** comes from a Greek word meaning 'spice'.

> **DID YOU KNOW?**
> The word **smelly** used to mean 'suspicious' as well as having a bad smell.

musty

- A truly repulsive or **repulsant** smell can **stink out** a room, or (if it is strong enough) the whole world of witches.
'Children smell!' she screamed. 'They stink out the vurld! Vee do not vont these children around here!'— THE WITCHES

- If someone **raises a stink** about something, it means that they complain or make a tremendous fuss about it.
'I know my father would raise a terrific stink if I told him the Headmistress had grabbed me by the hair and slung me over the playground fence.'— MATILDA

WHAT SMELLS REPULSANT?
- Some nasty-smelling things are: Mr Twit's unwashed **beard**, giants' **breath** (especially after eating **chiddlers**), George's **grandma**, **stink-bombs**.
'I'll bet it was she who put that stink-bomb under my desk here first thing this morning. The place stank like a sewer!'— MATILDA

- Farmers Boggis, Bunce and Bean also smell **foulsome** to foxes, and the cleanest of **chiddlers** are **smelly** to witches.
'The cleaner you happen to be, the more smelly you are to a witch... An absolutely clean child gives off the most ghastly stench to a witch,' my grandmother said.— THE WITCHES

foulsome foul fetid repulsant mildewed

DID YOU KNOW?
The word **waft** originally meant 'to carry by water', not to drift on the air.

SMELLING THINGS

- You can **sniff** or **scent** a smell, or **catch**, **detect** or **get a whiff** of it.
'Vot's going on down there?' shouted The Grand High Witch... 'Mildred's just got a whiff of dogs' droppings, Your Grandness!' someone called back to her.— THE WITCHES

- A smell can **drift** or **waft** gently towards you, or can **hang** in the air, like the musty smell around George's grandma.
He really hated that horrid old witchy woman... He wanted to blow away the witchy smell that hung about her in the next room.— GEORGE'S MARVELLOUS MEDICINE

- A strong smell might make you **choke** or **splutter**, or **make your eyes water**.
A fiery fearsome smell filled the kitchen. It made George choke and splutter.— GEORGE'S MARVELLOUS MEDICINE

- A very strong smell might **hit you in the nostrils**, like the **stink-waves** which witches can sense in the air.
The smell that drives a witch mad... comes oozing out of your skin in waves, and these waves, stink-waves the witches call them, go floating through the air and hit the witch right smack in her nostrils.— THE WITCHES

FIND OUT MORE!
What is odd about witches' **nostrils**? Find out in ALL ABOUT WITCHES in THE MAGICAL WORLD.

FIND OUT MORE!
Tastes can be **gloriumptious** and **repulsant** too! Find out more in ALL ABOUT FOOD.

filthy icky disgustive disgusting mouldy malodorous reeking smelly stinking rancid

Human-beaney Writing Hut

as blubbery as a blancmange

splendid similes

• Roald Dahl loved using **similes** to describe **faces** or **facial features**, especially **repulsant** ones. Augustus Gloop has a face **like a monstrous ball of dough** and Aunt Sponge looks **like a great white soggy overboiled cabbage**. Both of these similes compare a **human-beaney** face to **food**.

• What unappetising similes could you conjure up for a character's face or features? They might have a face *like lumpy porridge*, a nose *like a misshapen mushroom*, lips *as blubbery as a blancmange* or eyes *as watery as weak tea.*

• You can do the same for other **body parts** too. What about hands *as puffy as pastry* or spindly legs *like two sticks of rhubarb?*

redunculous rhymes

• The word **hirsute** (say her-*syoot*) means 'very hairy', so it is a perfect description for Mr Twit. It is also an excellent word to put in a **redunculous** rhyme or poem about Mr Twit (and hairiness generally), as it rhymes with useful words like *brute* (which Mr Twit is), *fruit* (which could be stuck in his beard) and *shoot* (which he does to birds). It also rhymes with *parachute* (like Mrs Twit's billowing petticoat). For example: *Mr Twit is so hirsute, he can use his beard as a parachute.*

• The word **squishous** rhymes with **delicious**, but also with **vicious** and **malicious**—and **vermicious** (which means 'worm-like'). Can you use some or even ALL of these in the same rhyme? For example: *Spaghetti is squishous and usually delicious—unless it's vermicious!*

• You can also make up your own words that end with *-ishous* or *-icious* to make an even more **redunculous** rhyme. What about *swishous* or *glishous,* or even *gloopicious?*

hirsute • brute

chocophile • snoozophile • chiddlerphobe

bish and trips

phizz-whizzing suffixes

Oxford ROALD DAHL Dictionary

- Matilda is a **bibliophile**, which means that she loves books. The ending (or **suffix**) *-phile* means 'someone who LOVES' a particular thing. For example, a **zoophile** loves animals and a **logophile** loves words (and of course dictionaries). You can make up your own *-phile* words, too. For example, a **chocolate** lover is a *chocophile*, and if you like having a *snooze* you are a *snoozophile*.

- The opposite of *-phile* is *-phobe*, which means 'someone who HATES' something. Roald Dahl hated **beards** and was a **pogonophobe**. What other words could you make with this hateful **suffix**? For example, Miss Trunchbull is a *chiddlerphobe*, as she hates her pupils. What might you call someone who hates **vegitibbles** or **homework** or **gym**?

wonky word play

- The Centipede eats **scrambled dregs** instead of **scrambled eggs**. The word **dregs** sounds like **eggs**, but means 'leftover rubbish', which sounds **disgusterous**! This type of funny mistake with words is called a **malapropism**. *'I've eaten fresh mudburgers by the greatest cooks there are, And scrambled dregs and stinkbugs' eggs and hornets stewed in tar.'* — JAMES AND THE GIANT PEACH

- To make your own munchable **malapropisms**, try swapping part of a food phrase so that it makes a funny joke. Remember to use a word that sounds like the word you are swapping. For example, your **malaprop menu** might include *screams on toast* (for *beans on toast*), or *bish and trips* (for *fish and chips*).

stroll + whistle = stristle

wondercrump wordbuilding

- Roald Dahl invented so many words that he didn't have space to use all of them in his stories! One of these **leftover** words that he invented is *strodel*, which is a blend of **stroll** and **yodel**, so it might mean to *yodel* while *strolling* along. What else could you do while strolling? Perhaps you could *stristle* (stroll and whistle) or *strunch* (stroll and munch).

- Roald Dahl based the word *chiddler* on **child**. Could you **invent** an alternative word for a **grown-up**? What about a *grump-up* (because they are often grumpy), or a *not-so-grown-up* (for someone who acts more childish than a *chiddler*)?

not-so-nice names

- Miss Trunchbull's first name is **Agatha**, but some **beastly** characters in Roald Dahl's stories don't have first names—or we don't know for certain what they are. Can you think of suitable names for **Mr and Mrs Twit**? Perhaps Mr Twit is secretly called *Dredrick Twit* and his wife is *Wickifrid Twit*.

- Or you could use **alliterative** names like *Trogothy* and *Trogetha Twit*. (Roald Dahl's words that begin with **trog-** always mean nasty things.) What might be the secret full names of Farmers **Boggis**, **Bunce** and **Bean**?

Trogothy & Trogetha Twit

ZIPPFETZ ALONG TO THE **WORLD OF WORDS** FOR MORE HOPSCOTCHY IDEAS FOR WRITERS AND STORYTELLERS!

peach

vegitibble

snozzberry

crockadow

newt butteryfly

blueberry

giraffe muckleberry glow-worm moonbeam

THE NATURAL WORLD

'They're the nicest creatures in the world!
Allow me to introduce them to you.'
— JAMES AND THE GIANT PEACH

DESCRIBING LANDSCAPE

THE COUNTRYSIDE

CAN BE: fertile, green, leafy, lush, rolling, wooded

CAN HAVE: fields, forest, wood, trees, meadow, moor, river, stream, footpath, hedgerow, cottage, farm
The world I lived in consisted only of the filling-station, the workshop, the caravan, the school, and of course the woods and fields and streams in the countryside around. — DANNY THE CHAMPION OF THE WORLD

• The trees and plants that grow in an area of land are its **vegetation**: *The vegetation in Giant Country is very sparse.*

HILLS AND MOUNTAINS

CAN BE: hilly, mountainous, steep or sheer; craggy, rocky, snow-capped

CAN HAVE: cliff or crag, ridge, slope, mountain stream, fjord, rocks, boulders, cave

• A series of hills or mountains is a **range**. A low-lying area between mountains is a **valley** or (in Scotland) a **glen**.
He leaped over a dozen rivers. He went rattling through a great forest, then down into a valley and up over a range of hills as bare as concrete. — THE BFG

• The top of a mountain is the **peak** or **summit** and the bottom is the **foot** or **foothills**. The front of a cliff is the **cliff face**.
'It is a tree called the Bristlecone Pine that grows upon the slopes of Wheeler Peak in Nevada, U.S.A.' — CHARLIE AND THE GREAT GLASS ELEVATOR

• Willy Wonka has a craggy **fudge mountain** in his factory, from which the Oompa-Loompas cut blocks of fudge.
A great, craggy mountain made entirely of fudge, with Oompa-Loompas (all roped together for safety) hacking huge hunks of fudge out of its sides. — CHARLIE AND THE GREAT GLASS ELEVATOR

• George's grandma wants him to eat **mountains** of cabbage every day, which is a gigantuous amount to eat!
'From now on, you must eat cabbage three times a day. Mountains of cabbage! And if it's got caterpillars in it, so much the better!' — GEORGE'S MARVELLOUS MEDICINE

DESERT OR WASTELAND

CAN BE: arid, bare, barren, desolate, parched, sandy, treeless

CAN HAVE: sand, rocks, boulders

• The extra-usual rocks in Giant Country are coloured blue.
Soon he was galloping over a desolate wasteland that was not quite of this earth. The ground was flat and pale yellow. Great lumps of blue rock were scattered around, and dead trees stood everywhere like skeletons. — THE BFG

UNDERGROUND

CAN BE: dank, damp, musty

CAN HAVE: cave or cavern, pit, tunnel

• The area under the Earth's surface is **subterranean**.
The Gnoolies who inhabit Minusland are a **subterrestrial** species.
'Do any other creatures live here, Mr Wonka?' 'Plenty of Gnoolies.' 'Are they dangerous?' 'If they bite you, they are. You're a gonner, my boy, if you're bitten by a Gnooly.' — CHARLIE AND THE GREAT GLASS ELEVATOR

FIND OUT MORE! What might you find inside a giant's **cave**? Find out in GIANT PLACES in THE MAGICAL WORLD.

rocky craggy sandy arid

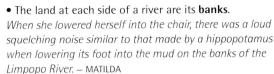

- The land at each side of a river are its **banks**.
When she lowered herself into the chair, there was a loud squelching noise similar to that made by a hippopotamus when lowering its foot into the mud on the banks of the Limpopo River. – MATILDA

- A small stream is a **brook** or (in Scotland) a **burn**.

- A falling stream of water is a **waterfall** or **cataract**. Willy Wonka's factory has a fantabulous river and waterfall of melted chocolate (as well as a steaming **lake** of hot caramel).
'The waterfall is most *important!' Mr Wonka went on. 'It mixes the chocolate! It churns it up! It pounds it and beats it! It makes it light and frothy!'* – CHARLIE AND THE CHOCOLATE FACTORY

- Other **areas of water** include: **canal**, **lake** or **loch**, **pond**, **pool**.

WHAT CAN WATER (AND CHOCOLATE) DO?

IT CAN: **flow** or **stream** along steadily
They were looking down upon a lovely valley. There were green meadows on either side of the valley, and along the bottom of it there flowed a great brown river.
– CHARLIE AND THE CHOCOLATE FACTORY

IT CAN: **cascade**, **gush**, **pour**, **rush** or **surge** strongly
All the time the water came pouring and roaring down upon them, bouncing and smashing and sloshing and slashing and swashing and swirling and surging and whirling and gurgling and gushing and rushing and rushing.
– JAMES AND THE GIANT PEACH

IT CAN: **dribble**, **drip**, **ooze** or **trickle** slowly
It was beginning to rain. Water was trickling down the necks of the three men and into their shoes. – FANTASTIC MR FOX

IT CAN: **slosh**, **splash**, **splish**, **splosh** or **swash** messily
And in every single tube the runny stuff was of a different colour, so that all the colours of the rainbow (and many others as well) came sloshing and splashing into the tub. – CHARLIE AND THE CHOCOLATE FACTORY

IT CAN: **bubble**, **gurgle**, **ripple**, **swirl** or **whirl** about
As we made our way out to the playground, my whole stomach began to feel as though it was slowly filling up with swirling water. – BOY

- **Human beans** can also **pour** and **stream** like water, when large numbers of them move along quickly in the same direction.
Every day of the week, hundreds and hundreds of children from far and near came pouring into the City to see the marvellous peach stone in the Park. – JAMES AND THE GIANT PEACH

RIVERS AND STREAMS

CAN BE: **clear**, **muddy** (or **chocolatey** in Willy Wonka's factory), **fast-flowing** or **rapid**
In the biggest brownest muddiest river in Africa, two crocodiles lay with their heads just above the water.
– THE ENORMOUS CROCODILE

- A river with a winding route might **wind its way** or **meander** (say me-*and*-er) along.

DID YOU KNOW?
The word **meander** comes from the River **Maeander** in ancient Phrygia (Turkey), which was famous for its twists and turns.

JUNGLES AND FORESTS

JUNGLES AND RAINFORESTS

CAN HAVE: coconut trees or coconut palms, creepers, vines, river, swamp

CAN BE: dense, lush, muddy, swampy, tangled, thick, tropical, verdant

 The Enormous Crocodile only *pretends* to be a **coconut tree** so that he can get close to children to gobble them up.
The Enormous Crocodile . . . arranged the branches and the coconuts so cleverly that he now looked exactly like a small coconut tree standing among the big coconut trees.
— THE ENORMOUS CROCODILE

• The tops of the trees in a jungle form a **canopy**. The plants that grow near the ground are the **undergrowth**.

• Roald Dahl uses a **metaphor** to describe Mr Twit's beard as a **hairy jungle**, because the hairs on his face grow as thickly as the plants in a jungle!

By sticking out his tongue and curling it sideways to explore the hairy jungle around his mouth, he was always able to find a tasty morsel here and there to nibble on. — THE TWITS

JUNGLE CREATURES

INCLUDE: crocodile, hippopotamus or hippo, lion, monkey, rhinoceros or rhino, snake, tiger, hornswoggler, snozzwanger, whangdoodle
'I'm the bravest croc in the whole river,' said the Enormous Crocodile. 'I'm the only one who dares to leave the water and go through the jungle to the town to look for little children to eat.'
— THE ENORMOUS CROCODILE

DID YOU KNOW?
The word **hippopotamus** comes from Greek words meaning 'river horse' and **rhinoceros** comes from Greek words meaning 'nose horn'.

FIND OUT MORE!
What does the BFG call a **hippopotamus** and a **rhinoceros**? Find out in GIANT LANGWITCH in THE MAGICAL WORLD.

lush
tropical
verdant

shady green cool

FIND OUT MORE!
The Red-Hot Smoke-Belching Gruncher lives in a forest too! See EXTRA-USUAL CREATURES in THE MAGICAL WORLD.

• **Muggle-Wump** and his family lived in the jungle before they were captured and forced to work in a circus.
Muggle-Wump and his family longed to escape from the cage in Mr Twit's garden and go back to the African jungle where they came from. – THE TWITS

• The **Oompa-Loompas** used to be **jungle dwellers** until they emigrated to work in Willy Wonka's factory (and to escape the **frightswiping** wildlife in **Loompaland**).
'And oh, what a terrible country it is! Nothing but thick jungles infested by the most dangerous beasts in the world —hornswogglers and snozzwangers and those terrible wicked whangdoodles.' – CHARLIE AND THE CHOCOLATE FACTORY

WOODS AND FORESTS

CAN HAVE: trees, shrubs, grass, wild flowers, moss, ferns, mushrooms, toadstools

CAN BE: cool, dense, green, leafy, shady

• The ground of a forest is the **floor** and the upper part is the **roof** or **treetops**. An open space in a wood or forest is a **clearing**.
Very very slowly, he walked forward into the great forest. Giant trees were soon surrounding him on all sides and their branches made an almost solid roof high above his head, blotting out the sky. – THE MINPINS

FOREST AND WOODLAND CREATURES

INCLUDE: badger, deer, field mouse, fox, hedgehog, mole, pheasant, rabbit, squirrel, stoat, weasel
Spectators all along the way Had come to watch and shout hooray, The field-mice, weasels, hedgehogs, stoats And rabbits in their furry coats All lined the route and waved their flags And picnicked out of paper-bags.
– RHYME STEW

• **Minpins** are also **forest dwellers**. They look like tiny **human beans** and live inside trees in the scary **Forest of Sin**.
'But . . . but . . . who are you?' Little Billy asked, taking care to speak very softly this time. 'We are the Minpins,' the tiny man said, 'and we OWN this wood.' – THE MINPINS

OTHER PLACES WHERE TREES GROW

INCLUDE: garden, grove, thicket, wood or woodland
Through the window, not so very far away, he could see the big black secret wood that was called The Forest of Sin. It was something he had always longed to explore. – THE MINPINS

• A large area planted with trees is a **plantation**.
'Look over there, my dear Giraffey, and you will see the only plantation of tinkle-tinkle trees in the entire country!'
– THE GIRAFFE AND THE PELLY AND ME

• An area planted with fruit trees, like Farmer Bean's apple trees, is an **orchard**. Willy Wonka has an **extra-usual** orchard of toffee-apple trees.
There were giant cog-wheels turning and mixers mixing and bubbles bubbling and vast orchards of toffee-apple trees and lakes the size of football grounds filled with blue and gold and green liquid, and everywhere there were Oompa-Loompas! – CHARLIE AND THE GREAT GLASS ELEVATOR

• If you are **out of the woods** you have managed to get out of trouble or danger, as if you had found your way out of a dark forest.
'If you think we're out of the woods yet, you're crazy!' shouted Grandma Georgina. – CHARLIE AND THE GREAT GLASS ELEVATOR

67

knotty
knobbly
gnarled
leafy

• Another name for a **chestnut tree** is a **conker tree**, because it produces hard shiny brown seeds called **conkers**.

It was lovely being high up there in that conker tree, all alone with the pale young leaves coming out everywhere around me. It was like being in a big green cave.
— THE WITCHES

DID YOU KNOW?
The word **conker** was originally a dialect word for 'snail shell', because the game of **conkers** was first played with snail shells.

EXTRA-USUAL TREES

• The **Big Dead Tree** is completely **leafless** because Mr Twit smears its branches with **HUGTIGHT** glue to trap birds.

• The **bong-bong tree** grows in **Loompaland** and has an edible **bark** which is useful for disguising the taste of caterpillars.

The Oompa-Loompas spent every moment of their days climbing through the treetops looking for other things to mash up with the caterpillars to make them taste better—red beetles, for instance, and eucalyptus leaves, and the bark of the bong-bong tree. — CHARLIE AND THE CHOCOLATE FACTORY

FIND OUT MORE!
The Giant Peach grows on a tree too! Find out more in FRUITS AND VEGETABLES.

• The **tinkle-tinkle tree** produces distinctive pink and purple **blossom** which is the sole diet of the **Geraneous Giraffe**.

PARTS OF A TREE

INCLUDE: root, trunk, treetop, bark, branch or bough, twig, leaf, blossom, catkin, cone, nut, fruit

The Monkey took off like an arrow, and a few seconds later he was high up in the branches of the walnut tree, cracking the nuts and guzzling what was inside. — THE GIRAFFE AND THE PELLY AND ME

• The amount of leaves that a tree has is its **foliage**: The Big Dead Tree has no foliage left at all.

• The juice inside a tree or plant is its **sap**. Willy Wonka uses the **sap** from a 400-year-old Bristlecone Pine to make **Vita-Wonk**.

ALL ABOUT TREES

TYPES OF TREE

INCLUDE: alder, ash, beech, cedar, chestnut, fir, fruit tree, hawthorn, hazel, oak, palm, pine, sycamore, walnut, willow

There were tall trees here and there on either side, oak and sycamore and ash and occasionally a sweet chestnut. Miss Honey . . . gave the names of all these to Matilda and taught her how to recognize them by the shape of their leaves and the pattern of the bark on their trunks. — MATILDA

DESCRIBING TREES

• A young tree is a **sapling**.

Then there was the tree-house which we built high up in the top of the big oak at the bottom of our field. And the bow and arrow, the bow a four-foot-long ash sapling, and the arrows flighted with the tail-feathers of partridge and pheasant. – DANNY THE CHAMPION OF THE WORLD

• A **deciduous** tree loses or sheds its leaves in autumn. An **evergreen** tree has leaves all year round. A tree that produces cones, like the ancient Bristlecone Pine, is a **conifer**.

'But what kind of a tree? Not the Douglas Fir. Not the Oak. Not the Cedar. No no, my boy. It is a tree called the Bristlecone Pine that grows upon the slopes of Wheeler Peak in Nevada, U.S.A.' – CHARLIE AND THE GREAT GLASS ELEVATOR

• The **bark** of a tree can be: **gnarled**, **knotty** or **knobbly**, **papery** or **smooth**.

• A branch with lots of leaves is **leafy** and one with no leaves is **leafless** or **bare**: *The branches of the Big Dead Tree are as bare as a witch's scalp!*

leafless

DID YOU KNOW?
The words **gnarled** and **knobbly** start with silent letters, but the first letters in these words were once pronounced, just like the K at the start of **Knid**.

WHAT CAN YOU SEE IN A TREE?

• **birds**, **bird nest**, **tree-house**, Mr Twit's **ladder**, **chiddlers** glued with HUGTIGHT, Minpins (but only if you are VERY lucky)

The next morning, when Mr Twit went out to collect the birds, he found four miserable little boys sitting in the tree, stuck as tight as could be by the seats of their pants to the branches. – THE TWITS

• If someone is **barking up the wrong tree**, they have the wrong idea about something, as if they were a dog chasing a cat in the wrong tree. (The BFG calls it **barking up the wrong dog** instead.)

'Of course,' the BFG said. 'But how is this helping us! I think you is barking up the wrong dog.' – THE BFG

WHAT CAN TREES DO?

THEY: **spread their branches** when they grow

An enormous oak tree stood overshadowing the cottage. Its massive spreading branches seemed to be enfolding and embracing the tiny building, and perhaps hiding it as well from the rest of the world. – MATILDA

 A giant can *pretend* to be a tree by spreading his arms out like branches.

'He is standing in the park in the dusky evening and he is holding great big branches over his head, and there he is waiting until some happy families is coming to have a picnic under the spreading tree.'
– THE BFG

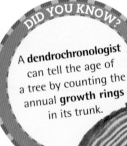

DID YOU KNOW?
A **dendrochronologist** can tell the age of a tree by counting the annual **growth rings** in its trunk.

THEY CAN: **shed their leaves** in the autumn (except for the Big Dead Tree which has no leaves left to shed)

Near the house you can see Mr Twit's work-shed. To one side there is The Big Dead Tree. It never has any leaves on it because it's dead. – THE TWITS

THEY CAN: **rock** or **sway** from side to side. Their leaves can also **rustle** in the wind.

The tree rocked from side to side, and everyone, even Mr Gregg, was afraid that the nest would fall down.
– THE MAGIC FINGER

• The BFG can hear trees **moan** when they are chopped down.

'If I is chopping an axe into the trunk of a big tree, I is hearing a terrible sound coming from inside the heart of the tree.' 'What sort of sound?' Sophie asked. 'A soft moaning sound,' the BFG said. – THE BFG

PLANTS AND FLOWERS

ALL ABOUT PLANTS

TYPES OF PLANT

`INCLUDE:` fern, flower, fungus, grass, heather, herb, ivy, lichen, moss, nettle, shrub, thistle, tree, vine, weed, wildflower

`CAN BE:` hardy, leafy, prickly, spiky, thorny, woody
On either side of the path there was a wilderness of nettles and blackberry thorns and long brown grass. — MATILDA

• Mrs Twit's favourite plants are **stinging-nettles** and **thistles**.
'I always grow plenty of spiky thistles and plenty of stinging-nettles,' she used to say. 'They keep out nasty nosey little children.' — THE TWITS

• A plant that grows in a pot (like Mr Hoppy's plants) is a **pot plant**.

stinging
spiky prickly thorny

TYPES OF FUNGUS

`INCLUDE:` mushroom, toadstool
Mrs Salt . . . was now kneeling right on the edge of the hole with her head down and her enormous behind sticking up in the air like a giant mushroom. — CHARLIE AND THE CHOCOLATE FACTORY

• Miss Trunchbull likes to insult her pupils by calling them **weeds** or **fungi** (say *fung*-gee).
'You ignorant little slug!' the Trunchbull bellowed. 'You witless weed! You empty-headed hamster! You stupid glob of glue!' — MATILDA

• The broad upper part of a mushroom or toadstool is called the **cap**.

SOME NAMES OF FLOWERS

INCLUDE: bluebell, buttercup, crocus, cowslip, daffodil, daisy, dandelion, foxglove, geranium, iris, lavender, orchid, poppy, primrose, rose, rhododendron, sunflower, tulip, violet

Graceful trees and bushes were growing along the riverbanks—weeping willows and alders and tall clumps of rhododendrons with their pink and red and mauve blossoms. In the meadows there were thousands of buttercups.
— CHARLIE AND THE CHOCOLATE FACTORY

• Willy Wonka makes edible **buttercups** (as well as grass) out of sugar.
'I could eat the whole field!' said Grandpa Joe, grinning with delight. 'I could go around on all fours like a cow and eat every blade of grass in the field!' 'Try a buttercup!' cried Mr Wonka. 'They're even nicer!' — CHARLIE AND THE CHOCOLATE FACTORY

PARTS OF A PLANT OR FLOWER

INCLUDE: root, stalk, stem, leaf, bud, petal, bloom, blossom, pollen, pod, seed, spine, thorn

• A single flower is a **bloom**, whereas **blossom** is a mass of flowers: *Giraffes are very fond of tinkle-tinkle blossom.*

• A single leaf of grass (or of swudge) is called a **blade**.
'The grass you are standing on . . . is made of a new kind of soft, minty sugar that I've just invented! I call it swudge! Try a blade! Please do! It's delectable!'
— CHARLIE AND THE CHOCOLATE FACTORY

• A handful of cut flowers is a **bunch** or **bouquet** (say boo-*kay*) and someone who sells or arranges cut flowers is a **florist**.
James began thinking about all the other children in the world and what they might be doing at this moment. . . . Some would be walking in cool woods and picking bunches of wild flowers. — JAMES AND THE GIANT PEACH

• The word **botanical** means 'to do with plants' and **floral** means 'to do with flowers'.

• If someone **turns over a new leaf**, they make a new start in life by promising to be good: *Will Miss Trunchbull ever turn over a new leaf?*

DESCRIBING PLANTS

• A word for plants in general is **vegetation**: *The vegetation in Giant Country is very sparse.*

• A plant that you can eat is an **edible** plant: *Is swudge edible? Of course it is!*

• A type of plant that farmers grow as food is a **crop**. *'They are very pleased when they have lots of Ladybirds in their fields . . . Because we gobble up all the nasty little insects that are gobbling up all the farmer's crops.'*
— JAMES AND THE GIANT PEACH

• A young plant is a **seedling** and a new growth is a **shoot**.

• A plant with sweet-smelling flowers or leaves is a **fragrant** or **scented** plant.

DID YOU KNOW?
Dandelion comes from French words meaning 'lion's teeth', because of the jagged shape of the plant's leaves.

DID YOU KNOW?
A scientist who studies plants is called a **botanist**.

stem blade swudge

WHAT CAN PLANTS DO?

THEY: **spring up** or **sprout** when they start to grow
At ten p. m. or thereabout, The little bean began to sprout. By morning it had grown so tall You couldn't see the top at all. — REVOLTING RHYMES

THEY: **climb** or **grow** upwards, or **creep** or **spread** over the ground

THEY: **bloom, blossom** or **bud** when they produce flowers or leaves
The next moment she was galloping full speed across the lawns and whinnying with excitement and the last we saw of her, she was burying her head in the beautiful pink and purple flowers that blossomed on the tops of the trees all around her. — THE GIRAFFE AND THE PELLY AND ME

THEY: **smell** or **give off a scent** when they flower

THEY: **flourish** or **thrive** when they are healthy

THEY: **droop, shrivel, wilt** or **wither** when they are not-so-healthy

• Hair can **sprout** like a plant too, meaning that it grows quickly or thickly (especially after eating **Hair Toffee** or taking **Wonka-Vite**).
But now the fringe of white hair was turning gold and all over the top of his head new gold hair was beginning to sprout, like grass. — CHARLIE AND THE GREAT GLASS ELEVATOR

ALL ABOUT GARDENS

• A small area of garden is a **plot** or **patch**.

• A person who tends plants in a garden is a **gardener**.
'I am not a slimy beast,' the Earthworm said. 'I am a useful and much loved creature. Ask any gardener you like.'
— JAMES AND THE GIANT PEACH

• A formal word for gardening is **horticulture**: *Mrs Twit is not very good at horticulture.*

• A garden that is not tended may be **overgrown** or **run wild**.

DID YOU KNOW?

Plants and flowers have special two-part Latin names which are used by people who grow or study them.

For example the word *polyflora* means 'many flowers' and *tintinnabulum* means 'a tinkling bell', so a possible name for the tinkle-tinkle tree would be *Tintinnabula polyflora*.

bud
bloom
blossom

overgrown

run wild

'Our Centipede will never move again. He will turn into a statue and we shall be able to put him in the middle of the lawn with a bird-bath on the top of his head.' – JAMES AND THE GIANT PEACH

WHAT DO GARDENERS DO (EXCEPT MRS TWIT)?

THEY: **plant** or **sow** seeds or seedlings

THEY: **nurture**, **tend** or **water** growing plants:
Miss Honey is a keen gardener and enjoys tending her roses.

THEY: **cut**, **mow** or **trim** the grass
Not more than a hundred yards away, through the tall trees in the garden, across the mown lawns and the tidy flower-beds, the massive shape of the Palace itself loomed through the darkness. – THE BFG

THEY: **prune** trees or shrubs with **clippers**
She flew up the drive and suddenly she saw Miss Honey in the front garden, standing in the middle of a bed of roses doing something with a pair of clippers.
– MATILDA

THINGS TO SEE IN A GARDEN (EXCEPT MRS TWIT'S)

INCLUDE: **grass, lawn, flower-bed, fruit trees; bird-bath, greenhouse, ladder, pond, garden shed** or **hut, tree house**
'What's he like, this Duke?' the Giraffe asked me. 'I don't know,' I said. 'But he's very very famous and very rich. People say he has twenty-five gardeners just to look after his flower-beds.'
– THE GIRAFFE AND THE PELLY AND ME

DID YOU KNOW?
Roald Dahl wrote his stories in a special **writing hut** at the bottom of his **garden**.

prune

clip

trim

tend

nurture

FRUITS AND VEGETABLES

ALL ABOUT FRUIT

TYPES OF FRUIT AND FRUIT TREE
INCLUDE: apple, banana, cherry, date, grape, grapefruit, lemon, lime, melon, orange, peach, pear, pineapple, plum, tomato

James's little face was glowing with excitement . . . He could see the peach swelling larger and larger as clearly as if it were a balloon being blown up. In half a minute, it was the size of a melon! — JAMES AND THE GIANT PEACH

luscious mushious

DID YOU KNOW?
The word **peach** comes from Latin words meaning 'Persian apple'.

• Willy Wonka's toffee apples grow on special **toffee-apple trees** that you can plant in your garden.

• An area planted with fruit trees, like the one that Farmer Bean owns, is an **orchard**.

winkleberry
puckleberry
snozzberry

muckleberry
strawbunkle

TYPES OF BERRY
INCLUDE: bilberry, blackberry, blueberry, bramble, cranberry, gooseberry, muckleberry, puckleberry, raspberry, snozzberry, strawberry or strawbunkle, twinkleberry, winkleberry

'The forest floor is safe at last for us to walk on! So now we can all go down to pick blackberries and winkleberries and puckleberries and muckleberries and twinkleberries and snozzberries to our hearts' content.' — THE MINPINS

• The spit of witches is **as blue as a bilberry**, which is a dark inky shade of blue.
'What is it, Grandmamma?' 'Their spit is blue.' 'Blue!' I cried. 'Not blue! Their spit can't be blue!' 'Blue as a bilberry,' she said. — THE WITCHES

• Willy Wonka uses **strawberries**, snozzberries and other fruits for making delectably **lickable wallpaper**.

DESCRIBING FRUIT

• Lemons, limes, oranges and grapefruit are **citrus** fruits.

• The skin on a fruit or vegetable is its **peel** and to **peel** it is to take its skin off. The **Centipede**'s friends suggest **peeling** him like a banana when he is coated with dried paint.
'It'll never come off,' the Earthworm said brightly. . . . 'We could try peeling him like a banana,' the Old-Green-Grasshopper suggested. — JAMES AND THE GIANT PEACH

• To squeeze a fruit (or a gum-chewing **chiddler**) to extract the juice is to **juice** or **de-juice** it.
'But Mr Wonka,' said Charlie Bucket anxiously, 'will Violet Beauregarde ever be all right again or will she always be a blueberry?' 'They'll de-juice her in no time flat!' declared Mr Wonka. — CHARLIE AND THE CHOCOLATE FACTORY

• Fruit **ripens** until it is **ripe** or ready to eat.
Immediately behind the caravan was an old apple tree. It bore lovely apples that ripened in the middle of September and you could go on picking them for the next four or five weeks. — DANNY THE CHAMPION OF THE WORLD

• It can taste: **juicy**, **luscious** or **mushious**, **sweet**, **sour** or **tart**.
'The whole floor of the forest is carpeted with wild strawberries, every one of them luscious and red and juicy-ripe. Go and see for yourself.' — THE MINPINS

TYPES OF VEGETABLE

INCLUDE: **beans** (except **human beans** and **jelly beans**), **cabbage**, **cauliflower**, **carrot**, frumpkin, **lettuce**, **parsnip**, **peas**, pigwinkle, **potato**, **pumpkin**, snozzcumber, **turnip**, **wurzel** or **mangel–wurzel**

Tortoise Number 2 had never eaten tender juicy lettuce leaves before. It had only had thick old cabbage leaves. It loved the lettuce and started chomping away at it with great gusto. – ESIO TROT

DID YOU KNOW?
The word **cabbage** comes from an old French word meaning 'head', so it is appropriate that Aunt Sponge's face looks like one.

wurzel snozzcumber frumpkin pigwinkle

• Vegetables that grow in the ground, like **parsnips** and **wurzels**, are **root vegetables**. It is very rude to call someone a **wurzel** (even if they look just like one).

There was no sign of Grandma. There was only a song-thrush sitting on one of the chimneypots, singing a song. The old wurzel's got stuck in the attic, George thought. Thank goodness for that. – GEORGE'S MARVELLOUS MEDICINE

• A frumpkin is like a **pumpkin** and is used to make scrumptious frumpkin pie—but neither frumpkins nor pigwinkles can grow in Giant Country as the soil is too dry. *'In this sloshflunking Giant Country, happy eats like pineapples and pigwinkles is simply not growing.'* – The BFG

DID YOU KNOW?
The **cacao bean** is a type of seed, not a vegetable. It grows on trees in tropical countries and is used to make cocoa and chocolate.

FIND OUT MORE!
Not all vegitibbles are delumptious! Read about slimacious snozzcumbers in GIANT FOOD AND DRINK in THE MAGICAL WORLD.

• The BFG's name for a vegetable is a vegitibble and **delumptious vegitibbles** are wonderveg. A person or giant who only eats vegetables (not meat or chiddlers) is a **vegetarian** or **vegan**.

FIND OUT MORE!
Why are giants afraid of **beanstalks**? Find out in ALL ABOUT GIANTS in THE MAGICAL WORLD.

• Some types of vegetable **bean** are **runner beans** and **string beans** (the BFG calls them **stringy beans**). The stem of a bean plant is a **beanstalk**. *'You can go looking into every crook and nanny. There is no human beans or stringy beans or runner beans or jelly beans or any other beans in here.'* – THE BFG

• Someone who is **full of beans** is full of energy and high spirits: *Willy Wonka is always cheerful and full of beans.*

• If someone **spills the beans**, they let you into a secret. (But when James spills the **magic beans**, he really does drop them on the ground!)

rhino

crockadowndilly

ALL ABOUT ANIMALS

WILD ANIMALS

INCLUDE: anteater, armadillo, badger, bat, crocodile or crockadowndilly, elephant, fox, frog, giraffe, hippopotamus or hippodumpling, lion, mole, monkey, mouse, newt, porcupine, rat, rhinoceros or rhinostossteriss, snake, squirrel, toad, wombat, zebra

What a prospect that was! I was off to the land of palm-trees and coconuts and coral reefs and lions and elephants and deadly snakes. – BOY

• A word for wild animals in general is **wildlife**: *Giant Country has some unusual wildlife as well as giants.*

• Crocodiles, snakes and tortoises are **reptiles**, which means that they are cold-blooded and lay eggs on land. Frogs, toads and newts are **amphibians**, which means that they live both on land and in water: *Lavender carries an amphibian to school in her pencil-box.*

• Mice, rats and squirrels are **rodents**, which means that they have large front teeth for **gnawing**: *Delayed Action Mouse-Maker Formula will turn children into rodents.*

• An animal that eats other animals (or **human beans**) is a **carnivore** and one that only eats plants is a **herbivore**. The **Enormous Crocodile** is a carnivore,

as he eats **chiddlers**, but the **Geraneous Giraffe**, who only eats **tinkle-tinkle** blossom, is a **herbivore**.

• Animals that are active at night are **nocturnal**: *Fantastic Mr Fox and his friend Badger are both nocturnal.*

DID YOU KNOW?
The word **reptile** comes from a Latin word meaning 'to creep'.

A scientist who studies reptiles and amphibians is called a **herpetologist**.

DID YOU KNOW?
An old name for a **giraffe** is camelopard, which comes from a Greek word meaning 'camel panther'.

FARM AND PET ANIMALS

INCLUDE: cat, cow, dog, goat, hamster, horse, mouse, pig, rabbit, sheep, tortoise

When he had finished, Mr Hoppy, in his enthusiasm, had bought no less than one hundred and forty tortoises and he carried them home in baskets, ten or fifteen at a time. – ESIO TROT

• Although **squirrels** are forest animals, a hundred of them work in Willy Wonka's factory shelling walnuts, and Veruca Salt wants one as a **pet** (which turns out to be a Very Bad idea).

'All I've got at home is two dogs and four cats and six bunny rabbits and two parakeets and three canaries and a green parrot and a turtle and a bowl of goldfish and a cage of white mice and a silly old hamster! I want a squirrel!' – CHARLIE AND THE CHOCOLATE FACTORY

stossteriss hippodumpling

FIND OUT MORE!
There is more wildlife to find in JUNGLES AND FORESTS and ALL ABOUT THE SEA—and some very extra-usual creatures in THE MAGICAL WORLD.

ANIMAL NAMES

• A female fox, like Mrs Fox, is called a **vixen** and the Small Foxes are **cubs**.
Mr Fox looked at the four Small Foxes and he smiled. What fine children I have, he thought. They are starving to death and they haven't had a drink for three days, but they are still undefeated. I must not let them down. — FANTASTIC MR FOX

• A young cat is a **kitten**, a young dog is a **puppy** and a young pig is a **piglet**.
Pig, peeping through the window, stood And yelled, 'Well done, Miss Riding Hood!' Ah, Piglet, you must never trust Young ladies from the upper crust.
— REVOLTING RHYMES

• A male horse is a **stallion** and a female horse is a **mare**. A young horse is a **foal** and a young cow is a **calf**.
Sergeant Samways . . . pedalled slowly, and there was a certain majesty in the way he held himself, with the head high and the back very straight, as though he were riding a fine thoroughbred mare instead of an old black bike. — DANNY THE CHAMPION OF THE WORLD

• The word **reptilian** means 'to do with reptiles' or 'like a reptile': *The Enormous Crocodile gave a reptilian grin.*

• The word **vulpine** means 'to do with foxes' or 'like a fox': *Fantastic Mr Fox has a clever vulpine brain.*

ANIMAL HOMES

INCLUDE: burrow, den, lair
Oh, lion dear, could I not make You happy with a lovely steak? Could I entice you from your lair With rabbit-pie or roasted hare?
— DIRTY BEASTS

• A fox lives in an **earth** and a badger lives in a **sett**.
Mr Fox turned to the Small Badger and said, 'Tell them they are invited to a Fox's Feast. Then bring them all down here and follow this tunnel back until you find my home!'
— FANTASTIC MR FOX

• A series of connected rabbit burrows underground is called a **warren**. Willy Wonka's Chocolate Factory is like a gigantuous **warren**, as it is full of winding corridors and passages.
The place was like a gigantic rabbit warren, with passages leading this way and that in every direction. — CHARLIE AND THE CHOCOLATE FACTORY

vulpine

ANIMAL BODIES

CAN HAVE: **horn** or **tusk, snout, muzzle, trunk, whiskers, jaws, claws, paws, hooves** or **trotters, fur, hide, coat** or **fleece, mane, scales, shell, spines** or **prickles, tail**

Bruno was getting smaller by the second. I could see him shrinking . . . Now his clothes seemed to be disappearing and brown fur was growing all over his body . . . Suddenly he had a tail . . . And then he had whiskers. — THE WITCHES

CAN BE: **furry, hairy, sleek, scaly, shaggy, spiny, spotted, striped, thick-skinned, wiry, woolly**

The foxes jumped. They looked up quickly and they saw, peeking through a small hole in the roof of the tunnel, a long black pointed furry face. 'Badger!' cried Mr Fox. — FANTASTIC MR FOX

'If you hadn't been so busy guzzling that sandwich,' I said, 'you would have noticed your hairy paws. Take a look at them.' Bruno looked down at his paws. He jumped. 'Good grief!' he cried. 'I am a mouse!' — THE WITCHES

• An animal's front legs are called **forelegs** and its back legs are **hind legs**: *Mr Fox's forelegs were digging away furiously.*

• Giraffes like the **Geraneous Giraffe** have a very long throat or **gullet**, which makes eating **Globgobblers** even more enjoyable.
The Globgobbler is an especially delicious sweet . . . and the moment you bite into it, all the perfumed juices of Arabia go squirting down your gullet one after the other. 'It's wonderful!' cried the Giraffe as a cascade of lovely liquid flavours poured all the way down her long long throat.
— THE GIRAFFE AND THE PELLY AND ME

• A formal name for an animal's **snout** is a **proboscis** (say proh-*baw*-siss). An elephant's proboscis is its **trunk**.
Trunky trotted over to the spot where the Enormous Crocodile was standing, and quick as a flash he wrapped his trunk around the Crocodile's tail and hoisted him up into the air. — THE ENORMOUS CROCODILE

• When **Badger lends a paw** with digging, it means that he is helping out. (A **human bean** would **lend a hand** instead.)
They dug on in silence. Badger was a great digger and the tunnel went forward at a terrific pace now that he was lending a paw. — FANTASTIC MR FOX

FIND OUT MORE! Witches have **claws** too! Find out more in ALL ABOUT WITCHES in THE MAGICAL WORLD.

ANIMAL SOUNDS

ANIMALS CAN: **bark, bellow, roar** or **trumpet** loudly. (Grandma Georgina can also trumpet as loudly as a **rhinostossteriss**.)

Grandma Georgina, in her red flannel nightgown with two skinny bare legs sticking out of the bottom, was trumpeting and spitting like a rhinoceros. — CHARLIE AND THE GREAT GLASS ELEVATOR

THEY CAN: **snarl, gnash** or **hiss** angrily

A ghoulish snarling ghastly sound Came up from somewhere underground, Then slimy tendrils tugged his coat And tried to fasten round his throat. — RHYME STEW

THEY CAN: **grunt, growl, snort** or **snuffle**

Captain Lancaster sat up front at his desk, gazing suspiciously round the class with his watery-blue eyes. And even from the back row I could hear him snorting and snuffling through his nose like a dog outside a rabbit hole. — DANNY THE CHAMPION OF THE WORLD

THEY CAN: **howl, whine** or **whimper** in pain

'Then at last, when everything is ready . . . phwisst! . . . and she swoops! Sparks fly. Flames leap. Oil boils. Rats howl. Skin shrivels. And the child disappears.' — THE WITCHES

• Horses and giraffes also **neigh** or **whinny**, cats **miaow** and frogs **croak**.
'Oh, my sainted souls!' gasped the Giraffe. 'Oh, my naked neck! I cannot believe what I am seeing!' The next moment she was galloping full speed across the lawns and whinnying with excitement. — THE GIRAFFE AND THE PELLY AND ME

FIND OUT MORE! Grown-ups can **bark** and **bellow** too! Find out more in DESCRIBING VOICES in THE WORLD OF HUMAN BEANS.

bark
bellow
growl
grunt
snort
snuffle

HOW DO ANIMALS MOVE?

scuttle slither slink

THEY CAN: **bound, leap, skip** or **spring** into the air
Suddenly, as though springs had been released in their legs, the three hungry Small Foxes and the ravenously hungry Badger sprang forward to grab the luscious food. – FANTASTIC MR FOX

THEY CAN: **crawl, crouch, slink, slither** or **scuttle** along the ground
'You call that walking?' cried the Centipede. 'You're a slitherer, that's all you are! You just slither along!' 'I glide,' said the Earthworm primly. – JAMES AND THE GIANT PEACH

THEY CAN: **gallop** or **stampede** quickly
Suddenly there was a tremendous whooshing noise. It was Humpy-Rumpy, the Hippopotamus. He came crashing and snorting out of the jungle. His head was down low and he was galloping at a terrific speed. – THE ENORMOUS CROCODILE

THEY CAN: **lumber, waddle** or **trot** along slowly
The Enormous Crocodile cursed the Roly-Poly Bird and waddled back into the bushes to hide. – THE ENORMOUS CROCODILE

THEY CAN: **paw, pad** or **stamp** on the ground
They stayed still, listening, and they could hear the Gruncher pawing the ground at the base of the tree with his giant hooves and snorting with greed. – THE MINPINS

THEY CAN: **stalk** or **pounce** on their prey
The Trunchbull started advancing slow and soft-footed upon Rupert in the manner of a tigress stalking a small deer. – MATILDA

WHAT ELSE CAN ANIMALS DO?

THEY CAN: **bite** or **sting** in attack or defence
Grandma didn't move either. 'I know a great many secrets,' she said, and suddenly she smiled. It was a thin icey smile, the kind a snake might make just before it bites you. – GEORGE'S MARVELLOUS MEDICINE

trot gallop stampede lumber waddle

DID YOU KNOW?
When an author like Roald Dahl writes about animals who talk or behave like **human beans** it is called **anthropomorphism.**

DID YOU KNOW?
A scientist who studies animals is a **zoologist**, and a doctor who treats animals is a **vet** (which is short for veterinary surgeon).

THEY CAN: **twitch** their noses and **sniff** to catch a scent
The front half of his body was now in the open. His black nose twitched from side to side, sniffing and sniffing for the scent of danger. – FANTASTIC MR FOX

SOME: **hibernate** in winter
When the colder weather came along in November, Mrs Silver would fill Alfie's house with dry hay, and the tortoise would crawl in there and bury himself deep under the hay and go to sleep for months on end without food or water. This is called hibernating. – ESIO TROT

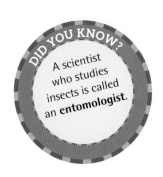

DID YOU KNOW?
A scientist who studies insects is called an **entomologist**.

spinnerets
butteryfly

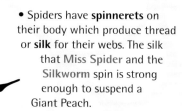

INSECTS AND MINIBEASTS

INCLUDE: ant, bee, beetle, bluebottle, **butterfly** or butteryfly, caterpillar, centipede, cricket, earthworm, glow-worm, grasshopper, ladybird, millipede, moth, silkworm, slug, snail, spider, wasp

What were they after? There was nothing down there. Nothing except the roots of the old peach tree . . . and a whole lot of earthworms and centipedes and insects living in the soil.
— JAMES AND THE GIANT PEACH

CAN HAVE: antennae or feelers, shell, wings

'If you want to know, I happen to be a "short-horned" grasshopper. I have two short feelers coming out of my head. Can you see them?' — JAMES AND THE GIANT PEACH

And next to the Spider, there was a giant Lady-bird with nine black spots on her scarlet shell. — JAMES AND THE GIANT PEACH

- Spiders have **spinnerets** on their body which produce thread or **silk** for their webs. The silk that Miss Spider and the Silkworm spin is strong enough to suspend a Giant Peach.

- Slugs and snails are **molluscs**, which means that they have a soft body and usually a shell.
You see, I now was sitting on A wonderfully ENORMOUS SNAIL! His shell was smooth and brown and pale, And I was so high off the ground That I could see for miles around. — DIRTY BEASTS

- Ants, bees and grasshoppers are **insects**, which means that they have six legs and a body divided into sections. Spiders are not insects, as they have eight (not six) legs.

- Insects and spiders are sometimes called **minibeasts** or **bugs**. The minibeasts in the Giant Peach are gigantuous— so they are really **not-so-minibeasts**.
An insect is usually something rather small, is it not? A grasshopper, for example, is an insect. So what would you call it if you saw a grasshopper as large as a dog? As large as a large dog. You could hardly call that an insect, could you? — JAMES AND THE GIANT PEACH

- Insects which are active at dawn and dusk, like crickets and moths, are called **crepuscular**.

INSECT LIFE CYCLE

- In the first stage of an insect's life, when it **hatches** from an egg, it is a **larva** or **grub**.
'Have you met the Trunchbull yet?' Hortensia asked . . . 'She hates very small children . . . She thinks five-year-olds are grubs that haven't yet hatched out.' — MATILDA

DID YOU KNOW?
The French word for **grasshopper** is sauterelle, which means 'little jumper'.

DID YOU KNOW?
In North America, a **ladybird** is called a ladybug.

• When a caterpillar changes into a **butterfly** or moth, it **metamorphoses** inside a hard case called a **chrysalis** (say *kriss*-a-liss).

'Your son Wilfred has spent six years as a grub in this school and we are still waiting for him to emerge from the chrysalis.' — MATILDA

hum
buzz
buzz
hum
drone
hum
drone
buzz
hum
drone
buzz

FIND OUT MORE!
Dreams also make a **buzzy-hum** noise. Find out more in ALL ABOUT DREAMS in THE MAGICAL WORLD.

INSECT SOUNDS

• Some insects make a **buzzing**, **humming** or **droning** sound. When **human beans** **buzz about** they bustle about in a hurry like busy bees.

Waiters were buzzing about all over the place, carrying plates and dishes. — THE WITCHES

• Grasshoppers **sing** or **chirp** by rubbing their hind legs against their wings. A formal word for this is **stridulating**. When the **Old-Green-Grasshopper** **stridulates** he makes music as sweet as a violin.

In the garden at home on summer evenings, he had listened many times to the sound of grasshoppers chirping in the grass, and he had always liked the noise that they made. — JAMES AND THE GIANT PEACH

'A real violin!' the Old-Green-Grasshopper cried. 'Good heavens, I like that! My dear boy, I am a real violin! It is a part of my own body!' — JAMES AND THE GIANT PEACH

DID YOU KNOW?
The word **centipede** is based on Latin and means 'a hundred feet', although many centipedes have fewer than a hundred legs. (The Centipede in the Giant Peach has only forty-two legs and wears twenty-one pairs of boots.)

The word **millipede** means 'a thousand feet' and is related to *million* and *millionaire*.

81

flock perch
roost

ALL ABOUT BIRDS

TYPES OF BIRD

INCLUDE: blackbird, buzzard, crow, dove, finch, jay, lark, magpie, nightingale or nightingull, owl, parrot, pigeon, raven, robin, Roly-Poly Bird, rook, seagull, skylark, sparrow, starling, swan, thrush, wren
They were surrounded by ducks, doves, pigeons, sparrows, robins, larks, and many other kinds that I did not know, and the birds were eating the barley that the boys were scattering by the handful. — THE MAGIC FINGER

• The Roly-Poly Bird is an extra-usual African bird with magnificent tail feathers who enjoys travelling (as well as playing tricks on Crocodiles and Twits).
Then one day, a truly magnificent bird flew down out of the sky and landed on the monkey cage. 'Good heavens!' cried all the monkeys together. 'It's the Roly-Poly Bird!'
— THE TWITS

• A group of birds is a **flock** and when birds **flock** together they gather in a large group.
The hundreds of silky white strings going upward from its stem were beautiful in the moonlight. So also was the great flock of seagulls overhead.
— JAMES AND THE GIANT PEACH

• A bird that eats small animals, such as mice, is a **bird of prey**. Some birds of prey are **eagles**, **hawks** and **kestrels**. (Grandma Josephine also *thinks* she is a **golden eagle** when she floats outside the force of gravity.)
We waited to see if the hawk would fly up again. He didn't, which meant he had caught his prey and was eating it on the ground. — DANNY THE CHAMPION OF THE WORLD

FARM AND GAME BIRDS
INCLUDE: chicken or hen, duck, goose, peacock, pheasant, turkey
They were in a huge shed and the whole place was teeming with chickens. There were white chickens and brown chickens and black chickens by the thousand! — FANTASTIC MR FOX

DID YOU KNOW?
An old name for a **flock** of crows is a *murder of crows*.

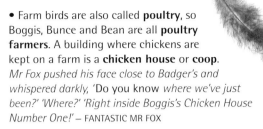

• Farm birds are also called **poultry**, so Boggis, Bunce and Bean are all **poultry farmers**. A building where chickens are kept on a farm is a **chicken house** or **coop**.
Mr Fox pushed his face close to Badger's and whispered darkly, 'Do you know where we've just been?' 'Where?' 'Right inside Boggis's Chicken House Number One!' – FANTASTIC MR FOX

• A male chicken is a **cock** or **cockerel**.
'Cock-a-doodle-do!' squawked the cockerel, shooting up into the air and coming down again. – GEORGE'S MARVELLOUS MEDICINE

• A group of geese is a **gaggle**: *Farmer Bunce owns a great gaggle of geese.*

YOUNG BIRDS

• A young bird is a **chick** or **nestling** and a family of chicks is a **brood**.
In less than a minute, the hen had shrunk so much it was no bigger than a new-hatched chick. It looked ridiculous. – GEORGE'S MARVELLOUS MEDICINE

• A group of eggs in a bird's **nest** is a **clutch**.
My father told me a nest with eggs in it was one of the most beautiful things in the world. I thought so too. The nest of a song-thrush, for instance, lined inside with dry mud as smooth as polished wood, and with five eggs of the purest blue speckled with black dots. – DANNY THE CHAMPION OF THE WORLD

BIRD BODIES

CAN HAVE: beak or bill, claws, talons or webbed feet, comb or crest, feathers, breast, tail, wings
All the other birds who had been sitting on the roof flew in to help, carrying paint-brushes in their claws and beaks. – THE TWITS

• A formal word for a bird's feathers is its **plumage**: *The Roly-Poly Bird has magnificent multi-coloured plumage.*

• The Gregg family grow **beaks** and **wings** after being zapped with the Magic Finger.
Mrs Gregg woke up. And when she saw Mr Gregg standing there on the floor, she gave a yell, too. For he was now a tiny little man! . . . And where his arms had been, he had a pair of duck's wings instead! – THE MAGIC FINGER

• The Pelican has a fantabulous Patented Beak with a sliding top and a bottom that acts as a bucket for window-cleaning.

> **DID YOU KNOW?**
> A scientist who studies birds is called an **ornithologist** and someone who enjoys watching birds in nature is a **bird-watcher**.

Suddenly, a second window was flung wide open and of all the crazy things a gigantic white bird hopped out and perched on the window-sill. I knew what this one was because of its amazing beak, which was shaped like a huge orange-coloured basin. – THE GIRAFFE AND THE PELLY AND ME

• The amount of food (or Marvellous Medicine) that a bird can hold in its beak is a **beakful**.
The brown hen stretched out its neck towards the spoon and went peck. It got a beakful of medicine. – GEORGE'S MARVELLOUS MEDICINE

BIRD SOUNDS

BIRDS CAN: **sing** or **warble** sweetly. A bird that sings is a **song-bird**. Although pelicans are not *usually* song-birds, they sing sweetly after chewing **Pishlet** sweets.
They had a splendid effect upon the Pelican, for after he had put one of them into his beak and chewed it for a while, he suddenly started singing like a nightingale. This made him wildly excited because Pelicans are not song-birds.
— THE GIRAFFE AND THE PELLY AND ME

THEY CAN: **cheep**, **chirp**, **tweet** or **twitter** happily
Not a cottage or a person was in sight, let alone a telephone. Some kind of bird started twittering in a tree farther down the road, otherwise all was silent. — BOY

THEY CAN: **screech** or **squawk** noisily
Sergeant Samways slammed the door, and suddenly there was the most infernal uproar inside the car as a dozen or more enormous pheasants started squawking and flapping all over the seats and round Mr Hazell's head. — DANNY THE CHAMPION OF THE WORLD

• Chickens also **cluck**, ducks (and the Greggs) **quack** and turkeys **gobble**.
George started telling his father about the magic medicine. While he was doing this, the big brown hen sat down in the middle of the yard and went cluck-cluck-cluck . . . cluck-cluck-cluck-cluck-cluck.
— GEORGE'S MARVELLOUS MEDICINE

• Parrots like **Chopper** can also **mimic** human speech.
Suddenly the parrot said, 'Hello, hello, hello.' It was exactly like a human voice. Matilda said, 'That's amazing! What else can it say?'
— MATILDA

• The sound that a bird makes is its **call** or **song**.
All the birds, too, I could name, not only by sighting them but by listening to their calls and their songs. — DANNY THE CHAMPION OF THE WORLD

• If someone is **all of a twitter**, they are feeling flustered and nervous, like a frightened bird.
Seated in a comfortable armchair in Mrs Silver's parlour, sipping his tea, Mr Hoppy was all of a twitter.
— ESIO TROT

FIND OUT MORE!
Grasshoppers can **chirp** too! Find out more in ALL ABOUT ANIMALS.

all of a twitter

Hello, hello, hello

WHAT CAN BIRDS (AND THE GREGGS) DO?

THEY CAN: **fly**, **dive**, **hover**, **soar**, **swoop** or **wheel** in the air
I looked where he was pointing and saw a kestrel hawk hovering superbly in the darkening sky above the ploughed field across the track. – DANNY THE CHAMPION OF THE WORLD

THEY CAN: **land** or **alight** on a branch, and **take off** or **take flight** into the air
Just then, a lovely blue swallow alighted on a branch not far away, and Little Billy saw a mother Minpin and her two children climb quite casually on to the swallow's back. Then the swallow took off and flew away with its passengers seated comfortably between its wings. – THE MINPINS

THEY CAN: **fluff**, **preen** or **ruffle** their feathers
'I've come for a holiday,' said the Roly-Poly Bird. 'I like to travel.' He fluffed his marvellous coloured feathers and looked down rather grandly at the monkeys. – THE TWITS

THEY CAN: **flap**, **flutter**, **spread** or **fold** their wings
'Oh! Oh! Oh! Oh' sobbed Mrs Gregg. 'This is witches' work!' cried Mr Gregg. And both of them started running around the room, flapping their wings. – THE MAGIC FINGER

Except for the swift fluttering of its wings, the hawk remained absolutely motionless in the sky. It seemed to be suspended by some invisible thread, like a toy bird hanging from the ceiling. Then suddenly it folded its wings and plummeted towards the earth at an incredible speed.
– DANNY THE CHAMPION OF THE WORLD

THEY CAN: **perch** or **roost** on a branch
'Here we go!' the Pelican whispered to me, and with a swish and a swoop he carried me up to the very top of the cherry tree and there he perched. – THE GIRAFFE AND THE PELLY AND ME

THEY CAN: **nest** or **build a nest** for their young
Underneath all the clamour that was going on I heard one witch in the back row saying to her neighbour, 'I'm getting a bit old to go bird's nesting. Those ruddy gruntles always nest very high up.' – THE WITCHES

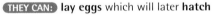

THEY CAN: **lay eggs** which will later **hatch**
'Come and watch this one!' he called out to Mrs Kranky. 'Come and watch us turning an ordinary chicken into a lovely great big one that lays eggs as large as footballs!'
– GEORGE'S MARVELLOUS MEDICINE

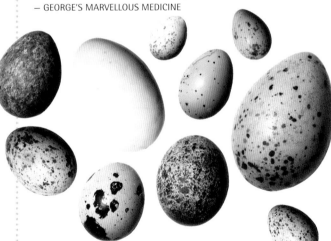

THEY CAN: **hop** on the ground or **peck** at food
Both birds turned their heads sharply at the drop of the raisin. Then one of them hopped over and made a quick peck at the ground. – DANNY THE CHAMPION OF THE WORLD

THEY CAN: **drop droppings** on beastly people like Mrs Twit
'What was that?' cried Mrs Twit. 'Some beastly bird has dropped his dirty droppings on my head!' – THE TWITS

• **Human beans** can **flock** too, meaning that they gather together in a large group like birds.
Meanwhile, tourists from all over the globe came flocking to gaze down in wonder at the nine horrendous man-eating giants in the great pit. – THE BFG

85

ALL ABOUT THE SEA

billow ripple swell bibble surge

AREAS OF SEA

• The large seas of the world are called **oceans**.
A strong current and a high wind had carried the peach so quickly away from the shore that already the land was out of sight. All around them lay the vast black ocean, deep and hungry. — JAMES AND THE GIANT PEACH

• A strip of water that reaches into the land from the sea or a lake is an **inlet**.

• A long narrow inlet of the sea between high cliffs, especially in Norway, is a **fjord** (say *fyord*).
There are no sandy beaches on the fjord. The rocks go straight down to the water's edge and the water is immediately deep. — BOY

DID YOU KNOW?
When Roald Dahl was a boy, he spent many happy holidays with his family in Norway, swimming and playing in the **fjords**.

• The bottom of the sea is the **seabed** or **sea floor**. The land at the side of the sea is the **shore** or **seaside**. James Henry Trotter grew up near the **seaside** and dreams of returning, but his beastly aunts refuse to take him.
'Oh, Auntie Sponge!' James cried out. 'And Auntie Spiker! Couldn't we all—please—just for once—go down to the seaside on the bus?' — JAMES AND THE GIANT PEACH

• A **beach** is a strip of sand or pebbles on the shore. Beaches can be **sandy** or **pebbly**.
There were always plenty of other children for him to play with, and there was the sandy beach for him to run about on, and the ocean to paddle in. — JAMES AND THE GIANT PEACH

DESCRIBING THE SEA AND SHORE

• The sea or waves can **billow**, **swell** or **surge**. Smaller waves can **ripple** or **bibble**.
Little waves were bibbling against the sides of the peach. — JAMES AND THE GIANT PEACH

WHAT CAN YOU DO IN THE SEA?

YOU CAN: **dive** into or **swim** in the sea
'The whole coast is dotted with tiny islands and there's nobody on them. We used to explore them and dive into the sea off the lovely smooth granite rocks.' — THE WITCHES

DID YOU KNOW?
The word **porpoise** comes from Latin words meaning 'sea pig'.

 Witches who spot **chiddlers** swimming in the sea may turn them into porpoises.

YOU CAN: **explore**, **paddle** or **picnic** on the shore

YOU CAN: **row** a boat, **paddle** a canoe or **sail** in a ship, yacht or Giant Peach
The giant peach, with the sunlight glinting on its side, was like a massive golden ball sailing upon a silver sea. — JAMES AND THE GIANT PEACH

• A ship that sails underwater is called a **submarine**, which means literally 'under the sea'.

DID YOU KNOW?
The word **yacht** (which rhymes with *hot*) comes from Dutch and originally meant 'a pirate ship'.

• If something smells or seems **fishy** to you, then you are suspicious or have doubts about it (as if it were a piece of fish that was starting to smell bad).
The Rat said, 'Ho! I do believe There's something fishy up your sleeve. It's obvious if the race was fair You'd have no chance against the Hare.'
— RHYME STEW

WHO LIVES IN OR BY THE SEA?

SEA CREATURES
INCLUDE: **fish**, **jellyfish**, **porpoise**, **seahorse**, **shark**, **slimy squiggler**, **starfish**, **turtle**, **whale**
'They must be some kind of fish,' said the Old-Green-Grasshopper. 'Perhaps they have come along to say hello.' — JAMES AND THE GIANT PEACH

• The BFG asks Sophie to stay **as still as a starfish**, which is very still indeed, so as not to startle passing dreams.
He handed the jar to Sophie and said, 'Please be still as a starfish now. I is thinking there may be a whole swarm of phizzwizards up here today.' — THE BFG

• Giants only *pretend* to be sea creatures to get close enough to **grabble** unsuspecting **human beans**.
'Sometimes,' the BFG said, 'they is swimmeling in from the sea like fishies with only their heads showing above the water, and then out comes a big hairy hand and grabbles someone off the beach.' — THE BFG

• Sea creatures are also called **marine** creatures: *The slimy squiggler is a marine creature that lives on the seabed.*

FIND OUT MORE!
Find out all about rivers (of water AND chocolate) in DESCRIBING LANDSCAPE.

as still as a starfish

SEA BIRDS
INCLUDE: **pelican**, **penguin**, **puffin**, **seagull**
This was the five hundred and first seagull, and the moment that James caught it and tethered it to the stem with all the others, the whole enormous peach suddenly started rising up slowly out of the water. — JAMES AND THE GIANT PEACH

FIND OUT MORE!
Find out what the Pelican's Patented Beak can do in ALL ABOUT BIRDS.

THE SKY AND OUTER SPACE

THE SKY BY DAY

CAN BE: **clear** or **cloudless**, **cloudy** or **overcast**

CAN HAVE: **clouds** (and **Cloud–Men**), **birds**, **kites**, **balloons** (sometimes carrying a **Twit**), flying **Giant Peach** (carried by seagulls), **rainbow**
They crouched very still on top of the peach, staring at the Cloud-Men. The whole surface of the cloud was literally swarming with them, and there were hundreds more up above climbing about on that monstrous crazy arch.
— JAMES AND THE GIANT PEACH

• Clouds (and **Cloud–Men**) can be: **billowy**, **fluffy**, **wispy**.
Once, deep in the hollow of a large billowy cloud, they spotted something that could only have been a Cloud-Men's city. — JAMES AND THE GIANT PEACH

Then the watchers on the peach saw one of the Cloud-Men raising his long wispy arms above his head and they heard him shouting, 'All right, boys! That's enough! Get the shovels!' — JAMES AND THE GIANT PEACH

FIND OUT MORE!
What else do Cloud–Men do? Find out in ALL ABOUT THE WEATHER.

wispy

fluffy

billowy

THE SKY AT NIGHT

CAN BE: **inky, moonlit, starry**
And clinging desperately to the end of the string, shouting and cursing with fury, was the huge hairy Cloud-Man. Up and up he went, swinging across the moonlit sky.
— JAMES AND THE GIANT PEACH

CAN HAVE: **moon, stars, shooting stars** or **meteors**
The night was very still. There was a thin yellow moon over the trees on the hill, and the sky was filled with stars.
— THE MAGIC FINGER

The three-quarter moon was well above the hills now, and the sky was filled with stars as we climbed back over the gate and began walking up the track towards the wood.
— DANNY THE CHAMPION OF THE WORLD

• A group of stars in the night sky is a **constellation**.

BEYOND THE EARTH

• The total of all planets, stars and galaxies in Space is the **cosmos** or **universe**.
'These Vermicious Knids are the terror of the Universe. They travel through space in great swarms, landing on other stars and planets and destroying everything they find.'
– CHARLIE AND THE GREAT GLASS ELEVATOR

• The area of Space beyond the Earth's **atmosphere** is called **outer space**.
Away in the distance, in the deep blue sky of outer space, they saw a massive cloud of Vermicious Knids wheeling and circling like a fleet of bombers. – CHARLIE AND THE GREAT GLASS ELEVATOR

• When an **asteroid** enters the Earth's atmosphere, it becomes a **meteor** or **shooting star**. When a Vermicious Knid enters the atmosphere, it **burns up** and becomes a Shooting Knid.

'Actually, they're not shooting stars at all,' said Mr Wonka. 'They're Shooting Knids. They're Knids trying to enter the Earth's atmosphere at high speed and going up in flames.' – CHARLIE AND THE GREAT GLASS ELEVATOR

• The BFG can turn his gigantuous ears like satellite dishes to pick up music from distant stars and galaxies.
'Sometimes, on a very clear night,' the BFG said ... 'I is sometimes hearing faraway music coming from the stars in the sky.' – The BFG

SUN, MOON AND PLANETS

• The word **lunar** means 'to do with the moon' and **solar** means 'to do with the sun'.

• The path followed by a planet around a sun, or a moon around a planet, is its **orbit**. A group of planets which orbit a sun is called a **solar system**.

• The planets in our solar system (in order from the Sun) are: **Mercury, Venus, Earth, Mars, Jupiter, Saturn, Uranus, Neptune.**

• The planet Vermes is not in our solar system (it is eighteen thousand four hundred and twenty-seven million miles away from Earth), so Vermicious Knids are from another solar system, and perhaps from another galaxy.

• The direction towards the moon is **moonward** and towards the sun is **sunward**, so the Enormous Crocodile is thrown **sunward** by Trunky.
He whizzed on and on. He whizzed far into space. He whizzed past the moon. He whizzed past stars and planets. Until at last ... With the most tremendous BANG the Enormous Crocodile crashed headfirst into the hot hot sun. – THE ENORMOUS CROCODILE

solar

sunward

moonward

lunar

89

WHO LIVES IN OUTER SPACE?

SPACE CREATURES

INCLUDE: **Martians**, **Poozas**, **quogwinkles**, **Vermicious Knids**

Here Mr Wonka paused and ran the tip of a pink tongue all the way around his lips. 'VERMICIOUS KNIDS!' he cried. 'That's what they were!' He sounded the K... K'NIDS, like that. – CHARLIE AND THE GREAT GLASS ELEVATOR

• A creature that comes from outer space is an **extra-terrestrial** or **alien life-form**.

• The **Poozas** are an **extinct** species of **moon-dwellers** or **lunar inhabitants**.

There used to be some rather nice creatures living on the moon a long time ago. They were called Poozas. But the Vermicious Knids ate the lot.
– CHARLIE AND THE GREAT GLASS ELEVATOR

• No **human bean** has ever seen a **quogwinkle** as they only visit Giant Country from outer space.

'I'll bet you is also finding it hard to believe in quogwinkles,' the BFG said, 'and how they is visiting us from the stars.' – THE BFG

SPACE LANGUAGES

• Willy Wonka pretends to speak **Martian** to the President and invents a string of rude words like **zoonk!** and **yubee luni!**

The next time Mr Wonka spoke, the words came out so fast and sharp and loud they were like bullets from a machine-gun. 'ZOONK-ZOONK-ZOONK- ZOONK- ZOONK!' he barked. – CHARLIE AND THE GREAT GLASS ELEVATOR

• **Vermicious Knids** communicate with **human beans** by forming letters with their bodies, but they only know how to spell one word: *SCRAM!*

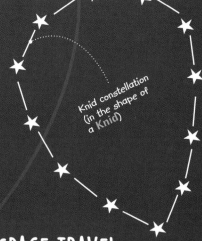

Knid constellation (in the shape of a **Knid**)

SPACE TRAVEL

TYPES OF SPACESHIP

INCLUDE: **space capsule**, **Great Glass Elevator, Space Hotel**

'Space capsules are made of special heat-proof metal, and when they make a re-entry, their speeds are reduced right down to about two thousand miles an hour.' – CHARLIE AND THE GREAT GLASS ELEVATOR

• The **Great Glass Elevator** is propelled by **booster-rockets** and suspended by an ingenious system of **skyhooks**.

• If you float in space or in orbit, you are **weightless** as you are outside the **pull of gravity**.

'We're outside the pull of gravity up here, Mr President. Everything floats. We'd be floating ourselves if we weren't strapped down.' – CHARLIE AND THE GREAT GLASS ELEVATOR

DID YOU KNOW?

The correct way to pronounce **Knid** is to sound the letter K at the start, as Willy Wonka does. Centuries ago, the silent letter K in words like **knight** and **knobbly** was pronounced, too.

Try saying *The K-night K-nocked his K-nobbly K-nees together* as fast as you can, being sure to pronounce all the letter Ks!

FIND OUT MORE!

What word describes the shape of a **Vermicious Knid**? Find out in SHAPES AND PATTERNS.

DON'T EAT US! (the Poozas) YuMMy! (The KniDs)

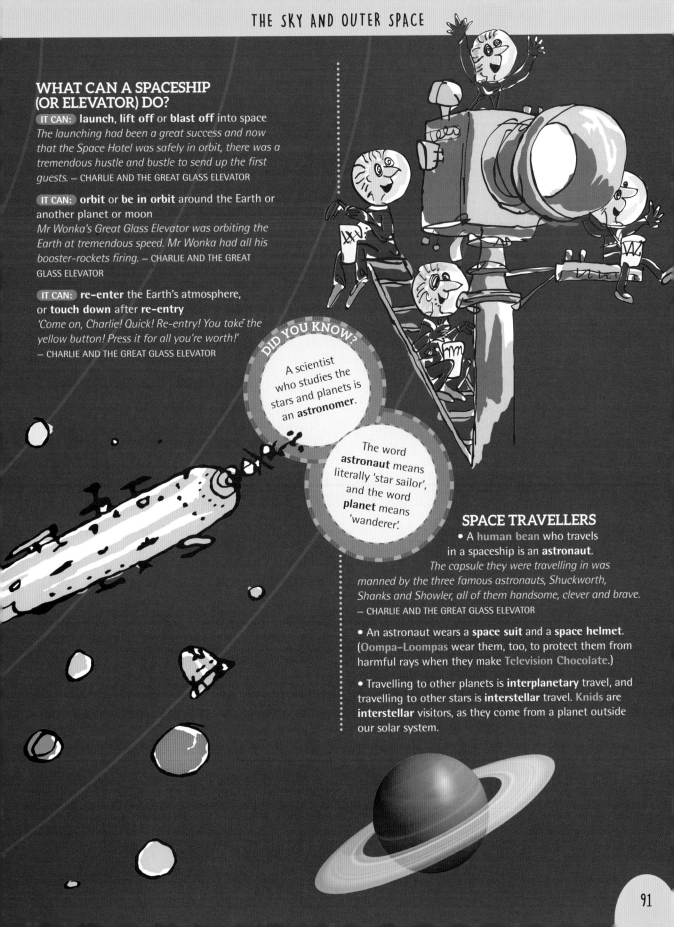

WHAT CAN A SPACESHIP (OR ELEVATOR) DO?

IT CAN: **launch**, **lift off** or **blast off** into space
The launching had been a great success and now that the Space Hotel was safely in orbit, there was a tremendous hustle and bustle to send up the first guests. — CHARLIE AND THE GREAT GLASS ELEVATOR

IT CAN: **orbit** or **be in orbit** around the Earth or another planet or moon
Mr Wonka's Great Glass Elevator was orbiting the Earth at tremendous speed. Mr Wonka had all his booster-rockets firing. — CHARLIE AND THE GREAT GLASS ELEVATOR

IT CAN: **re-enter** the Earth's atmosphere, or **touch down** after **re-entry**
'Come on, Charlie! Quick! Re-entry! You take the yellow button! Press it for all you're worth!' — CHARLIE AND THE GREAT GLASS ELEVATOR

DID YOU KNOW?

A scientist who studies the stars and planets is an **astronomer**.

The word **astronaut** means literally 'star sailor', and the word **planet** means 'wanderer'.

SPACE TRAVELLERS

• A **human** bean who travels in a spaceship is an **astronaut**.
The capsule they were travelling in was manned by the three famous astronauts, Shuckworth, Shanks and Showler, all of them handsome, clever and brave. — CHARLIE AND THE GREAT GLASS ELEVATOR

• An astronaut wears a **space suit** and a **space helmet**. (Oompa-Loompas wear them, too, to protect them from harmful rays when they make Television Chocolate.)

• Travelling to other planets is **interplanetary** travel, and travelling to other stars is **interstellar** travel. **Knids** are **interstellar** visitors, as they come from a planet outside our solar system.

DESCRIBING DAY AND NIGHT

TIMES OF DAY AND NIGHT

• The time during the day when the sun is in the sky is **daytime** and the time between evening and morning (when Violet Beauregarde has to stop chewing gum) is **night-time**.
'It's my most treasured possession now, this piece of gum is. At night-time, I just stick it on the end of the bedpost, and it's as good as ever in the mornings.' – CHARLIE AND THE CHOCOLATE FACTORY

• The time when the sun starts to **rise** in the morning is **dawn, daybreak** or **sunrise**.
An hour later, just before dawn, the travellers heard a soft whooshing noise above their heads and they glanced up and saw an immense grey batlike creature swooping down towards them out of the dark.
– JAMES AND THE GIANT PEACH

• The time when the sun starts to **set** in the evening is **dusk, twilight** or **sunset**. You can also call it **gloomness**.
'Why at twilight?' I asked. 'Because at twilight everything inside the wood becomes veiled and shady. You can see to move around but it's not easy for someone else to see you.'
– DANNY THE CHAMPION OF THE WORLD

• The time in the middle of the night, when witches and giants roam, is called the **witching hour**.
The witching hour, somebody had once whispered to her, was a special moment in the middle of the night when every child and every grown-up was in a deep deep sleep, and all the dark things came out from hiding and had the world to themselves. – THE BFG

DID YOU KNOW?
Old words for the evening **twilight** are gloaming and evengloam.

FIND OUT MORE!
Magical things happen during the **witching hour**! Find out more in THE MAGICAL WORLD.

• Something that happens **in the dead of night** happens in the very middle of the night, when everything is deadly quiet—which is the perfect time for the BFG to go **dream-blowing**.
'What does The BFG do with his powders after he has made them?' I asked. 'In the dead of night,' my father said, 'he goes prowling through the villages searching for houses where children are asleep.' – DANNY THE CHAMPION OF THE WORLD

DESCRIBING DAY

• The light that shines from the sun during the day is **daylight** or **sunlight**. When a person or tortoise **basks**, they lie or sit warming themselves in the sunlight.
They all sat in silence watching the sun as it came up slowly over the rim of the horizon for a new day. And when full daylight came at last, they all got to their feet and stretched their poor cramped bodies.
– JAMES AND THE GIANT PEACH

DESCRIBING NIGHT

- The light that shines from the moon and stars at night is **moonlight** and **starlight**.

- Moonlight can be: **eerie, ghostly, milky, pale** or **silvery**.
Gradually it grew darker and darker, and then a pale three-quarter moon came up over the tops of the clouds and cast an eerie light over the whole scene. – JAMES AND THE GIANT PEACH

- A night without moonlight is **moonless** or **pitch-black**.

 Witches can still *smell* you in the dark!
'A REAL WITCH has the most amazing powers of smell. She can actually smell out a child who is standing on the other side of the street on a pitch-black night.' – THE WITCHES

WHAT HAPPENS AT NIGHT?

- Most **giants** go hunting for **human beans**, while the BFG goes **dream-blowing**.
'They is just moocheling and footcheling around and waiting for the night to come. Then they will all be galloping off to places where people is living to find their suppers.' – THE BFG

- **Mr Fox** steals chickens and other farm birds to feed his family.
Every evening as soon as it got dark, Mr Fox would say to Mrs Fox, 'Well, my darling, what shall it be this time? A plump chicken from Boggis? A duck or a goose from Bunce? Or a nice turkey from Bean?' – FANTASTIC MR FOX

- The **Oompa-Loompas** work **late into the night** in the Chocolate Factory.
The faint shadows that sometimes appear behind the windows, especially late at night when the lights are on, are those of tiny people, people no taller than my knee . . .' – CHARLIE AND THE CHOCOLATE FACTORY

- If you are lucky enough to have one of Willy Wonka's **luminous lollies**, you can **eat** or **read in bed**.
Quickly, Charlie started reading some of the labels alongside the buttons . . . EXPLODING SWEETS FOR YOUR ENEMIES. LUMINOUS LOLLIES FOR EATING IN BED AT NIGHT. – CHARLIE AND THE CHOCOLATE FACTORY

- **Orphans** like Sophie must stay in bed for fear of the filthy old **fizzwiggler** Mrs Clonkers.
'The woman who ran it was called Mrs Clonkers and if she caught you breaking any of the rules, like getting out of bed at night or not folding up your clothes, you got punished' – THE BFG

OTHER DARK PLACES

INCLUDE: the cellar in Mrs Clonker's **norphanage**, the **Chokey** in **Crunchem Hall**

CAN BE: **dingy, gloomy, murky, pitch black** or **pitch dark, shadowy**
'She locked us in the dark cellar for a day and a night without anything to eat or drink.' 'The rotten old rotrasper!' cried the BFG. – THE BFG

'It's pitch dark and you have to stand up dead straight and if you wobble at all you get spiked either by the glass on the walls or the nails on the door.' – MATILDA

DID YOU KNOW?
The name of Miss Trunchbull's terrifying cupboard, the **Chokey**, comes from an Anglo-Indian word meaning 'police station' or 'prison'.

FIND OUT MORE!
Animals that are active at night, like **Mr Fox**, are **nocturnal**. Find out more in ALL ABOUT ANIMALS.

ALL ABOUT THE WEATHER

fridgy

fridging

frotsy

TYPES OF WEATHER

WARM OR DRY WEATHER

INCLUDES: sun or sunshine

CAN BE: sunny, warm, windless, balmy, hot, blazing, scorching

It was the first of October and one of those warm windless autumn mornings with a darkening sky and a smell of thunder in the air. — DANNY THE CHAMPION OF THE WORLD

COLD OR SNOWY WEATHER

INCLUDES: frost, hail, snow, snowstorm

CAN BE: chilly, freezing, fridgy or fridging, frosty or frotsy, icy, snowy

First came the snow. It began very suddenly one morning just as Charlie Bucket was getting dressed for school. Standing by the window, he saw the huge flakes drifting slowly down out of an icy sky that was the colour of steel. — CHARLIE AND THE CHOCOLATE FACTORY

WET OR WINDY WEATHER

INCLUDES: rain, clouds, fog, mist, breeze, gusts

CAN BE: rainy, cloudy, overcast, foggy, misty, blustery, breezy

Then came the rain. It rained and rained, and the water ran into the nest and they all got as wet as could be—and oh, it was a bad, bad night! — THE MAGIC FINGER

STORMY WEATHER

INCLUDES: storm, squall, thunder, lightning, gale, hurricane, cyclone, tornado, flood

CAN BE: stormy, thundery, torrential

A vast explosion filled the cave, Then thunder roared and lightning flashed And walls caved in and ceilings crashed! — RHYME STEW

• A single stroke of **lightning** is a **bolt** or a **flash**. **Vita–Wonk** works **as quick as lightning**, which means almost instantly.

'Vita-Wonk is as quick as lightning! The moment the medicine is swallowed—ping!—and it all happens!' — CHARLIE AND THE GREAT GLASS ELEVATOR

DID YOU KNOW?

A scientist who studies the weather is called a **meteorologist**.

frosty freezing snowy chilly icy

DESCRIBING SNOW AND ICE

• Snow can be: **crisp**, **feathery**, **powdery** or **slushy**.

• A single flake of snow is a **snowflake**. A sudden gust of wind and snow is a **flurry** and a driving storm of snow is a **blizzard**.

• **Cloud-Men** manufacture snow and frost using special **snow machines** and **frost factories** in the sky.
Once they passed a snow machine in operation, with the Cloud-Men turning the handle and a blizzard of snowflakes blowing out of the great funnel above – JAMES AND THE GIANT PEACH

• Snow that is beginning to melt or **thaw** is **slush** and snow mixed with rain is **sleet**.

• Hard icy snow is **hail** and a drop of hail is a **hailstone**.
'It's hailstones!' whispered James excitedly. 'They've been making hailstones and now they are showering them down on to the people in the world below!'
– JAMES AND THE GIANT PEACH

• A ball of snow that you make with your hands is a **snowball**. **Cloud-Men** eat **fried snowballs** which have to be cooked very quickly before they melt and turn to **slush**.
At the entrances to the caves the Cloud-Men's wives were crouching over little stoves with frying-pans in their hands, frying snowballs for their husbands' suppers.
– JAMES AND THE GIANT PEACH

• If you are scared, you say that your **blood freezes** or **turns to ice**—as it definitely would if you spotted a witch!
My blood turned to ice. I began to shake all over. I glanced frantically behind me for a back door to escape through. There wasn't one. – THE WITCHES

• A pointed piece of ice formed by dripping water is an **icicle**.
ALL OF YOU WILL BE INSTANTLY DEEP FROZEN. YOU HAVE FIFTEEN SECONDS TO SPEAK. AFTER THAT YOU WILL TURN INTO ICICLES. – CHARLIE AND THE GREAT GLASS ELEVATOR

teem *pelt* *spit* *pour*
drizzle *patter*

DESCRIBING RAIN AND CLOUDS

• A formal word for rain is **precipitation**: *There is very little precipitation in Giant Country.*

• A single drop of rain is a **raindrop**.
They saw it coming. It was quite easy to see because it wasn't just raindrops. It wasn't raindrops at all. It was a great solid mass of water that might have been a lake or a whole ocean dropping out of the sky on top of them.
— JAMES AND THE GIANT PEACH

• Light rain is **drizzle** or a **light shower**. Heavy rain is a **downpour** or a **heavy shower** (as happens when **Cloud–Men** turn on their **rain faucets**).
'On with the faucets!' it shouted. 'On with the faucets! On with the faucets!' Three seconds later, the whole underneath of the cloud seemed to split and burst open like a paper bag, and then—out came the water!
— JAMES AND THE GIANT PEACH

• A long period without rain (as happens in Giant Country) is a **drought** (rhymes with *shout*).

• Clouds can **roll** or **billow** in the wind and large areas of rolling cloud are called **billows**.
Hundreds of Cloud-Men's children were frisking about all over the place and shrieking with laughter and sliding down the billows of the cloud on toboggans. — JAMES AND THE GIANT PEACH

• When things **rain down** from the ceiling, they fall heavily like rain. A **shower** of something falls suddenly from above (as when tall giants bump into chandeliers).
A shower of glass fell upon the poor BFG. 'Gunghummers and bogswinkles!' he cried. 'What was that?' — THE BFG

• If you haven't **the foggiest idea** about something, you have no idea what is happening, as if you were wandering about in a cloud of fog.
'I've been digging around in circles for three days and nights and I haven't the foggiest idea where I am!'
— FANTASTIC MR FOX

DID YOU KNOW?
The word **faucet**, meaning 'tap', is mainly used in American English now, but it was once used in British English too.

WHAT CAN RAIN DO?

IT CAN: **pelt**, **pour** or **teem** down heavily
When the rainy seasons came and the water poured down in solid sheets and flooded the little dirt roads, I learned how to spend nights in the back of a stifling station-wagon with all the windows closed against marauders from the jungle.
— BOY

IT CAN: **drizzle**, **patter** or **spit** lightly. The sound of raindrops falling is the **patter** of rain.
He flung the entire handful way over the bushes into the clearing. They fell with a soft little patter, like raindrops on dry leaves, and every single pheasant in the place must have heard them fall. — DANNY THE CHAMPION OF THE WORLD

• Thunder also **roars** or **rumbles** and lightning **flashes**.

WHAT CAN WIND DO?

IT CAN: **blow**, **rush** or **whoosh** strongly
The wind rushing against Sophie's face became so strong that she had to duck down again into the blanket to prevent her head from being blown away. – THE BFG

IT CAN: **howl**, **scream** or **whistle** noisily
She crouched in the pocket and listened to the wind screaming past. It came knifing in through the tiny peep-hole in the pocket and whooshed around her like a hurricane. – THE BFG

IT CAN: **drop** or **die down** quietly
The wind didn't drop. And I will tell you something amazing. That kite stayed up there all through the night. – DANNY THE CHAMPION OF THE WORLD

• If someone **runs like the wind** they run VERY fast indeed (especially if they have just found a mouse in their shoe).
The maid let out a scream that must have been heard by ships far out in the English Channel, and she dropped the shoes and ran like the wind down the corridor. – THE WITCHES

DESCRIBING SEASONS

SPRING AND SUMMER
CAN BE: **fresh**, **spring-like**, **summery**
It all started on a blazing hot day in the middle of summer. – JAMES AND THE GIANT PEACH

• The months of spring and summer are **springtime** and **summertime**.
It was fine in summertime, but I can tell you that sitting out there on a snowy day in winter was like sitting in a fridge. – DANNY THE CHAMPION OF THE WORLD

AUTUMN AND WINTER
CAN BE: **autumnal**, **golden**, **wintry**
It was one of those golden autumn afternoons and there were blackberries and splashes of old man's beard in the hedges, and the hawthorn berries were ripening scarlet for the birds when the cold winter came along.
– MATILDA

whoosh

whistle

WHAT CAN SUNSHINE DO?

IT CAN: **shine** or **glow** brightly
The sun was shining brightly out of a soft blue sky and the day was calm. – JAMES AND THE GIANT PEACH

IT CAN: **blaze** or **beat down** strongly
There was not a sound anywhere, not even a breath of wind, and overhead the sun blazed down upon them out of a deep blue sky. – JAMES AND THE GIANT PEACH

IT CAN: **burn**, **parch** or **scorch** the ground (or giants' skin)
The giants were all naked except for a sort of short skirt around their waists, and their skins were burnt brown by the sun. – THE BFG

DID YOU KNOW?
In North America autumn is called **fall**, because it is the season when trees shed leaves. An earlier name for it was **the fall of the leaf**.

howl

97

ALL ABOUT TIME
MEASURING TIME

PARTS OF A DAY

• A **day** is divided into twenty-four **hours**. An **hour** is divided into sixty **minutes** and a **minute** is divided into sixty **seconds**.

'George!' came the awful voice from the next room. 'It's time for my medicine!' 'Not yet, Grandma,' George called back. 'There's still twenty minutes before eleven o'clock.' – GEORGE'S MARVELLOUS MEDICINE

TIMES OF DAY

• A **day** is divided into **morning**, **afternoon** and **evening**.

• The time at 12 o'clock in the middle of the day is **midday** or **noon**.

'Now what you have to do, Mrs Silver, is hold Alfie up to your face and whisper these words to him three times a day, morning, noon and night.' – ESIO TROT

• At 12 o'clock in the middle of the night it is **midnight**.
For several hours, there was complete pandemonium in the little house, and it must have been nearly midnight before Mr Bucket was able to get rid of them so that Charlie could go to bed. – CHARLIE AND THE CHOCOLATE FACTORY

• The early hours of the day are called the **small hours** or the **witching hour**.

DID YOU KNOW?
The phrase **o'clock** is short for **of the clock**.

FIND OUT MORE!
Find out what happens in the **witching hour** in THE MAGICAL WORLD.

PARTS OF A YEAR

• A **year** is divided into twelve **months** or 365 **days**. There are seven **days** in a **week** and fifty-two **weeks** in a **year**.
'Exactly how old are you, Matilda?' she asked. 'Four years and three months,' Matilda said. – MATILDA

• A **leap year** is a year which has an extra day at the end of **February**. It therefore has 366 **days** (instead of the usual 365) in total.

FIND OUT MORE!
For words to describe the **seasons** of the year see ALL ABOUT THE WEATHER.

MONTHS OF THE YEAR

ARE: January, February, March, April, May, June, July, August, September, October, November, December

• Willy Wonka invites the Golden Ticket winners to his factory on the first day of **February**.
'The first day of February!' cried Mrs Bucket. 'But that's tomorrow! Today is the last day of January. I know it is!' – CHARLIE AND THE CHOCOLATE FACTORY

DAYS OF THE WEEK

ARE: Monday, Tuesday, Wednesday, Thursday, Friday, Saturday, Sunday

• Every **Wednesday** Mr and Mrs Twit eat **Bird Pie** for supper.
'Then we must hurry,' said Muggle-Wump. 'Today is Tuesday and over there you can already see the revolting Mr Twit up the ladder painting sticky glue on all the branches of The Big Dead Tree.' – THE TWITS

• If something only happens **in a month of Sundays**, it will never happen at all (as no month has only Sundays in it). In Giant Country, you would say **a month of Mondays** instead.
The BFG looked down at her sadly and shook his head. 'She is never believing you,' he said. 'Never in a month of Mondays.' – THE BFG

DID YOU KNOW?
Monday is an Old English name meaning 'day of the moon', just as **Sunday** means 'day of the sun'.

Tuesday is named after *Tiw*, the Anglo-Saxon god of war, and **Saturday** is named after the Roman god *Saturn*.

Wednesday and **Thursday** are named after the Norse gods **Odin** and **Thor**, and **Friday** is named after the Norse goddess **Frigga**.

FEBRUARY

JANUARY

DEVICES THAT MEASURE TIME

INCLUDE: **alarm–clock, grandfather clock, watch, hour–glass, sundial, egg–timer**

• Rrroasted **alarm–clocks** are an essential ingredient in **Delayed Action Mouse-Maker Formula**.
'Here is what you do. You set your alarm-clock to go off at nine o'clock tomorrow morning. Then you rrroast it in the oven until it is crrrisp and tender.' – THE WITCHES

• A **grandfather clock** is a clock set in a tall wooden case, which can also be used as a table leg when a **jumbly** giant comes to breakfast.
'Now we shall make a table upon which this gentleman may eat his breakfast in comfort. Fetch me four very tall grandfather clocks. There are plenty of them around the Palace.' – THE BFG

EXTRA-USUAL TIME

• Time can **speed up** or **slow down** in these **extra–usual** ways.

• A dose of **Wonka-Vite** will make you **younger** by one year every second (so Time will seem to **go backwards**).
'It's a delicious sensation,' Mr Wonka said. 'And it's very quick. You lose a year a second. Exactly one year falls away from you every second that goes by!' – CHARLIE AND THE GREAT GLASS ELEVATOR

• A dose of **Vita-Wonk** will make you instantly **older** (so Time will seem to **jump forwards**).

• Someone who lives for an exceedingly long time, like a giant, is a **time-twiddler**.

SPENDING TIME

• To spend time doing nothing useful is to **waste time**.
'We mustn't waste time!' cried Muggle-Wump. 'Hurry up, hurry up!' – THE TWITS

• A short amount of time is a **jiffy** or (in Giant Country) a **mintick**.
In a jiffy he had dropped silently on to the flowerbed below. In another jiffy he was out through the garden gate.
– THE MINPINS

• When you do something **in the blink of an eye**, you do it very quickly. Willy Wonka says **in the twink of an eye** instead.
'We shall bring her back! We shall transform her into a blossoming blushing maiden in the twink of an eye!'
– CHARLIE AND THE GREAT GLASS ELEVATOR

• If you arrive at the right time, you are **on time** on **bang on time**. If you arrive before or after the right time, you are either **too early** or **too late**.
'We must enter the wood about fifteen minutes before sunset. If we arrive after sunset all the pheasants will have flown up to roost and it'll be too late.' – DANNY THE CHAMPION OF THE WORLD

• If you arrive like Charlie at ten o'clock **sharp**, you arrive at *exactly* ten o'clock.
'On this day, and on no other, you must come to the factory gates at ten o'clock sharp in the morning. Don't be late!' – CHARLIE AND THE CHOCOLATE FACTORY

in the twink of an eye

DESCRIBING LIGHT

SOME FORMS OF LIGHT

• A band of light is a **beam**, **ray** or **shaft** of light.
I switched on the torch. A brilliant beam of light reached out ahead of me like a long white arm. That was better. Now at any rate I could see where I was going.
– DANNY THE CHAMPION OF THE WORLD

FIND OUT MORE!
Faces can **beam** and **light up** too! Find out more in DESCRIBING FACES in THE WORLD OF HUMAN BEANS.

• A speck of light is a **glimmer**, **glint**, **sparkle** or **twinkle** of light.
Now that the entrance had been sealed up, there was not a glint of light inside the cave. All was black. – THE BFG

• An area of light is a **circle** or **pool** of light.

• A ray of light from the sun is a **sunbeam** and one from the moon is a **moonbeam**.
A brilliant moonbeam was slanting through a gap in the curtains. It was shining right on to her pillow. – THE BFG

• A quick burst of light is a **flash** and a strong intense burst is a **blaze**.
Just then, all in a blaze of light, The Magic Fairy hove in sight. – REVOLTING RHYMES

• The phrase **what the blazes** means 'what' or 'what on earth'—but grown-ups only say it when they are angry.
'What the blazes do you mean, madam?' shouted Mr Jenkins. 'My son isn't a mouse!' – THE WITCHES

TYPES OF LIGHT

NATURAL LIGHT
COMES FROM: **daylight, moonlight, starlight, sunlight** OR **glow-worms**
In the silvery moonlight, the village street she knew so well seemed completely different . . . Everything was pale and ghostly and milky-white.
– THE BFG

• Animals like the **Glow-worm** that emit natural light are **bioluminescent**.
'That crazy Glow-worm has gone to sleep with her light on!'
– JAMES AND THE GIANT PEACH

ARTIFICIAL LIGHT
COMES FROM: **candle, fire, flame, lamp, light bulb, torch**
My father put a match to the wick of the lamp hanging from the ceiling and the little yellow flame sprang up and filled the inside of the caravan with pale light. – DANNY THE CHAMPION OF THE WORLD

DID YOU KNOW?
The phrase **what the dickens** means the same as **what the blazes**—but it has nothing to do with the author *Charles Dickens* (or as the BFG calls him *Dahl's Chickens*).

DID YOU KNOW?
In North America an electric torch is called a **flashlight**.
'Each man will have a gun and a flashlight. There will be no escape then for Mr Fox'.
– FANTASTIC MR FOX

beam
blaze

HOW DOES LIGHT APPEAR?

BRIGHT OR STRONG LIGHT

CAN BE: bright, brilliant, harsh

A brilliant greenish light as bright as the brightest electric bulb was shining out of its tail and lighting up the whole room. – JAMES AND THE GIANT PEACH

• Things that are **luminous** glow in the dark, just like Willy Wonka's **LUMINOUS LOLLIES FOR EATING IN BED AT NIGHT**.

LOW OR GENTLE LIGHT

CAN BE: dim, diffused, muted, pale, soft, warm

The pale daylight that entered came from a single tiny window in the front wall, but there were no curtains. – MATILDA

• If something is **translucent**, like a phizzwizard, you can see light shining through it.

Sophie peered into the jar and there, sure enough, she saw the faint translucent outline of something about the size of a hen's egg. There was just a touch of colour in it, a pale sea-green, soft and shimmering and very beautiful. – THE BFG

dazzle

glow glisten

flash

flicker

DID YOU KNOW?

When a group of words that start with the same letters also mean similar things (for example **glimmer, glisten, glint** and **glitter**) it is called **phonaesthesia** (say fon-ess-theez-ya).

WHAT CAN LIGHT DO?

IT CAN: beam, blaze or shine strongly. Fires and candles also **burn** with light.

Every one of these 'creatures' was at least as big as James himself, and in the strange greenish light that shone down from somewhere in the ceiling, they were absolutely terrifying to behold.
– JAMES AND THE GIANT PEACH

IT CAN: glitter, sparkle or twinkle brightly

James could see a mass of tiny green things that looked like little stones or crystals . . . and there was a strange brightness about them, a sort of luminous quality that made them glow and sparkle in the most wonderful way. – JAMES AND THE GIANT PEACH

IT CAN: glimmer, glisten, glow or shimmer softly

Then a faint greenish light began to glimmer out of the Glow-worm's tail, and this gradually became stronger and stronger until it was anyway enough to see by.
– JAMES AND THE GIANT PEACH

IT CAN: dazzle or glare harshly

I kept the torch pointed to one side of him so as not to dazzle his eyes. – DANNY THE CHAMPION OF THE WORLD

IT CAN: flash suddenly or flicker on and off

It was like flashes of lightning. Little waves of lightning seemed to be flashing out of her eyes. – MATILDA

IT CAN: bathe, illuminate or light up a person or place

From the ceiling, huge lamps hung down and bathed the room in a brilliant blue-white light. – CHARLIE AND THE CHOCOLATE FACTORY

ALL ABOUT COLOURS

NAMES OF COLOURS

SHADES OF BLUE AND PURPLE

INCLUDE: navy, indigo, turquoise; lavender, mauve, violet

SEEN IN: blueberries (and blueberry-gum-chewers, like Violet Beauregarde), tinkle-tinkle tree blossom, witches' spit, Mr Wormwood's hair tonic
'Your whole nose has gone purple!' 'What do you mean?' said Violet, still chewing away. 'Your cheeks!' screamed Mrs Beauregarde. 'They're turning blue as well! So is your chin! Your whole face is turning blue!' – CHARLIE AND THE CHOCOLATE FACTORY

• Willy Wonka's tail coat is **plum-coloured**.

• Slightly blue or purple colours are **bluish** or **purplish**.

SHADES OF GREEN

INCLUDE: emerald, lime, mint, pea-green

SEEN IN: crocodiles, frogs and toads; glow-worms and grasshoppers; **frobscottle**, Willy Wonka's Mint Jujubes (which turn your teeth green too)
The toad said, 'Don't you think I'm fine? Admire these lovely legs of mine, And I am sure you've never seen A toad so gloriously green!' – DIRTY BEASTS

• Willy Wonka's trousers are **bottle green**.
'There's these three old birds in nightshirts floating around in this crazy glass box and there's a funny little guy with a pointed beard wearing a black top-hat and a plum-coloured velvet tail-coat and bottle-green trousers . . . ' – CHARLIE AND THE GREAT GLASS ELEVATOR

• Slightly green colours are **greenish**.

SHADES OF RED AND ORANGE

INCLUDE: crimson, pink, rose, ruby, scarlet

SEEN IN: Nine-Spotted Ladybirds, **Scarlet Scorchdroppers**, strawberries and **strawbunkles**, **trogglehumpers**, the **Inventing Room** door, **Oompa-Loompa** space suits
Inside the jar Sophie could see the faint scarlet outline of something that looked like a mixture between a blob of gas and a bubble of jelly. – THE BFG

• Slightly red or orange colours are **reddish** or **orangey**.

FIND OUT MORE!
Faces can turn **red**, **purple** and other **colours** too! Find out more in DESCRIBING FACES in THE WORLD OF HUMAN BEANS.

DID YOU KNOW?
The word **mauve** rhymes with **stove**. It comes from **malva**, the Latin name for the **mallow** plant, which has pink or purple flowers.

The root of the **mallow** plant was originally used to make **marshmallow** for sweets (or for pillows in Willy Wonka's factory).

SHADES OF YELLOW AND GOLD

INCLUDE: cream, gold or golden, lemon

SEEN IN: Giant Peaches, Golden Tickets, Wonka-Vite pills
Mr Wonka picked up the bottle from the bed and opened it and counted out fourteen of the little brilliant yellow pills. — CHARLIE AND THE GREAT GLASS ELEVATOR

• Slightly yellow colours are **yellowish** or **yellowy**. Shades of yellow can also be **buttery** or **creamy**.
The skin of the peach was very beautiful—a rich buttery yellow with patches of brilliant pink and red. — JAMES AND THE GIANT PEACH

• Gold, silver and bronze are **metallic** colours.

OTHER SHADES AND COLOURS

INCLUDE: black, brown, beige, grey, white

SEEN IN: chocolate rivers and waterfalls, George's grandma's teeth
George couldn't help disliking Grandma. She was a selfish grumpy old woman. She had pale brown teeth and a small puckered-up mouth like a dog's bottom. — GEORGE'S MARVELLOUS MEDICINE

• Slightly brown, grey or white colours are **brownish**, **greyish** or **whitish**.
They really were enormous, those pipes. There must have been a dozen of them at least, and they were sucking up the brownish muddy water from the river and carrying it away to goodness knows where. — CHARLIE AND THE CHOCOLATE FACTORY

FIND OUT MORE! For ways to describe **pitch-black** darkness, see DESCRIBING DAY AND NIGHT.

DESCRIBING COLOURS

• A type of a particular colour is a **hue** or **shade**.

• A small amount of a colour is a **tinge** or **tint**.

• Strong colours can be **dark**, **deep** or **rich**.
A rich blue smoke, the colour of peacocks, rose from the surface of the liquid, and a fiery fearsome smell filled the kitchen. — GEORGE'S MARVELLOUS MEDICINE

• Bright colours can be **brilliant**, **vibrant** or **zingy**.

• Colours that are unpleasantly bright or clashing, like those in Mr Wormwood's suit, are **garish**, **loud** or **lurid**.
In came Mr Wormwood in a loud check suit and a yellow tie. The appalling broad orange-and-green check of the jacket and trousers almost blinded the onlooker. — MATILDA

• Light colours can be **faded**, **muted**, **neutral**, **pale**, **pastel** or **soft**.
Sophie saw that under the cloak he was wearing a sort of collarless shirt and a dirty old leather waistcoat that didn't seem to have any buttons. His trousers were faded green and were far too short in the legs. — THE BFG

• Something with no colour at all is **colourless**: *The landscape of Dream Country is almost completely colourless.*

• A small patch of bright colour is a **splash** and a collection of bright colours (as in Mr Hoppy's flowers) is a **riot** of colour.
There were two loves in Mr Hoppy's life. One was the flowers he grew on his balcony. They grew in pots and tubs and baskets, and in summer the little balcony became a riot of colour. — ESIO TROT

COLOURFUL CREATURES AND THINGS

INCLUDE: George's Marvellous Medicine Number One, rainbows, Rainbow Drops, Roly-Poly Bird, zozimus

• Something which has many colours, like the Roly-Poly Bird, is **multicoloured** or **polychrome**.
The mixture was as thick as cream, and as he stirred and stirred, many wonderful colours rose up from the depths and blended together, pinks, blues, greens, yellows and browns. — GEORGE'S MARVELLOUS MEDICINE

• The colours of the **rainbow** are: red, orange, yellow, green, blue, indigo, violet. Your spit turns all seven colours after sucking Rainbow Drops.
There was a whole lot of splendid stuff from the great Wonka factory itself, for example the famous Willy Wonka Rainbow Drops—suck them and you can spit in seven different colours. — THE GIRAFFE AND THE PELLY AND ME

SHAPES AND PATTERNS

DESCRIBING SHAPES

TWO-DIMENSIONAL SHAPES

INCLUDE: circle, diamond, rectangle, square, star, triangle

CAN BE: circular or round, elliptical, oblong, oval or ovoid, rectangular, square, triangular

There it lay, this small oblong sea-green jellyish thing, at the bottom of the jar, quite peaceful, but pulsing gently, the whole of it moving in and out ever so slightly, as though it were breathing. – THE BFG

• A shape with six sides is a **hexagon** and one with eight sides is an **octagon**.

• Most sweets are **round** or **oval**, but Willy Wonka makes **square-shaped** sweets that *look round* (because they have faces painted on them).
On the next door, it said, SQUARE SWEETS THAT LOOK ROUND. 'Wait!' cried Mr Wonka, skidding suddenly to a halt. 'I am very proud of my square sweets that look round. Let's take a peek.' – CHARLIE AND THE CHOCOLATE FACTORY

THREE-DIMENSIONAL SHAPES

INCLUDE: cone, cube, cylinder, pyramid, sphere

CAN BE: conical, cubic, cylindrical, spherical

'First of all you dig a little hole in the ground. Then you twist a piece of paper into the shape of a cone and you fit this into the hole, hollow end up, like a cup.' – DANNY THE CHAMPION OF THE WORLD

• A half sphere is called a **hemisphere**.

DID YOU KNOW?
A creature that can change its shape, like a **Vermicious Knid**, is called a **shapeshifter**. Another word for changing shape is **morphing**, so you could say: Knids can morph into multiple monsters!

SPECIAL SHAPES

• Something shaped like an egg is **egg-shaped** or **oviform**. **Vermicious Knids** are naturally **oviform**, but they can also change shape to confuse their enemies.
It was a fearsome sight. The huge green egg-shaped Knids were grouping themselves into squadrons with about twenty Knids to a squadron. – CHARLIE AND THE GREAT GLASS ELEVATOR

• Something shaped like a sausage is **sausage-shaped**.
Two days before, the United States of America had successfully launched its first Space Hotel, a gigantic sausage-shaped capsule no less than one thousand feet long. – CHARLIE AND THE GREAT GLASS ELEVATOR

• Something shaped like the letter Y (for example) is **Y-shaped**, so the **Knids** that form the word **SCRAM** with their bodies are **S-shaped**, **C-shaped**, **R-shaped**, **A-shaped** and **M-shaped**.

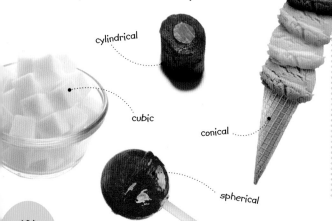

cylindrical

cubic

conical

spherical

DESCRIBING PATTERNS

PATTERNS WITH SPOTS

INCLUDE: dots, polka dots, spots

CAN BE: dotted or dotty, spotted or spotty

• **Spotted creatures** include: **ladybird, Pink-Spotted Scrunch** and **spotted whangdoodle.**
'The number of spots that a Ladybird has is simply a way of showing which branch of the family she belongs to. I, for example, as you can see for yourself, am a Nine-Spotted Ladybird.' — JAMES AND THE GIANT PEACH

• If you are **dotty about** something, it means that you like it very much. For example, Bruce Bogtrotter is **dotty** about chocolate cake, and mice are **dotty** about currant cake.
A fine currant cake is the favourite food of white mice. They are dotty about it. — THE WITCHES

PATTERNS WITH LINES

INCLUDE: checks, stripes, tartan

CAN BE: checked or chequered, striped or stripy, tartan, wavy, zigzag
Mr Wormwood . . . liked to wear jackets with large brightly coloured checks and he sported ties that were usually yellow or pale green. — MATILDA

• **Striped things** include: Grandpa Joe's **pyjamas** and **snozzcumbers.**
'Show him the ticket, Charlie!' shouted Grandpa Joe, who was still dancing around the floor like a dervish in his striped pyjamas. — CHARLIE AND THE CHOCOLATE FACTORY

OTHER PATTERNS

• A pattern with lots of flowers is **floral** or **flowery**.

• Something with an interesting pattern is **patterned**, like the **extra-usual** webs spun by Miss Spider.
'I can spin just as well as any Silkworm. What's more, I can spin patterns.' — JAMES AND THE GIANT PEACH

FIND OUT MORE!
The word **spotty** also means 'covered in itchy spots', which is what happens when you apply **spotty powder**. Find out more in DESCRIBING FACES in THE WORLD OF HUMAN BEANS.

FIND OUT MORE!
For more ways to describe **spotted whangdoodles** and **Pink-Spotted Scrunches**, see EXTRA-USUAL CREATURES in THE MAGICAL WORLD.

striped

stripy

dotted

spotted

spotty

wavy

zigzag

THINGS THAT GO UP

`INCLUDE:` **balloons**, **bubbles** (except in frobscottle), **Great Glass Elevator** (with **skyhooks**), **Giant Peach** (with seagulls)
Each balloon was on a long string and when it was filled with gas it pulled on its string, trying to go up and up. — THE TWITS

GOING DOWN

`THINGS CAN:` **descend**, **drop** or **fall downwards**. When you throw or kick a ball in the air it **descends** in an **arc** or a **parabola** (as do Miss Trunchbull's pupils).
Matilda, who was mesmerized by the whole crazy affair, saw Amanda Thripp descending in a long graceful parabola on to the playing-field beyond. — MATILDA

`THEY CAN:` **dive**, **plummet** or **plunge** downwards quickly
Round and round and upside down went the peach as it plummeted towards the earth, and they were all clinging desperately to the stem to save themselves from being flung into space. — JAMES AND THE GIANT PEACH

`THEY CAN:` **float** or **glide down** gently
As she floated gently down, Mrs Twit's petticoat billowed out like a parachute, showing her long knickers. — THE TWITS

ascend

climb rise

descend

plummet

plunge

FIND OUT MORE!
Find out what happens when there is no **gravity** in THE SKY AND OUTER SPACE.

ALL ABOUT DIRECTIONS

GOING UP

`THINGS CAN:` **ascend**, **climb** or **rise upwards**
Majestically . . . Like some fabulous golden balloon . . . The giant peach rose up dripping out of the water and began climbing towards the heavens. — JAMES AND THE GIANT PEACH

`THEY CAN:` **lift off** or **up** from the ground
As he spoke, the bed with the three old ones in it and Mr Wonka on top lifted gently off the floor and hung suspended in mid-air. — CHARLIE AND THE GREAT GLASS ELEVATOR

THINGS THAT GO DOWN

INCLUDE: burst balloons, **bubbles** (in **frobscottle**), **Great Glass Elevator** (without **skyhooks**), **Giant Peach** (without seagulls), rubbish (and Veruca Salt) in a **rubbish chute**

'But look! It's fizzing the wrong way!' Sophie cried. And indeed it was. The bubbles, instead of travelling upwards and bursting on the surface, were shooting downwards and bursting at the bottom. – THE BFG

GOING BACK AND FORTH

THINGS CAN: **advance** or **go forwards** or **forthwards**
'There is little point in teaching anything backwards. The whole object of life, Headmistress, is to go forwards.' – MATILDA

THEY CAN: **retreat** or **go backwards**
'Dear lady,' said Mr Wonka. 'This isn't a car on the motorway. When you are in orbit, you cannot stop and you cannot go backwards.' – CHARLIE AND THE GREAT GLASS ELEVATOR

• **Vermicious Knids** attack their enemies **backwards**, because their rear ends are more menacing than their fronts.
'They're shaped like enormous eggs and they're coming at us backwards!' 'Backwards?' cried the President. 'Why backwards?' 'Because their bottoms are even more pointy than their tops!' shouted Shuckworth. – CHARLIE AND THE GREAT GLASS ELEVATOR

• Something that moves to the side, like the **Great Glass Elevator**, goes **sideways**. Something that moves from one corner to the opposite corner goes **diagonally**.

DID YOU KNOW?
The word **elevator** is mainly used in American English. In British English the usual word is **lift**.

Roald Dahl lived some of his life in the USA and used several American words in his stories, such as **flashlight** and **pants** (meaning 'trousers' not underpants).

THE WRONG WAY ROUND (OR UP)

• Something that is turned the **wrong way round** is **back-to-front**. The words in tortoise language are written **backwards** or **back-to-front**.
'The other words are spelled backwards, too,' Mr Hoppy said. 'If you turn them round into human language, they simply say: TORTOISE, TORTOISE, GET BIGGER BIGGER!' – ESIO TROT

• The Vicar of Nibbleswicke has **Back-to-Front Dyslexia**, which means that he says some words **backwards** by mistake, like calling Miss Prewt *Miss Twerp*.

• Something that is turned the **wrong way up**, like Mr and Mrs Twit standing on their heads, is **upside down** or **topsy-turvy**. Mr Twit dreams of owning the world's first **Upside-down Monkey Circus**.
'We're UPSIDE DOWN!' gasped Mr Twit. 'We must be upside down. We are standing on the ceiling looking down at the floor!' – THE TWITS

DID YOU KNOW?
The word **awkward** originally meant 'the wrong way round' or 'upside down'.

topsy-turvy

upside down

Nature Writing Hut

swoop like seagulls

a crinkly old cauliflower

frost and ice not so nice

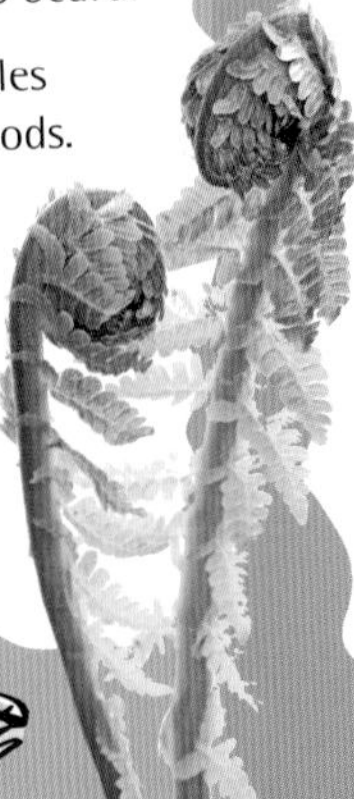

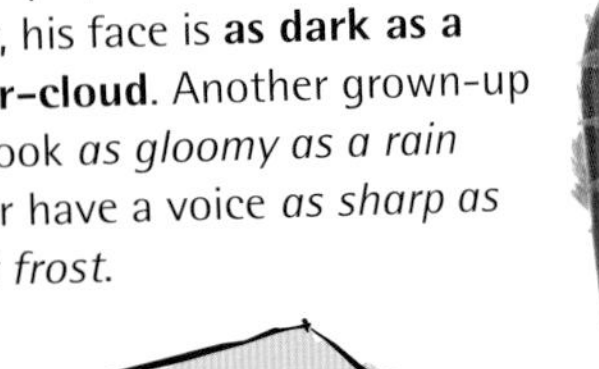

ingenious insults

• Roald Dahl's characters often insult each other with **vegitibble** names. Mrs Twit calls her husband a **rotten old turnip** and George calls his grumpy grandma an **old wurzel**, which is a type of wrinkly root vegetable.

Other fruits and **vegitibbles** make good **insults** for beastly grown-ups, too—and it is even better if you use **alliteration**! What about a *crinkly old cauliflower*, or a *prickly old parsnip*, or even a *soggy old sprout*?

splendid similes

• **Animals** and **birds** make splendid similes to describe how **human beans** move or sound. Miss Trunchbull stalks her pupils **in the manner of a tigress** and Willy Wonka moves his head and body **like a squirrel**. What other creature comparisons could you make?

A group of hungry **chiddlers** might swoop on a plate of sandwiches *like a flock of seagulls*, or an angry headmistress might bellow *like a raging rhinoceros*.

• The hills in Giant Country are **as bare as concrete**. What else could you compare **landscape** to? For example, a treeless hill could be *as bald as a boiled egg*, or a hill with bushes could be *as bushy as Mr Twit's beard*.

• You can use **weather** terms for similes to describe **human beans** or their moods. For example, when Mr Wormwood is angry, his face is **as dark as a thunder-cloud**. Another grown-up might look *as gloomy as a rain cloud* or have a voice *as sharp as a night frost*.

redunculous rhymes

• In the chant of the Cloud-Men, **freezes** rhymes with *sneezes* and **snow** rhymes with *go* and *blow*: '*Down they go! . . . Hail and snow! Freezes and sneezes and noses will blow!*' What other rhymes can you find for **weather** words to make your own chilly chant? For example: *Frost and ice! Not so nice! Hurl them down and don't think twice!*

trillipede • squillipede

phizz-whizzing suffixes

• Why not invent the name of a new **minibeast** based on **centipede** and **millipede**? For example, a minibeast with a *trillion* legs would be a *trillipede* and one with a *squillion* legs would be a *squillipede*.

dottycup • quogworm

sparky space creations

• The **Space Hotel** and **Great Glass Elevator** are ingenious inventions of Roald Dahl. You can invent your own space machine, too. It could be a familiar object that is adapted for space travel, such as a *Space Bathtub*, or a spaceship with an **extra-usual** shape, such as a *Space Doughnut*. Don't forget to draw a picture of your **spliffling** invention!

• Many **constellations** are named after animals or interesting objects because of the shape formed by the stars within them, for example *The Great Bear* and *The Plough*. Can you invent a new **constellation** based on a character or object in Roald Dahl's stories? For example: *The Evil Knid* constellation, or *The Great Snozzcumber*. When you have a good name, draw a picture plotting the stars that make up the shape.

Space Bathtub • The Great Snozzcumber

wondercrump wordbuilding

• Roald Dahl often blended words to make new creatures, for example the **quogwinkle** (a creature from outer space) is a blend of *quagmire* (a boggy marsh) and *winkle* (a type of shellfish). What other creatures could come from a boggy planet? What about a *quogworm*, a *quogodile* or even an ancient *quogosaur*?

• Some plants, like **buttercups** and **bluebells**, are named after the shape or colour of their leaves or flowers. What new plant names could you invent? For example, a plant with cup-shaped spotted flowers could be a *dottycup*. What would a *zebracup* look like, or a *snowbell*?

• What could you call the Enormous Crocodile when he pretends to be a **coconut tree**? He could be a *croconut* or *cocodile* tree, or perhaps a *croco-coco* tree!

Dlaor Lhad

speaking tortoise

• Anyone can speak or write **tortoise** language. Try writing your own name **back-to-front**, or the name of any of your friends, family or pets. Remember to reverse the order of letters in each word, but not the order of words in a name or sentence. For example, *Roald Dahl* in **esio trot** language would be *Dlaor Lhad* and *Matilda Wormwood* would be *Adlitam Doowmrow*. Try reading the names out, too—but go slowly like a tortoise!

ZIPPFIZZ ALONG TO THE WORLD OF WORDS FOR MORE RAZZTWIZZLING IDEAS FOR WRITERS AND STORYTELLERS!

foamy fiery fizz froth bubble boil swirl seethe

whisk fume fizzle stew stir swizzle

THE
MAGICAL
WORLD

*It was a brutal and bewitching smell,
spicy and staggering, fierce and frenzied,
full of wizardry and magic.*
— GEORGE'S MARVELLOUS MEDICINE

ALL ABOUT MAGIC

THINGS WITH MAGIC POWERS

INCLUDE: **amulet** or **talisman**, **crystal ball**, **magic beans** or **magic crystals**, **zozimus**

James could see a mass of tiny green things that looked like little stones or crystals, each one about the size of a grain of rice . . . 'There's more power and magic in those things in there than in all the rest of the world put together,' the old man said softly. — JAMES AND THE GIANT PEACH

• An animal that is kept by a witch because of its magic powers is a **familiar**, and a female cat kept as a familiar is a **grimalkin**. The **teeth** of an ancient Mexican **grimalkin** are an ingredient in Vita-Wonk.

Transformation

DID YOU KNOW?

The BFG is not the only story which takes place during the **witching hour**.

In William Shakespeare's play *Hamlet*, a ghostly scene happens in the very witching time of night.

MAGIC POWERS

• Magic powers are also known as **magical** or **supernatural** powers.

• The use of magic to make **extra-usual** things happen is **witchcraft** or **wizardry**.
'Some of us,' the old woman went on, 'have fire on our tongues and sparks in our bellies and wizardry in the tips of our fingers.' — GEORGE'S MARVELLOUS MEDICINE

• Witchcraft is also known as **sorcery**: *The Grand High Witch is an expert in every kind of sorcery.*

• When a **magic spell** turns a **human bean** into another creature (such as a mouse) it is called **transformation** or **metamorphosis**. When a witch or wizard changes into another creature it is called **shapeshifting**.
'The plain fact is,' my grandmother said, 'that your son Bruno has been rather drastically altered.' 'Altered!' shouted Mr Jenkins. 'What the devil d'you mean altered?' — THE WITCHES

• The time around midnight when witches are active and when magical things can happen is the **witching hour**.
The witching hour, somebody had once whispered to her, was a special moment in the middle of the night when every child and every grown-up was in a deep deep sleep, and all the dark things came out from hiding and had the world to themselves. — THE BFG

FIND OUT MORE!

Insects **metamorphose** too, and **Vermicious Knids** are good at **shapeshifting**! Find out more in THE NATURAL WORLD.

• The use of magic to foretell the future, for example with a **crystal ball**, is **fortune-telling** or **divination** and a person who does this is a **fortune-teller**.

• A **human bean** who seems to have magic powers is a **magician**. Willy Wonka is a **magician** with chocolate as he makes splendiferous creations that seem impossible to ordinary **human beans**.
'Clever!' cried the old man. 'He's more than that! He's a magician with chocolate! He can make anything—anything he wants!' – CHARLIE AND THE CHOCOLATE FACTORY

CASTING SPELLS

• Other words for a **magic spell** are **charm** and **incantation**. An evil spell is also a **curse** or **hex**.

• To **cast a spell** on someone is to **bewitch** or **enchant** them. To reverse a magic spell is to **undo** or **reverse** it:
Is there any way to undo the mouse-maker spell?

• A book of magic spells is a **spellbook**.
(PLEASE NOTE: this is NOT the same thing as a *spelling book*, which will only help you to spell words not to cast spells!)

FIND OUT MORE!
What kitchen **utensil** is used to mix magical zozimus? Find out in ALL ABOUT DREAMS.

• Something **bewitching** or **enchanting** is so powerful and unusual that it seems to cast a magic spell over you.
It was a brutal and bewitching smell, spicy and staggering, fierce and frenzied, full of wizardry and magic. – GEORGE'S MARVELLOUS MEDICINE

• If you are **spellbound** by something you are fascinated by it, as if my magic.
From the moment that the first note was struck, the audience became completely spellbound. – JAMES AND THE GIANT PEACH

• You can use a **magic wand** to cast spells, or (if you are lucky enough to have one) a **magic finger**.

• To wave a magic wand (or finger) is to **brandish** it. A quick wave of a wand is a **flick**, **swish** or **swoosh**.
Just then, all in a blaze of light, The Magic Fairy hove in sight, Her Magic Wand went swoosh and swish! 'Cindy!' she cried, 'come make a wish!' – REVOLTING RHYMES

• To make something disappear by using magic is to **magic it away**: *She magicked the creature away with a flick of her magic thumb.*

DID YOU KNOW?
The word **glamour** was originally a Scottish word meaning 'witchcraft' or 'magic'.

DID YOU KNOW?
An old name for a **magic wand** is a charming-rod.

or metamorphosis

bubble

boil

broth

froth

'Fiery broth

Foamy

Fume and

Fizzle

FIND OUT MORE!
For the
magic ingredients
in Wonka-Vite
and Vita-Wonk,
see EXTRA-USUAL
CREATURES.

MIXING POTIONS

• The instructions to make a **magic potion** are a **magic formula** (plural **formulae**) or **magic recipe**. The items listed in the formula are the **magic ingredients**.
'So yesterday I am personally prrree-paring a small qvantity of the magic formula in order to give to you a public demonstration.' – THE WITCHES

• Other words for a magic potion are **magic brew** and **magic broth**.

• To mix or prepare a magic formula is to **brew** or **concoct** it.
'Attention again!' The Grand High Witch was shouting.
'I vill now give to you the rrrecipe for concocting Formula 86 Delayed Action Mouse-Maker!' – THE WITCHES

• A magic potion can **boil**, **bubble**, **fizz** or **fizzle**, **foam**, **froth**, **seethe**, **simmer**, **smoke** or **stew**.
It was wonderful to stand there stirring this amazing mixture and to watch it smoking blue and bubbling and frothing and foaming as though it were alive. – GEORGE'S MARVELLOUS MEDICINE

• While it brews, you might **stir**, **swirl**, **swizzle** or **whisk** it.

• A large pot for brewing potions is a **cauldron** (although you can also try using an ordinary saucepan).
Back in the kitchen once again, George, with Mr Kranky watching him anxiously, tipped half a pint of engine oil and some anti-freeze into the giant saucepan. 'Boil it up again!' cried Mr Kranky. 'Boil it and stir it!' – GEORGE'S MARVELLOUS MEDICINE

and witch's brew

froth and riches blue

spume and spoondrift spray

swizzle shout hooray . . .'

DID YOU KNOW? The word **cauldron** comes from Latin *calidus* meaning 'hot' and is related to the words *calorie* and *scald*.

DID YOU KNOW? The three witches in William Shakespeare's play *Macbeth* chant the magic words:

Double double toil and trouble, fire burn and caldron bubble.

Their **magic ingredients** include eye of newt, toe of frog, wool of bat and tongue of dog.

TONGUE
of crocodile

EYE
of lizard

BEAK
of parrot

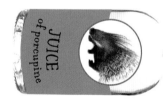

JUICE
of porcupine

MAGIC INGREDIENTS

INCLUDE: **tongue of crocodile, eye of lizard, beak of parrot, juice** (or **quill**) **of porcupine, skull of witch, spoonful of sugar, moonlight**

'Crocodile tongues!' he cried. 'One thousand long slimy crocodile tongues boiled up in the skull of a dead witch for twenty days and nights with the eyeballs of a lizard! Add the fingers of a young monkey, the gizzard of a pig, the beak of a green parrot, the juice of a porcupine, and three spoonfuls of sugar. Stew for another week, and then let the moon do the rest!'—JAMES AND THE GIANT PEACH

• You might add a **dash, drop, morsel, pinch, splash** or **touch** of an ingredient.

• You might **season** the brew—and perhaps (if you are Very Brave) **taste** or **sip** it.

• To help the magic, you might **chant** some **magic words** (preferably ones that rhyme) while the potion brews.

And suddenly, George found himself dancing around the steaming pot, chanting strange words that came into his head out of nowhere: 'Fiery broth and witch's brew Foamy froth and riches blue Fume and spume and spoondrift spray Fizzle swizzle shout hooray Watch it sloshing, swashing, sploshing Hear it hissing, squishing, spissing Grandma better start to pray.'—GEORGE'S MARVELLOUS MEDICINE

ALL ABOUT WITCHES

NAMES FOR WITCHES

INCLUDE: enchanter or enchantress, sorcerer or sorceress

• A male witch is a **wizard** or **warlock**. (But note that there are NO male **wizards** in Roald Dahl's stories: only female **witches**.)
I do not wish to speak badly about women. Most women are lovely. But the fact remains that all witches are women.
— THE WITCHES

• An old name for a witch is a **hag**, although now it usually means an ugly and nasty old woman, which is what Mrs Twit will become.

• An expert on witches is called a **witchophile** and someone who tracks down witches is a **witch hunter** or **witchfinder**.
'Are you a witchophile, Grandmamma?' 'I am a retired witchophile,' she said. 'I am too old to be active any longer.'
— THE WITCHES

FIND OUT MORE! Do **phizzwizards** have anything to do with wizards? Find out in ALL ABOUT DREAMS.

• A group of witches is called a **coven** (rhymes with *oven*): *Every year all the witches in Inkland hold a grand coven.*

• An animal, such as a cat, which accompanies a witch is called a **familiar**.

DESCRIBING WITCHES

SOME WEAR: cloak or robe, pointy hat, magical symbols

BEWARE: Real witches, including ALL witches in Roald Dahl's stories, wear Very Boring clothes.
REAL WITCHES dress in ordinary clothes and look very much like ordinary women. They live in ordinary houses and they work in ORDINARY JOBS. That is why they are so hard to catch. — THE WITCHES

SOME USE: broomstick, cauldron, magic potion, magic wand, spellbook.

• Some witches, including the **Grand High Witch** herself, are fantabulously old (perhaps as **ancient** as a **Bristlecone Pine**). They look **wizened**, **wrinkled**, **shrunken** or **shrivelled** with age.

• Some witches **croak** or **cackle** when they speak.

DID YOU KNOW? The word **wizard** comes from an old meaning of *wise* and originally meant 'a wise person'.

DID YOU KNOW? The word **coven** comes from Latin words meaning 'to come together' and is related to the words *convent* and *convention*.

sniff sniff sniff sniff

FIND OUT MORE! Does **langwitch** have anything to do with witches? Find out in GIANT LANGWITCH.

WITCH DISGUISES

• Some witches (including ALL witches in Roald Dahl's stories) are experts in **disguises**, which makes it Very Tricky to spot them.

THEY WEAR: gloves to hide their **claws**.
(If you suspect someone of being a witch, it is a good idea to ask them to **remove** their gloves.)

THEY WEAR: a **wig** to hide their **bald scalp**. This gives them an itchy **wig-rash**, which also makes them **scratch** a lot.

'The underneath of a wig is always very rough and scratchy ... It causes nasty sores on the head. Wig-rash, the witches call it. And it doesn't half itch.'– THE WITCHES

THEY WEAR: **pointed shoes** (which make them **limp**) to hide their **horrigustly** ugly **toeless feet**

'No toes!' I cried. 'Then what do they have?' 'They just have feet,' my grandmother said. 'The feet have square ends with no toes on them at all.'– THE WITCHES

THEY HAVE: **extra-usually** large **nose-holes** or **nostrils** which can sniff out **chiddlers**

THEY HAVE: **blue-coloured spit** which they use as writing ink

'Nobody can have blue spit!' 'Witches can,' she said. 'Is it like ink?' I asked. 'Exactly,' she said. 'They even use it to write with.' – THE WITCHES

• The **Grand High Witch** also wears a **face-mask** to hide her revoltingly **rotsome** features.

DID YOU KNOW?

The word **nostril** means literally 'nose hole' or 'nose piercing'. It is based on an old word *thirl* meaning 'pierce'.

DID YOU KNOW?

In Scotland, **chiddlers** who wear fancy dress on Halloween are called *guisers*, which is related to the word **disguise**.

THE GRAND HIGH WITCH

HAS: a **crumpled, wizened, shrunken, shrivelled, rotting, worm-eaten** face, which she hides behind a mask. You could also call it **maggotwise** or **rotsome**.
That face of hers was the most frightful and frightening thing I have ever seen . . . It was so crumpled and wizened, so shrunken and shrivelled, it looked as though it had been pickled in vinegar. — THE WITCHES

HAS: a **fiery** or **volatile** temper, which means that she often gets Very Cross

SHE: **rrrolls** the letter *R* when she speaks and pronounces the letter *W* like a *V*
'Classrooms vill all be svorrming with mice!' shouted The Grand High Witch. 'Chaos and pandemonium vill be rrreigning in every school in Inkland!' — THE WITCHES

SHE: **fries** any witch who annoys her (which is at least one witch per year). She does this by shooting **fiery sparks** from her eyes until her victim turns into a puff of smoke.

SHE: **screeches** at any witch who talks nonsense or **boshvollop**
'You blithering bumpkin!' screeched The Grand High Witch. 'You brrrainless bogvumper! . . . Never in my life am I hearing such a boshvolloping suggestion coming from a vitch!'
— THE WITCHES

SHE: **hatches** plans to **exterminate chiddlers**

WHAT DO WITCHES DO?

THEY: **cast a spell, put a curse on you, make themselves invisible** or **shapeshift** into another creature

THEY: **concoct** magic formulae or **brew** magic potions
'Delayed Action Mouse-Maker!' they chanted. 'She's done it again! Her Grandness has concocted yet another of her wondrous magic child-killers!' — THE WITCHES

rotsome

maggotwise

worm-eaten

FIND OUT MORE!
What magical **ingredients** go into spells and potions? Find out in ALL ABOUT MAGIC.

DID YOU KNOW?
In Ireland, witches were called eye-biters as they were thought to cast spells with their eyes.

THEY: **gather** ingredients, such as **gruntles'** eggs, to use in magic potions
'I'm getting a bit old to go bird's nesting. Those ruddy gruntles always nest very high up.' — THE WITCHES

THEY: try to **avoid being fried** themselves, by always obeying the **Grand High Witch** (and trying NOT to catch her fiery eye)

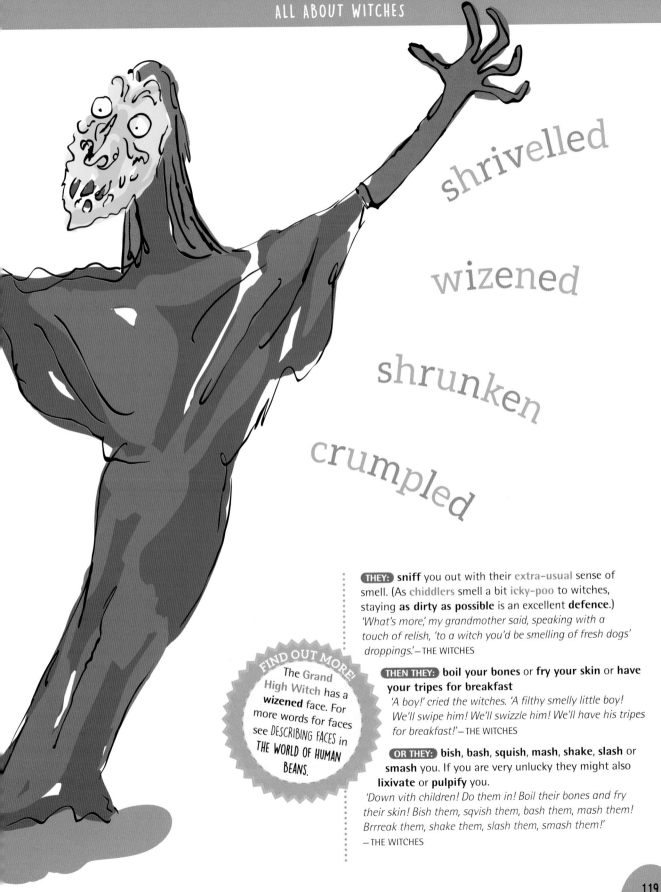

shrivelled

wizened

shrunken

crumpled

THEY: **sniff** you out with their **extra-usual** sense of smell. (As **chiddlers** smell a bit **icky-poo** to witches, staying **as dirty as possible** is an excellent **defence**.)
'What's more,' my grandmother said, speaking with a touch of relish, 'to a witch you'd be smelling of fresh dogs' droppings.'— THE WITCHES

FIND OUT MORE! The Grand High Witch has a **wizened** face. For more words for faces see DESCRIBING FACES in THE WORLD OF HUMAN BEANS.

THEN THEY: **boil your bones** or **fry your skin** or **have your tripes for breakfast**
'A boy!' cried the witches. 'A filthy smelly little boy! We'll swipe him! We'll swizzle him! We'll have his tripes for breakfast!'— THE WITCHES

OR THEY: **bish, bash, squish, mash, shake, slash** or **smash** you. If you are very unlucky they might also **lixivate** or **pulpify** you.
'Down vith children! Do them in! Boil their bones and fry their skin! Bish them, sqvish them, bash them, mash them! Brrreak them, shake them, slash them, smash them!'
— THE WITCHES

EXTRA-USUAL CREATURES

MAGICAL CREATURES

• Parts of these creatures are believed to have **magical properties**. This is Very Bad Indeed for them, as they are hunted by witches for making **magic potions**, which may lead to them becoming **endangered** or even **extinct**.
'Vun after the other you also mix in the following items: the claw of a crrrabcrrruncher, the beak of a blabbersnitch, the snout of a grrrobblesqvirt and the tongue of a catsprrringer!'
— THE WITCHES

• The **blabbersnitch** is a rare deep-sea creature with a distinctive **beak**, a bit like a dolphin or porpoise.

blabbersnitch

• The **catspringer** is a fast-moving creature that lives in a burrow, a bit like a mole or rabbit. Witches believe its **tongue** has magical properties.

• The **crabcruncher** is a creature that lives on high rocky cliffs. It has strong **claws** which are much prized by witches.
'We will spear the blabbersnitch and trap the crabcruncher and shoot the grobblesquirt and catch the catspringer in his burrow!' — THE WITCHES

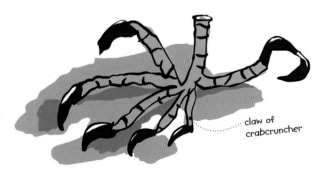

claw of crabcruncher

crabcruncher

• The **grobblesquirt** is a rare creature that lives on moorland. Its **snout** is thought to have magical properties.

• The **gruntle** is a bird that nests high up in tall trees (making it tricky for witches to find them). The eggs of the **gruntle** are added to **Delayed Action Mouse-Maker Formula**.
'Vhile the mixer is still mixing you must add to it the yolk of vun grrruntle's egg.' 'A gruntle's egg!' cried the audience. 'We shall do that!' — THE WITCHES

grobblesquirt

gruntle

WONKA-VITE CREATURES

• Willy Wonka's recipe for **Wonka-Vite** includes body parts from several **extra-usual** creatures. (Wonka-Vite should therefore NOT be taken by vegetarians.)

• The **proghopper** has a splendid **snout** which is a vital ingredient in **Wonka-Vite**.

• A **quadropus** is a sea creature like an octopus, but with four **tentacles** rather than eight, all of which are needed to make **Wonka-Vite**.

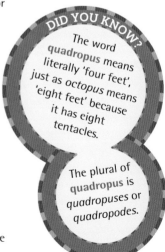

DID YOU KNOW?
The word **quadropus** means literally 'four feet', just as octopus means 'eight feet' because it has eight tentacles.

The plural of **quadropus** is quadropuses or quadropodes.

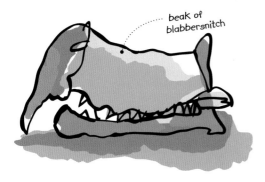

beak of blabbersnitch

DESCRIBING EXTRA-USUAL CREATURES

THEY CAN BE: amazing, **extraordinary, fantabulous, fantastic** or **fantastical, magical, marvellous, splendiferous, wonderful** or wondercrump, **wondrous**

'Nonsense,' said the Ladybird. 'We are now about to visit the most marvellous places and see the most wonderful things! Isn't that so, Centipede?' – JAMES AND THE GIANT PEACH

THEY CAN BE: bizarre, eccentric, funny, odd, **peculiar, puzzling, strange, surprising, weird, whimsical**

THEY CAN BE: dreadly, **fearsome, frightful, frightsome,** frightswiping, **monstrous, scary, terrifying**

'We knew that you would have to face Some frightful creatures up in space. We even thought we heard the crunch Of someone eating you for lunch.' – CHARLIE AND THE GREAT GLASS ELEVATOR

DID YOU KNOW?
A person who studies magical or legendary creatures is a **cryptozoologist**, which comes from Greek *kryptos* meaning 'hidden'.

• The red-breasted wilbatross is a rare type of bird. Unfortunately for the wilbatross, its **beak** is needed to make Wonka-Vite.

• The slimescraper is a rare creature that thrives in slimy places. It gathers slime and produces a natural substance called sprunge, which is a vital ingredient in Wonka-Vite. (It would therefore thrive next to a grobe, which is a slug-like creature that oozes slime.)

'At the witchy hour of gloomness, All the grobes come oozing home. You can hear them softly slimeing, Glissing hissing o'er the slubber, All those oily boily bodies Oozing onward in the gloam.' – CHARLIE AND THE GREAT GLASS ELEVATOR

• The tree-squeak and the whiffle-bird both lay **eggs** which are needed to make Wonka-Vite. Only the whites of tree-squeak eggs and the yolks of whiffle-bird eggs are used in the recipe.

slimescraper
whiffle-bird
skrock
giant curlicue

VITA-WONK CREATURES

INCLUDE: bobolink, giant curlicue, polly-frog, skrock, venomous squerkle, whistle-pig

• Willy Wonka needs parts of all these **ancient** and **long-lived** creatures to make Vita-Wonk, but no one else knows which parts as it is a Strictly Secret recipe.

'I tracked down THE WHISTLE-PIG, THE BOBOLINK, THE SKROCK, THE POLLY-FROG, THE GIANT CURLICUE, THE STINGING SLUG AND THE VENOMOUS SQUERKLE.' – CHARLIE AND THE GREAT GLASS ELEVATOR

• The cattaloo is a rare and ancient animal from South America whose **bones** are an ingredient in Vita-Wonk.

FIND OUT MORE!
There are even more extra-usual **creatures** to discover in Giant Country! Find out in GIANT PLACES.

LEGENDARY CREATURES

• The **cockatrice** (rhymes with *fleece*) is a legendary creature with the body and wings of a dragon and the head of a cockerel. It has a deadly stare and poisonous breath.

• The **oinck** is a very rare beast which may get its name from its deafening snort. The **Old–Green–Grasshopper** is mistaken for both a **cockatrice** and an **oinck**, so perhaps they look a bit similar.

FIND OUT MORE!
The word **oinck** also means the sound of a pig and is an example of **onomatopoeia**. Find out what this means in THE WORLD OF WORDS.

'That one's an Oinck!' screamed the Head of the Fire Department. *'I just know it's an Oinck!' 'Or a Cockatrice!'* yelled the Chief of Police. — JAMES AND THE GIANT PEACH

• A **dragon** is a legendary flying creature that breathes fire. It has scales on its body like a reptile and lays eggs. The **Centipede** is mistaken for a **dragon** (and other **curdbloodling** creatures) when he emerges from the Giant Peach.

'Look out!' they cried. *'It's a Dragon!' 'It's not a Dragon! It's a Wampus!' 'It's a Gorgon!' 'It's a Sea-serpent!' 'It's a Prock!' 'It's a Manticore!'* — JAMES AND THE GIANT PEACH

'I just know

• A **gorgon** is a legendary monster that has writhing and hissing snakes for hair.

• The **hippocampus** is a sea creature with the front legs of a horse and the tail of a dolphin. Its **hair** is a vital ingredient in Wonka-Vite.

• The **hippogriff** is a creature with the body of a horse and the wings and head of an eagle.

DID YOU KNOW?
The name **hippocampus** comes from Greek words meaning 'horse sea-monster' and is related to *hippopotamus*.

The French word for 'a seahorse' is *un hippocampe*.

• A snozzwanger is a deadly three-footed creature that lives in Loompaland. The Centipede is at first mistaken for a snozzwanger and a whangdoodle, probably because no one outside Loompaland has ever seen those creatures.

• The squerkle and the Pink-Spotted Scrunch are both **venomous** creatures. The squerkle spits poison and the Scrunch has a deadly bite (and a huge appetite).
I tracked down . . . THE STINGING SLUG AND THE VENOMOUS SQUERKLE who can spit poison right into your eye from fifty yards away.
— CHARLIE AND THE GREAT GLASS ELEVATOR

'We may see the venomous Pink-Spotted Scrunch Who can chew up a man with one bite. It likes to eat five of them roasted for lunch And eighteen for its supper at night.' — JAMES AND THE GIANT PEACH

it's an Oinck!'

• The **manticore** is a legendary creature with the body of a lion, a human head, sharp teeth and bat-like wings.

• A **unicorn** is a legendary creature like a horse with a long straight horn growing out of the front of its head. Part of a unicorn's **toe** is needed to make Wonka-Vite.

• The **wampus** (say *wom*-puss) is a legendary monster from North American folklore.

FRIGHTSWIPING CREATURES

• The hornswoggler and the whangdoodle are terrifying beasts that live in Loompaland and prey on Oompa-Loompas. The spotted whangdoodle is a rare species of whangdoodle with a patterned **hide** which is one of the ingredients in Wonka-Vite.
'And oh, what a terrible country it is! Nothing but thick jungles infested by the most dangerous beasts in the world—hornswogglers and snozzwangers and those terrible wicked whangdoodles.' — CHARLIE AND THE CHOCOLATE FACTORY

• The doodlewhang is a relative of the whangdoodle that likes to do things back-to-front. It is every bit as fearsome as the deadly boodlesniff.
Aladdin said, 'What if I meet Some brute that thinks I'm good to eat? A Gorgon or a Hippogriff? A Doodlewhang, a Boodlesniff?' — RHYME STEW

• The Giant Skillywiggler is an imaginary creature that Mr Twit invents to terrify his wife. It has teeth as sharp as screwdrivers and can bite off your nose and toes.
'Help!' screamed Mrs Twit, bouncing about. 'There's something in my bed!' 'I'll bet it's that Giant Skillywiggler I saw on the floor just now,' Mr Twit said.
— THE TWITS

FIND OUT MORE!
Willy Wonka's favourite **exclamations** are Great whistling whangdoodles! and Snorting snozzwangers! Find out more in ALL ABOUT SPEAKING in THE WORLD OF HUMAN BEANS.

• The Terrible Bloodsuckling Toothpluckling Stonechuckling Spittler is an imaginary monster that Little Billy's mother invents to scare him away from the Forest of Sin. The Red-Hot Smoke-Belching Gruncher is a fearsome monster that REALLY DOES live in the Forest of Sin and terrifies the Minpins who live there.
'The one waiting for you down there is the fearsome Gruncher, the Red-Hot Smoke-Belching Gruncher. He grunches up everything in the forest.'
— THE MINPINS

ALL ABOUT GIANTS

thirstbloody
murderful
horrigust

DESCRIBING GIANTS

• You can use all these words to describe **horrigust** giants—which are almost all giants in the world. (See JUMBLY GIANTS for the rarer kind.)

THEY LOOK: bogrotting, **disgusting** or disgusterous, **filthsome**, **foulsome**, **gross**, **gruesome**, **hideous**, **obscene**, **repulsant**, **revolting**, **ugly**
Once more he climbed the mighty bean. The Giant sat there, gross, obscene, Muttering through his vicious teeth (While Jack sat tensely just beneath).—REVOLTING RHYMES

THEY ARE: abominable, **bloodthirsty** or **thirstbloody**, **evil**, **fearsome**, grizzling, **horrigust**, **loathsome**, **malicious**, **monstrous**, murderful, **vile**
Then Sophie saw them. In the light of the moon, she saw all nine of those monstrous half-naked brutes thundering across the landscape together.—THE BFG

• When giants are in a **bad mood** (which is most of the time), they are **foul-tempered** or crotching.

• When they speak, giants **boom** loudly in voices that **rumble** like thunder. When they walk, they **clump** or **thump** heavily.
The creature came clumping into the cave and stood towering over the BFG. 'Who was you jabbeling to in here just now?' he boomed.—THE BFG

• All giants are **ancient** or **long-lived**, perhaps even **as old as the earth** (which would make them over 4.5 billion years old). A giant or other creature who lives for ever is said to be **immortal**.
'All I is knowing about myself is that I is very old, very very old and crumply. Perhaps as old as the earth.'—THE BFG

GIANT BODIES
ARE: burly, **hairy**, **hefty**, **hulking**, **towering**

CAN HAVE: unkempt hair, **piggy eyes**, **squashy-looking face**, **sprouting body hair**, **craggy yellow teeth**, **monstrous mouths** with **purple lips** and **rivers of spit** running down their chin
The Bloodbottler was a gruesome sight . . . There was black hair sprouting on his chest and arms and on his stomach. The hair on his head was long and dark and tangled.
—THE BFG

• All giants are **jumpsquifflyingly tall!** The giants in Giant Country are over fifty feet (or over fifteen metres) **tall**—which is taller than ten grown-ups standing on each other's shoulders. They have twice the **height** and double the **girth** of the BFG, who is only a snipsy twenty-four feet (or five grown-ups) tall.
'All of those man-eating giants is enormous and very fierce! They is all at least two times my wideness and double my royal highness!'—THE BFG

• Most giants in Giant Country wear only a **short cloth** around their waists, like a skirt. They are **bare-footed** and **bare-chested** (although their chests are also quite **hairy**).

WHAT DO GIANTS DO?

• Giants spend the day **lazing**, **loafing** or **moocheling** and **footcheling** around until night-time, when they can go **human-bean hunting**.
'What on earth are they doing?' Sophie asked. 'Nothing,' said the BFG. 'They is just moocheling and footcheling around and waiting for the night to come.' — THE BFG

• In the afternoon, giants enjoy a **snooze** or a **snozzle**. When they are **snoozling** or **snozzling** deeply, they start to **snortle** VERY LOUDLY. As he **snortles**, the **Fleshlumpeater** blows bubbles of spit which burst over his **repulsant** face.
'Those is just the giants snortling in their sleep,' the BFG said. 'I is a giant myself and I know a giant's snortle when I is hearing one.' — THE BFG

• When they are NOT **snoozling**, giants often start **squarreling** or **argying** with each other, or **bullying** the BFG because of his size.
In the bellowing thumping rough and tumble that followed, one sleeping giant after another either got stepped upon or kicked. Soon, all nine of them were on their feet having the most almighty free-for-all. — THE BFG

DID YOU KNOW?
The *Gigantes* (say jy-*gan*-teez) were a race of giants in ancient Greek mythology. Some were said to lie buried under the earth, causing volcanoes and earthquakes.

In Welsh folklore, *Gogmagog* was the last giant to have lived in the British Isles. It is said that he was thrown off a cliff during a wrestling match.

• Almost all giants (not just the **Bonecruncher**) like to crunch **human beans**, which makes an **earbursting** noise.
From somewhere high above the ground There came a frightful crunching sound. He heard the Giant mutter twice, 'By gosh, that tasted very nice. Although' (and this in grumpy tones) 'I wish there weren't so many bones.' — REVOLTING RHYMES

• Most giants have **squifflingly** sensitive **noses**, like witches. It is therefore an Excellent Plan to wash regularly so they will not be able to smell you (but unfortunately you will then be hunted by witches instead).

HOW DO GIANTS HUNT?

• When night falls, giants **gallop** or **zippfizz** around the world to find **human beans** to guzzle. (Each giant has a favourite **hunting ground** and a favourite method of hunting **human beans**.)

• A group of giants is called a **pack** when they are hunting or **zippfizzing** along (but not when they are just **snoozling**).
They were galloping in a pack, their necks craned forward, their arms bent at the elbows, and worst of all, their stomachs bulging. — THE BFG

• Some giants **snitch**, **snatch** or **kidsnatch chiddlers** from their beds in the **witching hour** of night.

• Other giants **swimmel** under water to get close enough to **grabble** their **victims** from the beach.
'Sometimes,' the BFG said, 'they is swimmeling in from the sea like fishies with only their heads showing above the water, and then out comes a big hairy hand and grabbles someone off the beach.' — THE BFG

FIND OUT MORE!
Which giant is called **Knochenknacker** in German? Find out in GLOBAL GOBBLEFUNK in THE WORLD OF WORDS.

snoozle

snortle

snozzle

moocheling

footcheling

JUMBLY GIANTS

• There is only ONE jumbly giant in Giant Country (but there may be others *elsewhere* that have yet to be discovered).

HE IS: amiable, benevolent, caring, friendly, good-natured, kind-hearted or kindly, thoughtful, unselfish

• Compared to other giants, he is snitchy, tiny, titchy, twiddly or extra-usually short (but he is still squacklingly tall compared to a human bean).

• He wears clothes that are so old they are faded, grubby, shabby or worn.
Sophie saw that under the cloak he was wearing a sort of collarless shirt and a dirty old leather waistcoat that didn't seem to have any buttons. His trousers were faded green and were far too short in the legs. — THE BFG

• He spends his time: picking and cooking snozzcumbers, dream-catching, delivering dreams to chiddlers, mixing dreams, writing labels for dream-bottles.

JUMBLY GIANT EARS

ARE: enormous, extra-usual, flexible, jumpsquiffling, propsposterous, swashboggling, super-sensitive

THEY CAN: flap, swivel, swiggle, wave or wiggle back and forth, in and out or to and fro
The Giant sat down and stared hard at Sophie. He had truly enormous ears. Each one was as big as the wheel of a truck and he seemed to be able to move them inwards and outwards from his head as he wished. — THE BFG

• They can pick up secret sounds, such as dreams whiffling past, ants and mice chittering, flowers and trees moaning, and music from the stars.
'You mean you can hear things I can't hear?' Sophie said. 'You is deaf as a dumpling compared with me!' cried the BFG. — THE BFG

• Sophie is able to crouch or recline in a crevice formed by the outer rim of the BFG's ear.
Sophie, still wearing only her nightie, was reclining comfortably in a crevice of the BFG's right ear. — THE BFG

propsposterous
swashboggling
ears
extra-usual
jumpsquiffling

FEE FI FO FUM

OTHER GIANTS

• A female giant is a **giantess** (although there are no female giants in Giant Country—as far as anyone knows). *'Whoever heard of a woman giant!' shouted the BFG, waving the snozzcumber around his head like a lasso. 'There never was a woman giant! And there never will be one. Giants is always men!'*—THE BFG

• Another name for a giant is an **ogre** and a female ogre is an **ogress**. The **yeti** or **Abominable Snowman** is a legendary ape-like giant that is said to live in the Himalayas.

• A **human bean** who kills giants is a **giant-killer**, like the legendary **Jack**, who climbs a magic **beanstalk** to reach a giant's castle.
'Jack is the only human bean all giants is frightened of,' the BFG told her. 'They is all absolutely terrified of Jack. They is all hearing that Jack is a famous giant-killer.'—THE BFG

• Some giants are famous for saying **FEE FI FO FUM** when they **catch the scent** of a **human bean** to eat.
A big deep voice, a rumbling thing That made the very heavens ring. It shouted loud, 'FEE FI FO FUM, I SMELL THE BLOOD OF AN ENGLISHMAN!'—REVOLTING RHYMES

DID YOU KNOW?
In the legend of 'Jack and the Beanstalk', Jack is given some magic beans, which his mother throws on the ground—a bit like James spilling the magic beans which make the Giant Peach grow.

FIND OUT MORE!
Human beans can be **jumbly** or **horrigust** too! Find out more in **THE WORLD OF HUMAN BEANS.**

DESCRIBING SIZE

GIANT-SIZED THINGS

INCLUDE: the BFG's **ears**, Enormous Crocodile, **enormous snail**, Giant Skillywiggler, **giants** (both **horrigust** and **jumbly**), **giant anteater**, **Giant Peach**

*You see, I now was sitting on
A wonderfully ENORMOUS SNAIL!
His shell was smooth and brown and
pale, And I was so high off the ground
That I could see for miles around.*
— DIRTY BEASTS

CAN BE: big, colossal, enormous, giant, gigantic or gigantuous, ginormous, great, huge, humungous, large, jumpsquiffling, mammoth, massive, overgrown, squackling, whopping, whoppsy

It was the sheer size of each one of them that boggled Sophie's brain most of all. They were simply colossal, far taller and wider than the Big Friendly Giant upon whose hand she was now sitting. — THE BFG

• A huge distance or area is also **immense** or **vast**: *The giant peach sailed across the vast Atlantic ocean.*

• A large room or space is also **generous** or **spacious**: *The BFG's cave was surprisingly spacious.*

• A large piece of something is a **chunk**, **hunk** or **lump**. *A great, craggy mountain made entirely of fudge, with Oompa-Loompas (all roped together for safety) hacking huge hunks of fudge out of its sides.* — CHARLIE AND THE CHOCOLATE FACTORY

colossal

gigantuous enormous

DID YOU KNOW?
The word **gigantic** originally meant 'to do with giants'—so *The BFG* is literally a **gigantic** story!

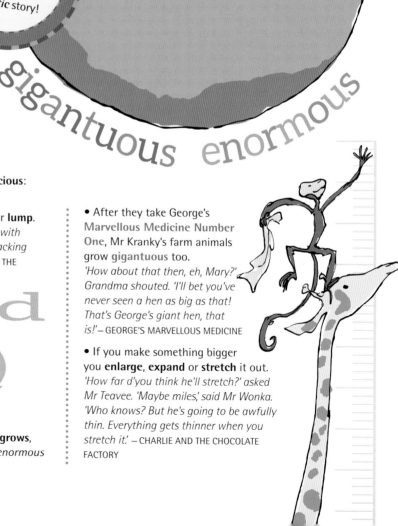

• After they take George's **Marvellous Medicine Number One**, Mr Kranky's farm animals grow **gigantuous** too.
'How about that then, eh, Mary?' Grandma shouted. 'I'll bet you've never seen a hen as big as that! That's George's giant hen, that is!' — GEORGE'S MARVELLOUS MEDICINE

• If you make something bigger you **enlarge**, **expand** or **stretch** it out.
'How far d'you think he'll stretch?' asked Mr Teavee. 'Maybe miles,' said Mr Wonka. 'Who knows? But he's going to be awfully thin. Everything gets thinner when you stretch it.' — CHARLIE AND THE CHOCOLATE FACTORY

extend
swell

BECOMING BIGGER
• When something becomes bigger, it **expands**, **grows**, **increases** or **swells**: *Violet had swollen into an enormous blueberry!*

• If you make something wider you **broaden** or **widen** it. If you make it longer you **extend**, **lengthen** or **stretch** it. When a **stretchy** creature like a **Knid elongates**, it becomes longer and thinner.
Then the three remaining creatures began stretching themselves all at the same time, each one elongating itself slowly upward, growing taller and taller. — CHARLIE AND THE GREAT GLASS ELEVATOR

SNIPSY THINGS

INCLUDE: chiddlers (or any **human bean** compared to a giant), Charlie Bucket's **house**, Miss Honey's **cottage**, micies, **minibeasts**, Minpins and their houses, **puddlenuts**

CAN BE: **little**, **microscopic**, midgy, **miniature**, minuscule, **minute** (rhymes with *newt*), **small**, snitchy, **teeny**, **tiny**, titchy, **twiddly**, **wee**
'I is guzzling you nice and slow!' the Fleshlumpeater was saying to the soldier in his hand. 'Then I is guzzling ten or twenty more of you midgy little maggots down there!' — THE BFG

• A small piece of something is a **fragment**, **particle** or **speck**.
'You call that unharmed?' snapped Mrs Teavee, peering at the little speck of a boy who was now running to and fro across the palm of her hand, waving his pistols in the air. — CHARLIE AND THE CHOCOLATE FACTORY

BECOMING SMALLER

• When something becomes smaller, it **shrinks**, **decreases** or **contracts**. Mrs Twit only *thinks* she is shrinking because Mr Twit tricks her into believing she has the Dreaded Shrinks.
'You're shrinking, woman!' said Mr Twit . . . 'You're shrinking fast! You're shrinking dangerously fast! Why, you must have shrunk at least a foot in the last few days!' — THE TWITS

FIND OUT MORE! There are **minibeasts** galore to explore in ALL ABOUT ANIMALS in THE NATURAL WORLD.

DID YOU KNOW? The word **minuscule** (say *min*-is-kyool) originally meant 'in lower-case letters' (not in capital letters).

• If you make something smaller you **shrink** or **compress** it. If you make something shorter you **shorten** or **condense** it.

• Something that is more snipsy is **snipsier** and the most snipsy thing is the **snipsiest**: *The BFG is snipsier than the other giants, but he is still gigantuous to Sophie!*

MEASURING SIZE

• When you measure how **long** something is, you measure its **length** or measure it **lengthways**. The opposite of long is **short**.
The tunnel began to grow longer and longer. It sloped steeply downward. Deeper and deeper below the surface of the ground it went. — FANTASTIC MR FOX

• When you measure how **high** or **tall** something is, you measure its **height**. The opposite of high is **low** and the opposite of tall is **short**: *All the tables in the Palace were too low for the BFG.*

• When you measure how **wide** or **broad** something is, you measure its **width** or **breadth**. The opposite of wide is **narrow**.
'The Chokey,' Hortensia went on, 'is a very tall but very narrow cupboard. The floor is only ten inches square so you can't sit down.' — MATILDA

• When you measure across the widest part of a circle, you measure its **diameter**. The cake that Bruce Bogtrotter guzzles is a whoppsy eighteen inches in diameter!

OTHER SIZES

INCLUDE: **average**, **medium-sized**, notsobig, **biggish**, **smallish**
Mr Fox laughed and began pulling more bricks out of the wall. When he had made a biggish hole, he crept through it. — FANTASTIC MR FOX

• The largest size or amount of something is the **maximum** and the smallest is the **minimum**.
'And then I shall make absolutely sure you are sent to a reformatory for delinquent girls for the minimum of forty years!' — MATILDA

FIND OUT MORE! Human beans are **tall** and **short**, too! Find out more in ALL ABOUT BODIES in THE WORLD OF HUMAN BEANS.

GIANT PLACES

DESCRIBING GIANT COUNTRY

• The **landscape** in Giant Country is **desert** or **wasteland**.

IT IS: **arid**, **bare**, **barren**, **desolate**, **dry**, **dusty**, **parched**, **treeless**

Sophie peeped over the rim of the ear and watched the desolate landscape of Giant Country go whizzing by. They were certainly moving fast. — THE BFG

• The ground is **dotted**, **scattered** or **strewn** with rocks and boulders.

• The colours of the landscape (with **yellow** earth and **blue** rocks) make it look **alien** or **unearthly**.
He went rattling through a great forest, then down into a valley and up over a range of hills as bare as concrete, and soon he was galloping over a desolate wasteland that was not quite of this earth. — THE BFG

CREATURES OF GIANT COUNTRY

• The **crumpscoddle**, **humplecrimp**, **scotchhopper** and **wraprascal** are very common creatures in Giant Country, but no **human bean** has ever seen them—so you will have to *imagine* what they look like.

• A **cattypiddler** is a wild cat-like creature that lives in Giant Country. A **fizzlecrump** is a creature that can move as fast as a giant running at top speed.
'Be careful to hang on tight!' the BFG said. 'We is going fast as a fizzlecrump!' — THE BFG

• The **slime-wangler** is a creature found in Giant Country which is edible but not pleasant to eat, as it tastes like a **snozzcumber**. It may be related to the **slimescraper** which is found outside Giant Country.

• The **vindscreen viper** is a deadly snake whose fangs are an ingredient in **Wonka-Vite**. Vindscreen vipers are found in Giant Country and giants are very scared of being bitten by them.

FIND OUT MORE!
Roald Dahl often uses **alliteration** in his similes and invented words, such as **vindscreen viper**. You can find many more in THE WORLD OF WORDS.

DESCRIBING A CAVE

• The top of a cave is the **roof** and the bottom is the **floor**. The sides of a cave are the **walls**.

• The entrance to a cave is also called the **mouth**.
As soon as he was inside, he stopped and turned and rolled the great stone back into place so that the entrance to his secret cave was completely hidden from outside. — THE BFG

• Voices and other sounds can **echo** or **roll around** inside a cave (which makes them even more curdbloodling and scary).
'Ha!' shouted the Giant, walking forward and rubbing his hands together. 'What has us got here?' His booming voice rolled around the walls of the cave like a burst of thunder. — THE BFG

• A large deep cave, like the one the BFG lives in, is a **cavern**. A network of caves with connecting passages is a **labyrinth**.

• A human bean or giant who lives in a cave is a **cave-dweller** or **troglodyte**: *The BFG is a cave-dwelling giant.*

• Willy Wonka tracks down an ancient **cave-dwelling grimalkin** for his recipe for Vita-Wonk.

INSIDE A CAVE

IT FEELS: damp, dank, dark, eerie, gloomy, murky, musty

YOU CAN SEE: cracks, crevices, fissures, nooks and crannies (or crooks and nannies)

• A rocky spike which hangs like an **icicle** from the roof of a cave is a **stalactite** and one which rises up from the floor is a **stalagmite**.

• The **walls** of a cave can be: **rough**, **rocky** or **stony**; **smooth**, **clammy** or **slimy**.

• The walls of the BFG's cave are **lined** with stacks of shelves.
The walls on either side were lined with shelves, and on the shelves there stood row upon row of glass jars. There were jars everywhere. They were piled up in the corners. They filled every nook and cranny of the cave. — THE BFG

• Some other ancient caves are covered with **cave paintings** or carvings called **petroglyphs**.

FIND OUT MORE!
There are also **crevices** in the BFG's gigantuous ears! Find out more in ALL ABOUT GIANTS.

DID YOU KNOW?
The word **petroglyph** comes from Greek *petra* meaning 'rock' or 'stone'. It is related to **petrify**, which means literally 'to turn into stone'.

The words **stalactite** and **stalagmite** are based on a Greek verb meaning 'to drip'.

131

ALL ABOUT DREAMS

DESCRIBING DREAMS

ringbellers

• Dreams can be: **vivid, lifelike, realistic, surreal**: *The BFG gives the Queen a very vivid dream.*

• Something you see in a dream or daydream is a **vision**. Something you think you see that is not real is an **illusion** or a **hallucination**.

• A dream or dreamlike experience that you have while you are awake is a **daydream, fantasy** or **reverie**, and when you have one of these, you are **daydreaming**.
'Attention, please! Attention, please! Don't dare to talk! Don't dare to sneeze! Don't doze or daydream! Stay awake! Your health, your very life's at stake!'
— CHARLIE AND THE GREAT GLASS ELEVATOR

• When you dream or daydream, you use your **imagination** or your **mind's eye**.

GOOD DREAMS
CAN BE: amazing, exciting, fantabulous, marvellous, phizz–whizzing, splendiferous, wondercrump, wonderful

• The good dreams that the BFG catches are **ringbellers** and **winksquifflers**, and the VERY best, MOST splendiferous dreams are **golden phizzwizards**.
'It's a winksquiffler!' he whispered with a thrill in his voice. 'It's . . . it's . . . it's . . . it's even better. It's a phizzwizard! It's a golden phizzwizard!'
— THE BFG

BAD DREAMS
CAN BE: awful, disturbing, frightful, frightswiping, horrendous, horrigust, terrifying, unsettling

• A bad dream is a **nightmare** and the REALLY bad or **nightmarish** dreams that the BFG catches are **bogthumpers, grobswitchers** and **trogglehumpers**.
'I is catching a frightsome trogglehumper!' he cried. *'This is a bad bad dream! It is worse than a bad dream! It is a nightmare!'*
— THE BFG

trogglehumpers

golden

DID YOU KNOW?
The word **nightmare** comes from an old word *mare,* which meant an evil spirit that caused bad dreams (a kind of ancient **trogglehumper**).

grobswitchers winksquifflers phizzwizards bogthumpers

CATCHING DREAMS

• When he goes **dream–hunting** (in Dream Country), the BFG takes with him a dream–catcher, which is a long pole with a net on the end.

• **Dream Country** is where all the dreams in the world start. It is a flat **treeless** land of cold air and swirling mists, where nothing grows except grey grass.

• Dreams make a **buzzy–hum** sound like insects, but only the BFG can hear them with his **extra–usual** ears.
'Every dream in the world is making a different sort of buzzy-hum music. And these grand swashboggling ears of mine is able to read that music.' – THE BFG

• After catching a dream, the BFG **seals** it in a tight-lidded jar or dream–bottle, which he carries in his **suitcase** and then **stores** in his **cave**.

DID YOU KNOW?
Some **human beans** also use **dreamcatchers**, which are small hoops decorated with feathers and beads, with a mesh inside to catch bad dreams.

DID YOU KNOW?
The ancient Greek god of dreams, *Morpheus*, lived in a cave like the BFG and could appear in dreams in disguise.

• When he is ready to deliver his dreams, the BFG goes **dream-blowing** (at the **witching hour** of night). He **pours** each dream into the end of a long trumpet called a dream–blower and then blows through it to send the dream into the ears of sleeping chiddlers (or a sleeping Queen).
'If you is really wanting to know what I am doing in your village,' the BFG said, 'I is blowing a dream into the bedroom of those children.' 'Blowing a dream?' Sophie said. 'What do you mean?' 'I is a dream-blowing giant,' the BFG said.
– THE BFG

MIXING DREAMS

• Dreams are made of a mysterious magical substance called zozimus. The BFG uses an old **egg-beater** to mix parts of dreams together.
'Dreams is not like human beans or animals. They has no brains. They is made of zozimus.' – THE BFG

DID YOU KNOW?
The word *zozimus* sounds a bit like *Zosimos*, which was the name of an ancient Greek-Egyptian alchemist who made magical potions.

• If you **beat**, **stir** or **whisk** zozimus it will start to form **bubbles**, **froth** or **foam**. **Flashes** of colour will also **burst**, **explode** or **collide** with each other.
The BFG . . . started turning the handle very fast. Flashes of green and blue exploded inside the jar. The dreams were being whisked into a sea-green froth – THE BFG

• Dreams look: **blob-like**, **jellyish**, **oval**, **sea-green**.
Sophie sat watching him but said nothing. Inside the big jar, lying on the bottom of it, she could clearly see about fifty of those oval sea-green jellyish shapes, all pulsing gently in and out, some lying on top of others, but each one still a quite separate individual dream. – THE BFG

GIANT FOOD AND DRINK

WHAT DO GIANTS EAT?

• **Murderful** giants, like the **Bloodbottler** and the **Fleshlumpeater**, eat **human beans**, especially **chiddlers** (but never other giants).

'If any one of them is waking up, he will gobble you down before you can say knack jife,' the BFG answered, grinning hugely. 'Me is the only one what won't be gobbled up because giants is never eating giants.' — THE BFG

• A giant who gobbles **human beans** (as opposed to other types of bean) is a **cannybull** or a **cannybully** giant. You can also say **man-eating** or **man-gobbling** giant.

The Giant let out a bellow of laughter. 'Just because I is a giant, you think I is a man-gobbling cannybull!' he shouted. — THE BFG

• The BFG is NOT a **cannybully** giant. As he only eats snozzcumbers, which are **vegitibbles**, he is a **vegetarian** giant. (However he is *only* a vegetarian until he has breakfast with the Queen and starts to eat sausages and other kinds of **grabble**.)

'That was only one titchy little bite,' the BFG said. 'Is you having any more of this delunctious grabble in your cupboard, Majester?' — THE BFG

• A formal word that means **'human–bean-eating'** is **anthropophagous** (say an-throw-*poff*-a-guss): *All giants except the BFG are anthropophagous.*

FIND OUT MORE!

There are words to describe all kinds of **grabble** in ALL ABOUT FOOD in THE WORLD OF HUMAN BEANS.

splutter

spit   slurp

swallop

HOW DO GIANTS EAT?

THEY: **gobble, guzzle, swallop** or **swollop** greedily
'In eight hours those nine blood-thirsty brutes will be galloping off to gobble up another couple of dozen unfortunate wretches. They have to be stopped.' — THE BFG

THEY: **crunch, grunch, munch, chomp** or **slurp** noisily
'Bonecrunching Giant crunches up two whoppsy-whiffling human beans for supper every night! Noise is earbursting! Noise of crunching bones goes crackety-crack for miles around!' — THE BFG

THEY: **spit, slabber** or **splutter** messily
'It's filthing!' he spluttered, speaking with his mouth full and spraying large pieces of snozzcumber like bullets in Sophie's direction. — THE BFG

pop pop pop pop pop pop

slabber

ALL ABOUT FROBSCOTTLE

IT IS: **bubbly, fizzy, sparkling, effervescent, green**
'Here is frobscottle!' he cried, holding the bottle up proud and high, as though it contained some rare wine. 'Delumptious fizzy frobscottle!' he shouted. — THE BFG

IT WILL: **bubble, fizz** or **froth**. The bubbles **travel downwards** (NOT up) until they **burst** or **pop**

YOU CAN: **glug, gurgle, take a swig** (or **swiggle**) when you drink it

IT TASTES: **delicious** or **delumptious, jumbly, sweet**
Very gently the BFG tipped the bottle forward and poured some of the fabulous frobscottle down her throat. And oh gosh, how delicious it was! It was sweet and refreshing. It tasted of vanilla and cream, with just the faintest trace of raspberries on the edge of the flavour. — THE BFG

IT MAKES YOU: **whizzpop** or make **whizzpoppers** (which is perfectly fine in Giant Country but NOT in front of the Queen)
'BFG,' she said, 'there is no frobscottle here and whizzpopping is strictly forbidden!' 'What!' cried the BFG. 'No frobscottle? No whizzpopping? No glumptious music? No boom-boom-boom?' — THE BFG

FIND OUT MORE!
What is frobscottle called in French and German? Find out in GLOBAL GOBBLEFUNK in THE WORLD OF WORDS.

ALL ABOUT SNOZZCUMBERS

• A **snozzcumber** has **skin** or **peel** on the outside and **flesh** or **pulp** on the inside. The pulp is **embedded** with **seeds**.

• The skin is covered or **encrusted** with **knobbles** or **knurls** and is **banded** with black-and-white **stripes**.

• The **shape** of a **snozzcumber** is like that of a cucumber, which is called **cucumiform**. Its **girth** or **diameter** is **gigantuous** (with a **circumference** as great as a perambulator).
It was as thick around its girth as a perambulator. It was black with white stripes along its length. And it was covered all over with coarse knobbles. — THE BFG

• The **skin** outside is **knobbly** and **ridged**, **striped** or **stripy**.
The BFG put an arm into the sack and pulled out a gigantic black and white striped object the size of a man. 'Snozzcumbers!' he cried. — THE BFG

• The **pulp** inside is **gooey**, **gloopy**, **mushy**, **pulpy**, **slimy** or **viscous**.
The snozzcumber . . . had large seeds in the middle, each one as big as a melon. They were embedded in soft slimy stuff. — THE BFG

EATING A SNOZZCUMBER

• To prepare a **snozzcumber**, you can **peel**, **de-seed**, **chop**, **slice** or **mash** it. (But whatever you do, it will still taste **disgusterous**.)

YOU CAN: **crunch**, **munch**, **nibble** or **peck** when you eat it. Afterwards you can **spit**, **splutter** or **spray** it in all directions.
Sophie took a small nibble. 'Uggggggggh!' she spluttered. 'Oh no! Oh gosh! Oh help!' She spat it out quickly. 'It tastes of frogskins!' she gasped. 'And rotten fish!' — THE BFG

IT TASTES: **disgusterous**, **filthing**, **foulsome**, **loathsome**, **repulsant**, **rotsome**
'So this is the filthing rotsome glubbage you is eating!' boomed the Bloodbottler, holding up the partly eaten snozzcumber. 'You must be cockles to be guzzling such rubbsquash!' — THE BFG

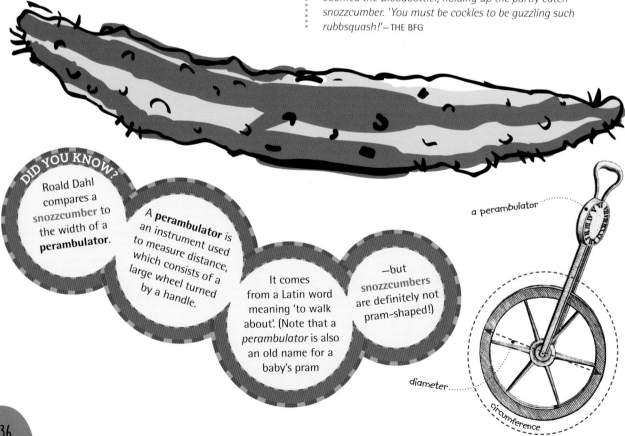

DID YOU KNOW?

Roald Dahl compares a **snozzcumber** to the width of a **perambulator**.

A **perambulator** is an instrument used to measure distance, which consists of a large wheel turned by a handle.

It comes from a Latin word meaning 'to walk about'. (Note that a *perambulator* is also an old name for a baby's pram

—but **snozzcumbers** are definitely not pram-shaped!)

a perambulator

diameter

circumference

rotsome

pulpy

repulsant

gloopy

gooey

foulsome

filthing

FIND OUT MORE!
Are **snozzwangers** related to **snozzcumbers**? Find out by looking up EXTRA-USUAL CREATURES!

loathsome

disgusterous

137

GIANT LANGWITCH

SPEAKING SQUIGGLY

• Some giants speak a special language or langwitch that is only spoken in Giant Country. It is also called speaking squiggly. (This is not the same as speaking while eating Squiggly Spaghetti, which is unheard of in Giant Country.)
'I know it is bones,' the BFG said. 'But please understand that I cannot be helping it if I sometimes is saying things a little squiggly.' – THE BFG

• Some human beans call giant language gobblefunk. However, gobblefunk has a different meaning for giants, who use it as a verb meaning 'to mess around' or 'muddle up'.
'There is something very fishy about Wales.' 'You means whales,' Sophie said. 'Wales is something quite different.' 'Wales is whales,' the Giant said. 'Don't gobblefunk around with words.' – THE BFG

• Giant langwitch may be a dialect, or else an ancient form of English, as many of the words are similar to human-beaney words. They may differ by a few letters (like norphanage and vegitibble) or have a different ending (like rotsome).

• Words with squiggly endings include: disgusterous (for *disgusting*), frightsome (for *frightful*), gigantuous (for *gigantic*), healthsome (for *healthy*) maggotwise (for *maggoty*), murderful (for *murderous*), repulsant (for *repulsive*) and wondercrump (for *wonderful*).

• The BFG also says idioms a bit squiggly, such as **bark up the wrong dog** instead of **bark up the wrong tree**.

SQUIGGLY SPOONERISMS

• Giant langwitch is full of spoonerisms and malapropisms. Although these are funny to human beans, most giants do not mean to be funny when they say them (so it is best not to laugh if you meet a squiggly-speaking giant).

• A spoonerism is when you swap the sounds at the start of two or more words, so that *skipping and jumping* becomes jipping and skumping and *disastrous catastrophe* becomes catasterous disastrophe.
'Catasterous!' cried the BFG. 'Upgoing bubbles is a catasterous disastrophe!' – THE BFG

• Other giant spoonerisms include: buckswashling (for *swashbuckling*) and curdbloodling (for *bloodcurdling*).

FIND OUT MORE! What do giants say in other countries? Find out in GLOBAL GOBBLEFUNK in THE WORLD OF WORDS.

hide and sneak
jipping and skumping

SQUIGGLY WORDS AND PHRASES
• In Giant Country, you would say exunckly (not **exactly**) when you agree, and redunculous (rather than **ridiculous**) when you disagree.
'It's a funny thought,' Sophie said. 'Exunckly,' the BFG said. – THE BFG

• Giants go forthwards rather than **forwards**.
'I is galloping forthwards and backwards from Giant Country every night to blow my dreams into little chiddlers' bedrooms.' – THE BFG

• Some squiggly names for creatures include: crockadowndilly, hippodumpling and rhinostossteriss.

DID YOU KNOW? The word crockadowndilly is a blend of crocodile and daffodowndilly, which is a dialect word for a daffodil.

• A malapropism is when you say a different word from the one you mean, so that it makes a funny mistake. For example, in a puddle instead of *in a muddle*, hide and sneak instead of *hide and seek* and skin and groans instead of *skin and bones*.
'Is you helping me to find this Palace?' the BFG asked. 'I has never dared to go hide and sneaking around London in my life.' – THE BFG

• Other giant malapropisms include: bellypopper (for *helicopter*), human bean (for *human being*) and rotton-wool (for *cotton-wool*).

'Your brain is full of rotten-wool.' 'You mean cotton-wool,' Sophie said. 'What I mean and what I say is two different things,' the BFG announced rather grandly. — THE BFG

• When the BFG says **crook and nanny** (for *nook and cranny*) and calls *Charles Dickens* by the name **Dahl's Chickens**, he is using both a **spoonerism** AND a **malapropism** at the same time.

GIANT RUDE WORDS

GIGANTUOUS INSULTS

• There are LOTS of **rude words** in giant **langwitch**, because giants are very angry and shout at each other most of the time. They especially like to **hurl insults** at the BFG, because he is so much smaller than they are.

• **Insulting adjectives** which mean **small** or **insignificant** include: **piffling, prunty, runty, squimpy, squinky, troggy.**

• **Insulting nouns** which mean 'a small or insignificant person (or giant)' include: **grobsquiffler, pigswiller, pogswizzler, scumscrewer, squiddler, swinebuggler, swishfiggler.**
The other giants stood around, waiting for the fun to start. 'Now then, you little grobsquiffler!' boomed the Fleshlumpeater. — THE BFG

'You little swinebuggler!' roared the Bloodbottler. 'You little pigswiller!' He rushed at the BFG and smashed what was left of the snozzcumber over his head. — THE BFG

• The **unjumbly** giants also call the BFG a **bottle-wart** because they think it is silly to collect bottles of dreams.
The Bloodbottler pointed a finger as large as a tree-trunk at the BFG. 'Runty little scumscrewer!' he shouted. 'Piffling little swishfiggler! Squimpy little bottle-wart! Prunty little pogswizzler! — THE BFG

GIGANTUOUS CURSES

• Giant **langwitch** includes lots of explosive **expletives** or **curses** to shout out loud when things are going badly.

THEY SAY: I'm bopmuggered!, I'm crodsquinkled!, I'm fluckgungled!, I'm flushbunkled!

OR: I'm goosegruggled!, I'm gunzleswiped!,

I'm slopgroggled!, I'm splitzwiggled!, I'm swogswalloped!
The finest sight of all was to observe those nine hideous brutes squirming and twisting about . . . as they tried to free themselves from their ropes and chains. 'I is flushbunkled!' roared the Fleshlumpeater. 'I is splitzwiggled!' yelled the Childchewer. 'I is swogswalloped!' bellowed the Bonecruncher. — THE BFG

THEY SAY: gunghummers and bogswinkles! when they bump into something
A shower of glass fell upon the poor BFG. 'Gunghummers and bogswinkles!' he cried. 'What was that?' — THE BFG

OR: mince my maggots or swipe my swoggles when they get a nasty surprise
'Oh no!' he cried. 'Oh mince my maggots! Oh swipe my swoggles!' 'What's the matter?' Sophie asked. 'It's a trogglehumper!' he shouted. — THE BFG

FIND OUT MORE! For **buckswashling** **blends** like **delumptious** and **dreadly**, see the WORD INVENTING ROOM in THE WORLD OF WORDS.

'Gunghummers and bogswinkles!'

Magical
Writing Hut

as wriggly as a wraprascal

a whole bottle of fizzy frobscottle...

splendid similes

• The BFG can run **as fast as a fizzlecrump**, which is phizz-whizzingly fast! What other similes can you make with Giant Country creatures, using **alliteration** too? For example, something could be as slippery as a slime-wangler or as wriggly as a wraprascal.

• How green is **frobscottle**? It could be: as green as a grasshopper or as green as a Mint Jujube. Willy Wonka's trousers are **bottle-green**, so perhaps they are as green as a bottle of frobscottle.

• What could you compare to a **snozzcumber**? Something could be as slimy as a snozzcumber, as stripy as snozzcumber skin, or even as knobbly as the knurls on a snozzcumber.

redunculous rhymes

• As **frobscottle** rhymes with **bottle**, you can make up a funny rhyme about drinking it. For example: *If you glug a whole bottle of fizzy frobscottle your tummy will bubble—and then there'll be trouble!*

gazillipus • snozzcumberophagous

If you glug

phizz-whizzing suffixes

• You can make up your own multi-legged creatures, based on the words **quadropus** and **octopus**. How many feet or tentacles would a *centipus* have, for example? Or what about a *gazillipus*?

• The word **anthropophagous** means 'man-eating'. You can add *-phagous* to other food words to make new adjectives for eaters. For example a *bananaphagous* creature only eats bananas, and the BFG is a *snozzcumberophagous* giant!

names for thingalings

- An old-fashioned word for an **egg-beater** is a *froth-stick*. Can you think of another name for the BFG's **egg-beater**? What about a *dream-swirler* or a *whirlyzoz*?

- The BFG calls a frying-pan a *sizzlepan* because of the sizzling sound that it makes. What name could you give to a witch's **cauldron** or a magic saucepan? For example, it could be a *bubblepot* or a *spellpot*.

blabbersnore •

slurpersnitch

wondercrump wordbuilding

- To make the name blabbersnitch, Roald Dahl may have joined together *blabber* meaning 'chatter' and *snitch* meaning 'steal'! Can you swap one half of this name with another word to make a new creature with different habits? For example, what would a *blabbersnore* do, or a *slurpersnitch*?

- To make **doodlewhang**, Roald Dahl swapped around the parts of **whangdoodle**: a word which he had also invented. You can make new creature names in this way too, from the ones that Roald Dahl invented (see EXTRA-USUAL CREATURES for ideas). What about a *squirtlegrob* or a *swogglehorn* or a *sniffleboo*?

whirlyzoz • **bubblepot**

crazy collective nouns

- There is no special name for a bunch or bundle of snozzcumbers—but you can invent one! You could use a word that describes what a snozzcumber looks or feels like, for example *a knobblement* or *a slimation of snozzcumbers*: *The BFG keeps a whole knobblement of snozzcumbers in his cupboard.*

- You can use Roald Dahl's invented words as names of **collective nouns** too. For example, in giant language, the word **snoozle** means 'to sleep soundly' and **snortle** means 'to snore', so a group of sleeping giants could be *a snoozle of giants* or *a snortle of giants*.

a snoozle of giants

a snortle or snoozle of giants

jelly beans • **belly jeans**

wonky word play

- The phrase **every nook and cranny** means every possible corner or hiding place. The BFG swaps the words around and says *crook and nanny* instead. This type of funny mistake with words is called a **spoonerism**.

- Try making your own **spoonerisms** by swapping the sounds at the start of two words. For example, you could say *belly jeans* instead of *jelly beans*, or *whack and blight* instead of *black and white*.

ZIPPFIZZ ALONG TO THE WORLD OF WORDS FOR MORE HOPSCOTCHY IDEAS FOR WRITERS AND STORYTELLERS!

inky-booky

spoonerism

wigglish rhyming babblement

simile

storyteller

limerick gobblefunk

onomatopoeia langwitch

alliteration

THE WORLD OF WORDS

'It is the most scrumdiddlyumptious story.'
— THE BFG

All about language

using idioms

An **idiom** is a phrase that means something more than the simple meaning of the words. For example:

• If you are **full of beans** you are full of **phizz-whizzing** energy, like Willy Wonka. This is NOT the same as being full of **human beans**, which is what giants are after a hunting expedition.

• If you are **all ears** you (probably) do not have **gigantuous** ears like the BFG. It means that you are listening very carefully, like **Mr Fox** listening for the farmers.

• If you jump **out of the frying-pan into the fire** you leave one tricky situation only to end up in another. In Giant Country you would say **out of the sizzlepan into the fire**.

• If you **go the whole hog** you put your whole heart and spirit into doing something, as Matilda always does.
Matilda said, 'Never do anything by halves if you want to get away with it. Be outrageous. Go the whole hog.' – MATILDA

• If you have **a close shave** (something Mr Twit never has) you have a very narrow escape from danger.

• If you **come out of your shell** you become less shy and more confident, like Alfie poking his head out to eat lettuce.

• If something **drives you up the wall** it makes you very annoyed and angry. If it drives you far enough up the wall, you might end up upside-down on the ceiling like Mr and Mrs Twit.

• If you are **out of the woods** you are no longer in danger. This is doubly true if you have managed to escape from the **Forest of Sin** before being eaten by the **Red-Hot Smoke-Belching Gruncher**.

> **DID YOU KNOW?**
> Roald Dahl once got a school report which said he was 'a persistent muddler' (a bit like the BFG).

full of human beans

full of beans

playing with words

• A **pun** is a joke based on two words that sound the same but have different meanings, for example the *hair* on Mr Twit's beard is different from a *hare* in the woods. Words like these are called **homophones**. Willy Wonka is a genius at making **puns** as well as confectionery, as in his recipe for Wonka-Vite.
TWO HAIRS (AND ONE RABBIT) FROM THE HEAD OF A HIPPOCAMPUS . . . THE HIDE (AND THE SEEK) OF A SPOTTED WHANGDOODLE. — CHARLIE AND THE GREAT GLASS ELEVATOR

• A **malapropism** is when you use a wrong (and funny) word that sounds similar to the word you mean, as when the Centipede says scrambled dregs instead of *scrambled eggs*. The word **malapropism** is named after *Mrs Malaprop*, a character in an 18th-century play who made funny mistakes with words.
'I've eaten fresh mudburgers by the greatest cooks there are, And scrambled dregs and stinkbugs' eggs and hornets stewed in tar.' — JAMES AND THE GIANT PEACH

• A **spoonerism** is when you swap around the first letters of two words, as when Willy Wonka says mideous harshland instead of *hideous marshland*. The word **spoonerism** is named after *William Spooner*, an Oxford academic who was famous for muddling his words.
'In the quelchy quaggy sogmire, In the mashy mideous harshland, At the witchy hour of gloomness, All the grobes come oozing home.' — CHARLIE AND THE GREAT GLASS ELEVATOR

FIND OUT MORE!
The BFG is famous for **spoonerisms!** Find out more in GIANT LANGWITCH in THE MAGICAL WORLD.

collective nouns

A **collective noun** is a name for a group of things, people or animals. For example:

• a **bask** of crocodiles or a **bouquet** (say boo-*kay*) of pheasants

• a **colony** of newts or a **coven** (rhymes with *oven*) of witches
There was a muddy pond at the bottom of Lavender's garden and this was the home of a colony of newts. — MATILDA

• a **flock** of birds (or a **flight** of birds when they are flying): *A flight of seagulls carried the peach over the ocean.*

• a **gaggle** of geese or a **gang** of Cloud-Men

• a **herd** of hippodumplings or a **horde** of Knids

• a **pod** of porpoise or pelicans or a **pack** of giants

• a **tower** of giraffes or a **troop** of monkeys. (Note that **troupe** is a different word meaning a group of acrobats, but Muggle-Wump and his family are both a **troop** AND a **troupe**.)

a troop of monkeys

WHY NOT TRY?

• Human beans have been inventing collective nouns for hundreds of years, but there are still more to be invented. What about a *bellow* or *thunder of headmistresses*, or a *gloop of chocolatiers*?

• Why not use a Roald Dahl word to make an extra-usual collective noun? For example, you might say a zippfizz of hunting giants or a glissing of slimy grobes.

All about writing

describing things

marvellous metaphors

A **metaphor** is used to describe one thing as if it were something else. For example:

• A **mountain** of food, such as potato or cabbage (with or without caterpillars), is a large pile of it on a plate.
'From now on, you must eat cabbage three times a day. Mountains of cabbage! And if it's got caterpillars in it, so much the better!' – GEORGE'S MARVELLOUS MEDICINE

• A **river of spit** is a gushing stream of saliva running down a chin (usually of a giant). If it is a LOT of spit, you could say a **torrent** or a **cascade** of spit or saliva. (Note that it is hard to see any rivers of spit on Mr Twit's face, as they are hidden by the **forest** of beard.)
Craggy yellow teeth stuck out between the two purple frankfurter lips, and rivers of spit ran down over the chin. – THE BFG

• A **sea** of tortoises (or witch scalps) is a large area of them that stretches before you.
Mr Hoppy turned and ran from the balcony into the living-room, jumping on tip-toe like a ballet-dancer between the sea of tortoises that covered the floor.
– ESIO TROT

splendid similes

Similes use the words **as** or **like** to compare two things. For example:

• The spit of witches is **as blue as a bilberry**. Note that when Violet turns **blue as a blueberry** this is not strictly a simile, as she really IS turning into a blueberry.
'It's turning blue!' screamed Mrs Beauregarde. 'Your nose is turning blue as a blueberry!' – CHARLIE AND THE CHOCOLATE FACTORY

a sea of tortoises

glissing

quelchy

squelchy

slubber

• The morning sky in Giant Country is **as red as blood**, which means it is a deep dark shade. The mention of blood also makes it sound sinister and threatening.

• If you are ill or afraid (for example after seeing a giant) you might turn **as white as paper** or **as white as a sheet**.
'Mary! You've gone as white as a sheet! Are you feeling ill?' – THE BFG

• Similes are very useful for describing extra-usual things, such as a giant's body. The Bloodbottler has gigantuous fingers that are **as large as a tree trunk** and the BFG's long-legged strides are **as long as a tennis court**.

using sound-effects
onomatopoeia

• **Onomatopoeic** (say on-o-mat-o-*pee*-ik) words sound like the thing they describe, for example **crash**, **crunch**, **swish**, **swoosh**, **whizz** and **whoosh**.
It was deafening in his ears, this fearsome swooshing whooshing whiffling panting noise. Woomph-woomph, it went. Woomph-woomph, woomph-woomph! – THE MINPINS

• Animal sounds are often **onomatopoeic**, like **oink**, **quack**, **snarl** and **snort**. (Note that an oinck is also an extra-usual creature which may be named after the sound it makes.)

DID YOU KNOW?
Blithering is an old-fashioned word that means 'talking nonsense'. It originally comes from Old Norse.

• Roald Dahl also invented new **onomatopoeic** words, such as glissing (which slimy grobes do) and quelchy (for squelchy mud).
You can hear them softly slimeing, Glissing hissing o'er the slubber, All those oily boily bodies Oozing onward in the gloam. – CHARLIE AND THE GREAT GLASS ELEVATOR

lickswishy alliteration

• When you put words together that start with the same sound, you are using **alliteration**.
The witches gasped. They gaped. They turned and gave each other ghoulish grins of excitement. – THE WITCHES

• Alliteration is phizz-whizzingly effective for insults, such as *blithering bumpkin* or *muddleheaded mugwump*.
'But my dear old muddleheaded mugwump,' said Mr Wonka, turning to Mrs Bucket. – CHARLIE AND THE GREAT GLASS ELEVATOR

• When the Enormous Crocodile crashes into the sun, he is **sizzled up like a sausage**—which uses **alliteration**, **onomatopoeia** (*sizzle*) AND a **simile** (*like a sausage*)!
With the most tremendous BANG the Enormous Crocodile crashed headfirst into the hot hot sun. And he was sizzled up like a sausage! – THE ENORMOUS CROCODILE

Blithering bumpkin!

WHY NOT TRY?

• How many **alliterative** words can you fit into a single sentence? Use Roald Dahl's extra-usual words, and invent your own words and names, to make it as propsposterous as possible! For example: *A Martian and a mideous manticore were madly munching on mushious marshmallows on a mizzly morning in May.*

Word inventing room

method no.1: buckswashling blends

A **blend** or **portmanteau word** combines the meanings of two other words. For example:

• **chortle** is a blend of **chuckle** and **snort**. The word was invented and first used by Lewis Carroll.
Charlie Kinch started chuckling and chortling so much he nearly drove off the track. — DANNY THE CHAMPION OF THE WORLD

• **churgle** is a blend of **chuckle** and **gurgle**
The fact that it was none other than Boggis's chickens they were going to eat made them churgle with laughter every time they thought of it. — FANTASTIC MR FOX

• **delumptious** is a blend of **delicious** and **scrumptious**: *a bottle of delumptious fizzy frobscottle.*

• **dreadly** is a blend of **dread** and **deadly**
'The teeth of the dreadly viper is still sticking into me!' he yelled. 'I is feeling the teeth sticking into my anklet!' — THE BFG

• **fantabulous** is a blend of **fantastic** and **fabulous**
'Whoopee!' cried the witches, clapping their hands. 'You are brilliant, O Your Grandness! You are fantabulous!' — THE WITCHES

• **griggle** is a blend of **grin** and **giggle**
Sophie couldn't stop smiling. 'What is you griggling at?' the BFG asked her, slightly nettled. — THE BFG

• **jabbel** is a blend of **jabber** and **babble**
The creature came clumping into the cave and stood towering over the BFG. 'Who was you jabbeling to in here just now?' he boomed. — THE BFG

DID YOU KNOW?
The term **portmanteau word** was invented by Lewis Carroll, who created many words of that type, including **galumph** (from gallop and triumph) and **slithy** (from slimy and lithe).

A **portmanteau** was originally a type of folding suitcase with two parts.

• **mushious** is a blend of **mushy** and **delicious**
'It's luscious, it's super, It's mushious, it's duper, It's better than rotten old fish. You mash it and munch it, You chew it and crunch it! It's lovely to hear it go squish!' — THE ENORMOUS CROCODILE

• **sogmire** is a blend of **soggy** and **quagmire**
'In the quelchy quaggy sogmire, In the mashy mideous harshland, At the witchy hour of gloomness, All the grobes come oozing home.' — CHARLIE AND THE GREAT GLASS ELEVATOR

• **splongy** is a blend of **splodge** and **spongy**: *a sticky splongy pudding.*

• **swallop** is a blend of **swallow** and **gulp** or **gollop**: *Bruce Bogtrotter swalloped the whole cake!*

swallow +

method no.2: creative compounds

A **compound** is a bit like a **blend**, but it joins two words together without losing any letters, so it is easy to work out what it means. For example, a **mudburger** is a *burger* made from *mud* and a **slugburger** is made from *slugs*.

• a **buzzy-hum** is a sound that both buzzes and hums

• **grimesludge** is thick grimy sludge or mud

• a **lickswishy** sweet is pleasant to lick and swish about with your tongue

lick + swish = lickswishy

gulp = swallop

• a **sizzlepan** is a pan in which things sizzle when you cook them

• You can also make an old compound *sparkier* by replacing one of the parts with a different word. For example, **kidnap** becomes kidsnatch, **extraordinary** becomes extra-usual and **chatterbox** becomes natterbox.

'Spiders is also talking a great deal. You might not be thinking it but spiders is the most tremendous natterboxes.' – THE BFG

method no.3: squiggly syllables

You can add an extra **syllable** in the middle of a word to make a new one. For example:

• insert *igg* in **giraffe** to make jiggyraffe, or *y* in **butterfly** to make butteryfly

'I is never showing myself to human beans … If I do, they will be putting me in the zoo with all the jiggyraffes and cattypiddlers.' – THE BFG

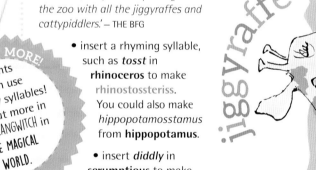

jiggyraffe

FIND OUT MORE!
Giants often use squiggly syllables! Find out more in GIANT LANGWITCH in **THE MAGICAL WORLD.**

• insert a rhyming syllable, such as *tosst* in **rhinoceros** to make rhinostossteriss. You could also make *hippopotamosstamus* from **hippopotamus**.

• insert *diddly* in **scrumptious** to make **scrumdiddlyumptious**. You could also make *glorididdlyumptious* from gloriumptious or *yumdiddlyummy* from **yummy**.

WHY NOT TRY?

• Other syllables to try are: *idd* or *iddle*, *iff* or *iffle*, *iggle*, *ogg* or *oggle*. For example: a *splendiddorous* dream, a *horriffendous* nightmare.

method no.4:
spliffling suffixes

You can add a **suffix** to the end of a word to make a new one. For example:

• add **–proof** to make a word meaning 'able to withstand', as in **Knidproof** *The Great Glass Elevator is shockproof, waterproof, bombproof, bulletproof and Knidproof! So just relax and enjoy it.'* — CHARLIE AND THE GREAT GLASS ELEVATOR

• add **–able** to make a word meaning 'able to be' or 'easy to', as in **bishable**, **squishable** and **lickable** *'Lovely stuff, lickable wallpaper!' cried Mr Wonka, rushing past.* — CHARLIE AND THE CHOCOLATE FACTORY

• add **–ful** to make a word meaning 'full of', as in **murderful**: *a slimeful snozzcumber.*

• add **–ish** to make a word meaning 'rather like', as in **greenish**, **jellyish** and **nightmarish**

• add **–less** to make a word meaning 'without' or 'lacking', as in the **Ladderless Window-Cleaning Company**

• add **–like** to make a word meaning 'like' or 'like a': *a Knid-like evil stare.*

Ladderless Window-Cleaning Company

-proof -able -ful -ish -less -like -some -wards -ly -y

• add **–some** to make a word meaning 'full of or producing', as in **filthsome**, **foulsome**, **healthsome** and **venomsome**

• add **–wards** to make a word meaning 'in the direction of', as in **earthwards** or **forthwards**: *The Great Glass Elevator was hurtling earthwards.*

• add **–y** or **–ly** to make a word meaning 'of or like', as in **human-beaney**, **witchy** and **wormy**

likes and dislikes

• add **–phile** (say *file*) to make a word meaning 'someone who loves or studies', as in **witchophile** *'Are you a witchophile, Grandmamma?' 'I am a retired witchophile,' she said. 'I am too old to be active any longer.'* — THE WITCHES

• add **–phobe** (say *fobe*) to make a word meaning 'someone who hates or fears': *Matilda is a bibliophile but her dad is a bibliophobe.* A fear or hatred of something is a **phobia.**

• add **–ologist** to make a word meaning 'an expert in': *Willy Wonka is a chocophile AND a chocolatologist!* (PLEASE NOTE: a **meteorologist** is an expert in weather, not meteors.)

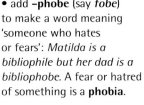

FIND OUT MORE! For words with Latin **prefixes**, like **interstellar**, see WORDS FROM AROUND THE WORLD (AND BEYOND).

method no.5: propsposterous opposites

You can add these **prefixes** to the start of a word to make an **opposite** word meaning 'not':

• add **un-**, as in **unblinking**, **unfriendly** or **unhairy**. For example, *an ungrumpy grandma, an unjumbly giant*. (In giant langwitch you can also add **um-**, as in **um-possible**.)

As you know, an ordinary unhairy face like yours or mine simply gets a bit smudgy if it is not washed often enough, and there's nothing so awful about that. — THE TWITS

'Redunculus and um-possible,' the BFG said. 'They is going two times as fast as me and they is finishing their guzzle before we is halfway.' — THE BFG

• add **dis-** or **mis-**, as in **dishonest** and **misspell** or **dispunge** and **mispise**

'Here is the repulsant snozzcumber!' cried the BFG, waving it about. 'I squoggle it! I mispise it! I dispunge it!' — THE BFG

• add **non-** or **not-so-**, as in **nonsense** and **Notsobig One**

'I never eat children,' the Notsobig One said. 'Only fish.' — THE ENORMOUS CROCODILE

method no.6: plussy parts of speech

• add **-ly** to make an **adverb**, such as extra-usually, phizz-whizzingly, **slowly**, squifflingly

One second later . . . slowly, insidiously, oh most gently, the great peach started to lean forward and steal into motion. — JAMES AND THE GIANT PEACH

• add **-ness** to make a **noun**, such as disgusterousness, gloomness, scrumdiddlyumptiousness, **sparkiness**, **stretchiness**

'So what we'll do, we'll put him in a special machine I have for testing the stretchiness of chewing-gum!' — CHARLIE AND THE CHOCOLATE FACTORY

• add **-er** to make a **comparative**, such as **grislier**, jumblier, rotsomer, **thirstier**

'We shall get thinner and thinner and thirstier and thirstier, and we shall all die a slow and grisly death from starvation.' — JAMES AND THE GIANT PEACH

• add **-est** to make a **superlative**, such as glummiest, **muddiest**, troggiest

In the biggest brownest muddiest river in Africa, two crocodiles lay with their heads just above the water. — THE ENORMOUS CROCODILE

scrumdiddlyumptiousness

'I mispise it!
I dispunge it!'

scrum

WHY NOT TRY?

• Add a suffix to a blend or other invented word to make a double-invention! For example, a grigglesome joke is one that makes you griggle.

• Try making the **opposite** of a Roald Dahl **opposite**, by taking the prefix away (to make a **positive**). For example, as disgustive means 'disgusting' and dispunge means 'dislike', then gustive will mean 'delicious' and punge will mean 'like': *Everyone punges chocolate sponge!*

truncheon + bull = **Trunchbull**

FIND OUT MORE! What is Miss Trunchbull's **name** in French and Italian? Find out in GLOBAL GOBBLEFUNK.

Names and naming

naming characters

Many of Roald Dahl's **characters** have names that suit their personalities, like Mr and Mrs *Twit*. This type of funny name is called an **aptronym**.

• Miss **Honey**'s name suggests that she has a sweet nature, like the taste of honey.

• Mr **Hoppy** sounds light-footed and fun, and Mrs **Silver** sounds soft and sparkling (compared to, for example, Mr *Clumpy* and Mrs *Mud*).

• Miss **Trunchbull**'s name sounds like a blend of *truncheon* (a type of stick for hitting people) and *bull* or *bully*, so it suits her very well.

• Willy **Wonka**'s surname sounds a bit like *wonky*, like one of his dottier ideas or inventions.

• Violet **Beauregarde**'s surname means 'beautiful look' in French (although she looks not-so-beautiful when chewing gum).

• Augustus **Gloop** sounds as if he enjoys slurping gloopy food like melted chocolate (which he does).

• **Veruca Salt** sounds like *verruca*, which is a painful wart you can get on your foot, and her surname tells you she is Not Sweet at all.

• The name **Oompa-Loompa** may be based on *oompah*, as the **Oompa-Loompas** like to sing and make music. Roald Dahl originally called them *Whipple-Scrumpets*, but later changed his mind.

gloopy Gloop

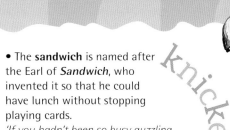

naming places

• **Crunchem Hall** sounds like *crunch 'em*, which is probably what Miss Trunchbull would like to do to her pupils.

• **Inkland** is the name that the **Grand High Witch** gives to England. She calls English people or things **Inklish** (which suggests that they like to write and use a lot of ink).
'All over Inkland, in everrry school in Inkland, noise of snapping mouse-trrraps vill be heard!'
— THE WITCHES

• **Loompaland** is named after the **Oompa–Loompas** who live there (or perhaps they are named after the land they come from). If Miss Trunchbull's pupils were named after their school, they would be called *Crunchemers*.

• Planet **Vermes** has a Latin name meaning 'worms' and the **Vermicious Knids** who live there are invertebrates, like worms.

excellent eponyms

An **eponym** is a word that is named after the **human bean** who invented or used the thing it describes.

• **Cardigans** and **wellington boots** are named after the Earl of *Cardigan* and the Duke of *Wellington*, because they once wore clothes of a similar design.
The Queen, now fully dressed in a trim skirt and cashmere cardigan, entered the Ballroom holding Sophie by the hand. — THE BFG

• The **sandwich** is named after the Earl of *Sandwich*, who invented it so that he could have lunch without stopping playing cards.
'If you hadn't been so busy guzzling that sandwich,' I said, 'you would have noticed your hairy paws.' — THE WITCHES

• **Knickers** is short for **knickerbockers**, which are a type of knee-length trousers. They are named after *Diedrich Knickerbocker*, a character in a book by the American author Washington Irving.
The small girl smiles. One eyelid flickers. She whips a pistol from her knickers.
— REVOLTING RHYMES

• When something **mesmerizes** you, it grips your attention. The word comes from an 18th-century German doctor, Franz Anton *Mesmer*, who developed a type of hypnosis.
There are times when something is so frightful you become mesmerized by it and can't look away. I was like that now. — THE WITCHES

• An **eponymous** character is one whose name is the title of the book, like *Matilda* or the *BFG*.

WHY NOT TRY?

• Use **alliteration** to make a memorable name, like *Bruce Bogtrotter* or *Willy Wonka*.

• Create a character based on one of Roald Dahl's **invented words**, for example *Mr Moochel* or *Miss Footchel*.

• Make an **eponym** from a Roald Dahl character name. For example a stylish top hat could be called a *wonka*, or old-fashioned breeches or gym knickers could be called *trunchbulls*.

Rhymes and rhyming words

some types of rhyme

• A piece of writing with lines that **rhyme** is a **poem** or **verse** and someone who writes or **composes** verse is a **poet**: *Roald Dahl was a poet as well as a splendid storyteller.*

• A **couplet** is a pair of rhyming lines which are often part of a longer poem. The **Oompa-Loompas** always chant in couplets.
'Augustus Gloop! Augustus Gloop!
The great big greedy nincompoop!'
— CHARLIE AND THE CHOCOLATE FACTORY

DID YOU KNOW?
Roald Dahl kept a **rhyming dictionary** in his writing hut to help him find rhymes for his poems.

• A **limerick** is a funny poem with five lines and a strong rhythm. Matilda enjoys reading limericks and also writes her own.
Reluctantly Matilda stood up and very slowly, very nervously, she recited her limerick:

'The thing we all ask about Jenny
Is, "Surely there cannot be many
Young girls in the place
With so lovely a face?"
The answer to that is, "Not any".'
— MATILDA

• The words to a **song**, such as the one the **Centipede** sings, are the **lyrics** (say *lir*-icks).
Whereupon, the Centipede . . . suddenly burst into song: 'I've eaten many strange and scrumptious dishes in my time, Like jellied gnats and dandyprats and earwigs cooked in slime.' — JAMES AND THE GIANT PEACH

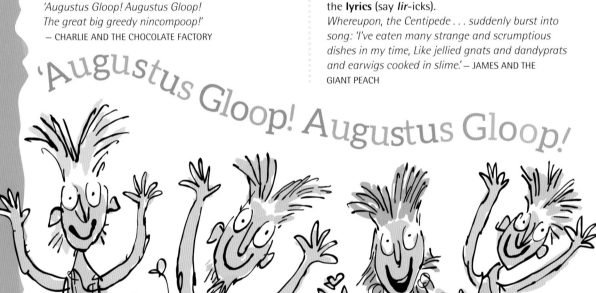

'Augustus Gloop! Augustus Gloop!

The great big greedy nincompoop!'

rhyming words

• Here are some of Roald Dahl's favourite **word endings** and some words that **rhyme** with them —including some that he invented. If you run out of **rhyming words** for your own poems, you can invent some new ones too!

-abble and -ibble

• babble, dabble, grabble, scrabble

• bibble, dribble, nibble, quibble, scribble, squibble, vegitibble

-ickle and -icky

• fickle, pickle, prickle, tickle, trickle

• icky, picky, sticky, tricky

The shoe was long and very wide. (A normal foot got lost inside.) Also it smelled a wee bit icky. (The owner's feet were hot and sticky.) — REVOLTING RHYMES

-iddle and -iddly

• fiddle, middle, riddle, squiff-squiddle, switchfiddle, twiddle, whiffswiddle

• diddly, fiddly, tiddly, twiddly

-iffle and -iffy

• piffle, pigspiffle, sniffle, swishwiffle, whiffle

• iffy, jiffy, sniffy, whiffy

-iggle and -iggly

• biffsquiggle, giggle or griggle, squiggle, swiggle, swishfiggle, wiggle, wriggle

• giggly, squiggly, wiggly, wriggly

-itious or -icious

• ambitious, delicious, fictitious, malicious, squishous, superstitious, vermicious, vicious

-izz and -izzle

• fizz, gee-whizz, whizz, zippfizz

• drizzle, fizzle, frizzle, sizzle, squizzle, swizzle

Then dad cries, 'Golly-gosh! Gee-whizz! Oh cripes! How hot this porridge is! Let's take a walk along the street Until it's cool enough to eat.' — REVOLTING RHYMES

-oggle and -oggy

• boggle, crodswoggle, goggle, squoggle, toggle

• boggy, doggy, foggy, froggy, groggy, soggy, troggy

-umptious and -ummy

• delumptious, frumptious, glumptious, gloriumptious, grumptious, presumptious, scrumptious, scrumdiddlyumptious

• crummy, dummy, glummy, plummy, scrummy, tummy, yummy

-uscious and -ushy

• luscious, mushious

• hushy, mushy, nailbrushy, slushy

extra-usual rhymes

• Using extra-usual rhymes can make your poems *sparkier*. For example, Roald Dahl rhymes *garden hose* with *armadillo's toes* and *eyes ablaze* with *mayonnaise*.

garden hose armadillo's toes

• Rhymes for chiddler include: cattypiddler, squinky squiddler and time-twiddler.

• Rhymes for frobscottle include: axolotl (a Mexican newt), bluebottle and full throttle.

axolotl

WHY NOT TRY?

• **add** an extra letter in the middle of a rhyme word to make a new one, for example *gloggle* (from **goggle**) or *snizzle* (from **sizzle**)

• **add** new letters before a word ending, for example *frumpicious* (from **–icious**) or *horrumptious* (from **–umptious**)

• make a **rhyming compound** (a word with two parts that rhyme), like Oompa-Loompa and oozy-woozy. What about an *iffy-whiffy* smell or *ushy-mushy* porridge?

Words from around the world (and beyond)

You can find all the words below in Roald Dahl's stories, but they originally come from many different countries—just like the ingredients in Willy Wonka's factory!

words from European languages

• **caterpillar** (or as giants say **cattlepiddler**) is thought to come from an old **French** word meaning 'hairy cat'

• **piano** is short for *pianoforte*, an **Italian** word meaning 'quiet (and) loud', because a piano can be played quietly or loudly (except when a giant is using it as a chair)

'It's been a rough morning,' the Queen said. 'First I had a horrid nightmare, then the maid dropped my breakfast and now I've got a giant on the piano.' – THE BFG

• **porcupine** comes from old **French** words meaning 'prickly pig'

But by the way, I think I know why porcupines Surround themselves with prickly spines. It is to stop some silly clown From squashing them by sitting down. – DIRTY BEASTS

• **spaghetti** means literally 'little strings' in **Italian**. There is a thinner type of pasta called *vermicelli* (say ver-mi-*chell*-ee) which means 'little worms'—just like Mrs Twit's recipe.

• **ugly** comes from an **Old Norse** (Viking) word meaning 'to dread', so it is no wonder that **chiddlers** dread Mrs Twit

• **umbrella** comes from an **Italian** word meaning 'a little shade', because it was originally a sun-shade (not a weapon, as Mrs Gloop seems to think)

'You monster!' she shrieked, pointing her umbrella at Mr Wonka as though she were going to run him through. – CHARLIE AND THE CHOCOLATE FACTORY

umbrella = a little shade

spaghetti = little strings

words from other languages

pyjamas = leg clothing

- **caravan** comes from **Persian** and originally meant 'a group of people travelling across a desert', not a house on wheels like Danny's

- **chocolate** comes from the **Nahuatl** (Mexican) word *chocolatl*, because chocolate was first created and drunk in ancient Mexico
'The cacao bean,' Mr Wonka continued, 'which grows on the cacao tree, happens to be the thing from which all chocolate is made.' — CHARLIE AND THE CHOCOLATE FACTORY

- **giraffe** comes from an **Arabic** word meaning 'fast-walker', like a Geraneous Giraffe trotting towards a tinkle-tinkle tree

- **pyjamas** comes from **Urdu** and **Persian** words meaning 'leg clothing'. It originally meant loose trousers tied at the waist, not striped nightclothes like Grandpa Joe's pyjamas.

- **shampoo** comes from a **Hindi** word meaning 'to press or massage', just as Mr Wormwood does every day with his purple hair tonic

- **sherbet** comes from an **Arabic** word meaning 'a drink' and was originally a cooling drink of fruit juices, not a fizzy powder to slurp
The sweet-shop of my dreams would be loaded from top to bottom with Sherbet Suckers and Caramel Fudge and Russian Toffee and Sugar Snorters.
— THE GIRAFFE AND THE PELLY AND ME

- The word **zoonk** is **Martian** (according to Willy Wonka) and probably means something very rude.
The next time Mr Wonka spoke, the words came out so fast and sharp and loud they were like bullets from a machine-gun. 'ZOONK-ZOONK-ZOONK-ZOONK-ZOONK!' he barked. — CHARLIE AND THE GREAT GLASS ELEVATOR

FIND OUT MORE!
Some spliffling **suffixes** come from Greek and Latin too! Find out more in the WORD INVENTING ROOM.

words based on Greek or Latin

- **astronaut** comes from **Greek** words meaning 'star sailor'
'They can't possibly be astronauts.' 'What makes you say that?' 'Because at least three of them are in nightshirts!' — CHARLIE AND THE GREAT GLASS ELEVATOR

- **crocodile** (both Enormous and Notsobig) comes from a **Greek** word meaning 'worm of the stones'

- **pelican** probably comes from a **Greek** word meaning 'axe', because of its strong beak—although the window-cleaning Pelly has an extra-usual beak which slides rather than snaps open and shut

- **thesaurus** comes from a **Greek** word meaning 'treasure-house', because a thesaurus is like a treasure chest of interesting words: *I do enjoy dipping into my Roald Dahl Thesaurus!*

all about prefixes

- If a word starts with one of these Greek or Latin **prefixes**, you can tell what part of its meaning will be.

- **anti-** means 'against', as in the **anti-freeze** which George adds to his medicine (to make his grandma less frosty)

- **bi-** means 'two', as in **binoculars** or **biciruclers** (which have two lenses)

- **inter-** means 'between', as in **interstellar** meaning 'between the stars': *Quogwinkles are interstellar travellers.*

- **multi-** means 'many', as in **multicoloured**: *the multicoloured feathers of the Roly-Poly Bird.*

- **tele-** means 'far or distant', as in **telekinesis**, which is the power Matilda has to move things at a distance

- **trans-** means 'across or through', as in **transatlantic**: *the transatlantic voyage of the Giant Peach.*

Global gobblefunk

Roald Dahl's stories have been translated into more than fifty languages, and so have the words that he invented, which are sometimes called **gobblefunk**. Some of the **dillions** of different **gobblefunk** words are listed here—but you can also come up with your own!

dream words

• A **trogglehumper** is a **troglogoblo** in Italian and **jorobanoches** ('night nuisance') in Spanish.

• A **ringbeller** is a **tintinnarello** in Italian and **campanillo** in Spanish.

• A **golden phizzwizard** is a **bouille de gnome dorée** ('golden gnome face') in French.

• **zozimus** is called **susimusss** in Spanish and **whirligigum** in Scots.

giant names

• The **Bloodbottler** is called **Blodgulperen** in Norwegian.

• The **Bonecruncher** is called **Knochenknacker** in German.

• The **Gizzardgulper** is called **Slaverslorper** in Scots.

• The German BFG calls the Queen **Ihre Mayonnaise** ('Your Mayonnaise') instead of **Your Majester**.

zozimus *(English or Inklish)* susimusss *(Spanish)* whirligigum *(Scots)*

FIND OUT MORE! Roald Dahl invented over 300 words of *gobblefunk*! There are more to explore in GIANT LANGWITCH in THE MAGICAL WORLD.

snozzcumbers & frobscottle

- A snozzcumber is a cetrionzolo in Italian, pepináspero in Spanish and snoscymbr in Welsh.

- A bottle of frobscottle is Blubberwasser in German, fripsdripper in Frisian and gasipum in Spanish. In French it is called frambouille because it tastes like raspberries (*framboises*).

- A whizzpopper is a flitspopper in Dutch, rummlypump in Scots and popotraque in Spanish.

creature names

- A blabbersnitch is a blablapif in French and a grobblesquirt is a cochon de vin ('wine pig').

- A humplecrimp is a humphlebumfle in Scots and a scotch-hopper is a hobbity-bobbity.

- Human beans are called blodau dynol ('human flowers') in Welsh and hommes de terre in French, which means 'earth men' but is also a pun on *pommes de terre* meaning 'potatoes'.

- Miss Honey is Mlle Candy in French.

- George Kranky is Georges Bouillon ('George Broth') in French.

- Aunts Sponge and Spiker are Schwamm und Spitzig in German and Spugna e Stecco in Italian.

- Miss Trunchbull is Mlle Legourdin ('Miss Cudgel') in French and la Spezzindue ('Breaks in half') in Italian.

- Mr and Mrs Twit are les Gredins ('the Rogues') in French.

FIND OUT MORE! Trunchbull and *Twit* are both aptronyms. Find out what this means in NAMES AND NAMING.

el Superzorro

(Spanish)

character names

- Bruce Bogtrotter is Bruce Boufetout ('Bruce Eat-all') in French.

- Fantastic Mr Fox is el Superzorro in Spanish and Mr Cadno Campus in Welsh.

- Augustus Gloop is Augustus Glupsch (say *gloopsh*) in German.

- The Grand High Witch is la Reina de les Bruixes ('Queen of the Witches') in Catalan and la Strega Suprema in Italian.

WHY NOT TRY?

- Think of a related word in a language that you know (or look one up in a dictionary) and then play with the start or ending. For example, to translate snozzcumber, start with a word meaning 'cucumber', like French concombre or Italian cetriolo or Spanish pepino.

- You could also translate gobblefunk words into Oompa-Loompish or Martian—or invent your own language. It could be a back-to-front language like esio trot, or something even more brain-boggling.

STORIES ARE GOOD FOR YOU.

Roald Dahl said,

'IF YOU HAVE GOOD THOUGHTS THEY WILL SHINE OUT OF YOUR FACE LIKE SUNBEAMS AND YOU WILL ALWAYS LOOK LOVELY.'

We believe in doing good things.
That's why ten percent of all Roald Dahl income* goes to our charity partners. We have supported causes including: specialist children's nurses, grants for families in need, and educational outreach programmes. Thank you for helping us to sustain this vital work.

Find out more at roalddahl.com

The Roald Dahl Charitable Trust is a registered UK charity (no. 1119330).
*All author payments and royalty income net of third-party commissions.